Transnational Politics in Central America

UNIVERSITY PRESS OF FLORIDA

Florida A&M University, Tallahassee
Florida Atlantic University, Boca Raton
Florida Gulf Coast University, Ft. Myers
Florida International University, Miami
Florida State University, Tallahassee
New College of Florida, Sarasota
University of Central Florida, Orlando
University of Florida, Gainesville
University of North Florida, Jacksonville
University of South Florida, Tampa
University of West Florida, Pensacola

Transnational Politics in Central America

Luis Roniger

University Press of Florida

Gainesville

Tallahassee

Tampa

Boca Raton

Pensacola

Orlando

Miami

Jacksonville

Ft. Myers

Sarasota

First cloth printing, 2011
First paperback printing, 2013

Library of Congress Cataloging-in-Publication Data
Roniger, Luis, 1949–
Transnational politics in Central America / Luis Roniger.
p. cm.
Includes bibliographical references and index.
ISBN 978-0-8130-3663-2 (cloth: alk. paper)
ISBN 978-0-8130-4445-3 (pbk.)
1. Central America—Politics and government—1979– 2. Transnationalism. I. Title.
JL1410.R66 2011
327.728—dc22   2011011166

The University Press of Florida is the scholarly publishing agency for the State University
System of Florida, comprising Florida A&M University, Florida Atlantic University, Florida
Gulf Coast University, Florida International University, Florida State University, New College
of Florida, University of Central Florida, University of Florida, University of North Florida,
University of South Florida, and University of West Florida.

University Press of Florida
15 Northwest 15th Street
Gainesville, FL 32611-2079
http://www.upf.com

To Shuli, my partner in this lifelong
transnational and multicultural journey

.

Contents

Illustrations

Tables

Graphs

Preface

Central America is a small region uniting the continental masses of North and South America and an isthmus that separates the Pacific Ocean from the Caribbean Sea. It is a region of impressive volcanic chains, extraordinary nature, ancient archeological sites, colonial and modern cities, and extensive rural hinterlands. In spite of its small dimensions when compared to other regions of the globe, it is a highly differentiated area, host to varied ecosystems and multiple societies and cultures, as well as the seat of seven sovereign countries that have maintained close yet often tension-ridden relationships since their political independence.

This book aims to provide an understanding of the transnational dynamics of Central America. I approach transnationalism as the extension of human activities and institutions across nation-state boundaries, which creates political, sociological, and cultural dynamics not confined by state borders. In tracing the transnational dynamics of Central America, the book analyzes the connected history, close and dynamic interrelations, crossings and mutual impact of the countries of the isthmus on one another, in addition to their geopolitical interdependence and a series of common challenges they have faced in the international arena.

Analytically, *Transnational Politics in Central America* draws attention to long-term trends in the region, stressing the existence of transnational dynamics before and beyond the current stage of globalization. It claims that regional, transnational processes have been operating far back in time, long before the relocation of assembly plants by capitalist corporations and before the massive migration of individuals escaping repression in the 1980s or looking for sources of livelihood in the 1990s and 2000s.

From this perspective, the reader will realize that transnationalism is not coterminous with globalization, which often refers to the removal of barriers to free trade, finance, and investment leading to the reorganization of production. Likewise, the study of transnationalism cannot be reduced to economic and migration processes, even if these are highly important. Social orientations, political culture in a broad sense—which includes narrative constructions, discourse, and practices—and institutional design are also central to an inquiry of transnationalism in Central America, as anywhere else. Stressing and integrating these somehow neglected aspects in the study of isthmian transnational development will accordingly have general theoretical implications for students of transnationalism in other parts of the globe.

In order to follow the changing transnational dynamics of these countries, the book builds bridges between historical analyses and recent developments in the social sciences, particularly on the relationships between politics and the construction of collective identities. As such, it relies on the work of social scientists and historians and is written with a deep respect for studies attempting a reconstruction of the past, turning it into a less "alien territory." I do not know if the findings presented here are all satisfactory and will stand the scrutiny of further research, but I am fully convinced that the issues raised are challenging and deserve serious consideration.

Writing in the early 1990s, Ralph Lee Woodward Jr. opened a comprehensive review article on works dealing with the unity and diversity of Central America with the following observation:

> Most scholarly writing on Central America continues to focus on the individual states rather than on the entire region. The political fragmentation of the past century and a half has long since established state sovereignty and conditioned outsiders and natives alike to think in city-state terms and to recognize the obvious differences among the isthmian peoples. Local elites have found it convenient, in protecting special privileges best defended at the local level, to encourage notice of this diversity.[1]

Since Woodward's remark, under the impact of the regional peace processes, globalization, the transition to democracy throughout the isthmus, and the relative progress in the establishment of regional institutions, more attention has been given to the analysis of pan–Central American problems and challenges beyond the state level.[2]

Nonetheless, many excellent books on the region continue to be mostly geared to the framework of analysis of the individual states, their projects and policy impact on societies and ethnicities, their implications for inclusion and exclusion from the perspective of individual nations, and their dynamics of representation and participation.

Needless to say, the state level constitutes a most important aspect of these societies' development, as states have remained crucial actors in both the internal and international scene. In the words of Forrest Colburn and Arturo Cruz, "the nation-states that have been built in the isthmus are inviolable."[3] And yet, such perspective needs to be complemented and intertwined with the analysis of transnational trends affecting these societies beyond the boundaries of state sovereignty or the dimension of intervention by hegemonic powers or capitalist forces.

This book is an attempt to bridge between these perspectives and transnationalism in the study of Central America. As such, it traces the dialectical tug-of-war that unfolded between the process of distinct state consolidation and processes of transnational engagement and disengagement in the region. Neither one of these processes obliterated the dynamic unfolding of the other, as reflected in the ebbs and flows of transnational politics in Central America.

I would like to express my gratitude to the Mellon Foundation for its support of this research and to the Institute of Advanced Studies (IAS) in Jerusalem for its hospitality. I completed this work while being a Fellow at the IAS during the spring and summer of 2009 as a member of the research group on Challenging Liberal Democracy in Latin America. The comments and criticisms by the researchers there contributed to the refinement of some of the arguments of this work. I owe special thanks to Judit Bokser, David Coates, Sergio DellaPergola, James Dunkerley, Shmuel N. Eisenstadt, Wei-chin Lee, Thomas Legler, David Lehmann, Raanan Rein, Shuli Roniger, Mario Sznajder, Deborah Yashar, Leon Zamosc, Lisbeth Zimmermann, and the anonymous readers of earlier versions for their comments on various parts of this work. The research assistance of Melissa Velarde, James Merrick, Adam Parker, and Orly Haimovich and the meetings with Sara Bivin have been highly important in preparing early versions of the typescript, and I am grateful to them.

Also instrumental have been the meetings, readings, and discussions conducted with students at Wake Forest University in 2007 and 2008 and presentations at various meetings, particularly at the Truman Research Institute for the Advancement of Peace in the Spring of 2008 and at the IPSA world congress in Santiago, Chile, in July 2009. I am also grateful to the directors and staff of the following institutions and libraries: the Library of the Iberoamerican Institute of the Prussian Heritage Foundation in Berlin, the International Institute of Social History in Amsterdam, the Centre d'information et d'études sur les migrations internationales in Paris, the

Mount Scopus Library at the Hebrew University of Jerusalem, the Library of Congress in Washington, and the National Library in San José, Costa Rica, for their assistance.

Thanks are also due to The Americas Barometer by LAPOP (the Latin American Public Opinion Project) of Vanderbilt University for permission to use information from the datasets in graphs 14.3, 14.4, 14.5, and 14.6 and to the International Human Rights Law Institute of De Paul University, Chicago, for permission to reproduce with some additions a table published originally in David E. Guinn and Elissa Steglich, *In Modern Bondage: Sex Trafficking in the Americas* (2003, p. 25). The map of Central America was prepared by Tammy Soffer. Tamar Golan-Lev, Idan Saragosti, and Eldad Saragosti converted the graphs into Adobe Illustrator. Morgan Miller assisted in preparing the index. The photographs were taken by the author.

Introduction

Could a Honduran be president of El Salvador? Could a Guatemalan be minister of foreign affairs not only of his country but also of Costa Rica? Could the same individual serve as a diplomatic representative of Costa Rica in El Salvador and also, later on, as a representative of El Salvador in Peru? Could militias and armies operate freely in neighboring countries to support one political faction over others? Why did children in Guatemalan schools sing an anthem to Central America together with their national anthem until well into the twentieth century? All this happened in Central America, and much more: in the 1830s and 1840s it was not uncommon for cities in Honduras to place themselves under the protection of Guatemala or El Salvador. In the 1850s the key "national" war launched against a U.S. citizen serving as president of Nicaragua was fought by transnational forces. Up to the late nineteenth century there were attempts at political reunification in the region. Likewise, in the 1910s and 1920s a movement of activists drawn from all over the isthmus tried to rekindle the vision of a united Central American nation. In the twentieth century, constitutional provisions allowed Central American individuals to naturalize, reside, and work in the other countries, while local citizens, migrants, students, and sojourners were often politically activated and radicalized by incoming exiles from sister nations.

This book is an attempt to make sense of these and other regional trends by indicating that we need to approach Central America with a Janus-faced perspective: trying to understand the process of fragmentation into separate nation-states along with lingering transnational dynamics. Following this dual perspective, readers will be able to follow findings that may seem puzzling from a state-centered perspective. Why did five of these countries find it hard to define distinct dates for their independence? Why did rulers in one country often feel they had to intervene in the other countries of the region in order to retain control of their own states? How can we explain the intermittent yet recurrent attempts at regional reunification? How could exiles from one country fulfill key public roles or be triggers of social movements in the other countries of the region? Conversely, we also should understand why these countries went separate ways, established distinct states, and constructed different national identities, if early on they were rather indistinguishable in terms of language, religion, or other primordial identities. How can we explain their dismemberment into separate states in the early nineteenth century and why they could not disengage fully thereafter, thus triggering from time to time new attempts at reunification, at least institutionally? How did transnational migration and the construction of a transnational diaspora affect regional identity? How do globalization and regionalism intertwine? How can these states in close proximity confront transnational illicit markets and criminality? How do interstate institutions and transnational involvement affect each other?

This work analyzes the transnational dynamics of Central America. This is a region that includes Guatemala, Belize, El Salvador, Honduras, Nicaragua, Costa Rica, and Panama. These countries share a close geographical relationship and historical background, a geopolitical interdependence, and challenges in the international arena.

Traditionally, the social sciences and particularly political science and international relations have focused attention on these countries from either a nation-state perspective or from the perspective of international intervention. From the first perspective, analyses have traced the distinctive constitution of the countries, following closely the national rhetoric of these states. From the latter perspective, scholars have recognized the impact of hegemonic powers in the international arena effecting regime change, as in Central America in the 1980s. Yet, a third, transnational dimension has become increasingly evident, as when civil wars became entangled with international intervention during the last phase of the cold war or, more recently, as these countries have been beleaguered by transnational migration, narcotrafficking, and illicit networks.

The book claims that this transnational dimension has been present in the region since early times and most clearly since the colonial period, affecting political and social processes at the national level. This analytical perspective highlights the interplay between states and non-state actors in the local, the regional, and the international arenas and attempts to assess developmental and transnational theories used in making sense of regional dynamics.

Five major factors stand out behind the selection of Central America as the core of this book. First, from a geopolitical perspective, the isthmus is a region composed of small republics standing in relative proximity to one another and thus prone to be affected by political processes in the neighboring societies and polities.

Second, the core states of Central America trace their origins back to the disintegration of a single state, established in the early nineteenth century, on the basis of a previous colonial jurisdiction. Accordingly, research can trace the evolving construction of separate nation-states and the intricate transnational connections of each such state and society with the other states and societies in the region as processes unfolding in parallel, affecting and impinging on one another.

Third, Central America is a region fit for the study of political and social change on a regional level due to its strategic location as a natural interoceanic bridge in the Americas, paying attention to transnational factors complementing the balance between domestic factors and international factors at work within the sphere of influence of a hegemonic state.

Fourth, during the cold war period, Central America was beleaguered by national and transnational wars and human rights crises, with a shift in the 1990s toward democratization and market openings, thus providing a good vantage point on the transnational dimensions of regime and socioeconomic change.

Last but not least, the study of Central America enables a close look at the challenges that small nation-states face in the global arena, especially under the lingering effects of violence, poverty, and transnational criminality.

All these lines of analysis call for a transnational approach to the region. Bringing these factors together, the book traces some of the central trends in the political and sociological history of these states. It introduces alternative approaches for interpreting the social and political development of these states, in terms that go beyond their important though not exclusive relationship with a hegemonic superpower, be it Spain in colonial times, Britain in early independence, or more recently the United States.

Chapters are arranged thematically while carrying forward historical developments, reaching from late colonial times through independence toward contemporary issues and challenges. Chapter 1 reviews the burgeoning recognition of transnationalism as a dimension of analysis distinguished from both nation-state and global perspectives, identifying transnational issues of special relevance for the study of Central America. Readers may choose to skip this chapter and return to it once they have read other parts of the book and attain a sense of the range of transnational issues and developments in the region.

Chapter 2 presents a general background of the Central American isthmus, identifying the early geographic and demographic factors shaping low levels of integration affecting the progressive formation of distinct territorial domains within the region.

The short-lived attempt at political unification of the early nineteenth century followed by balkanization are analyzed in chapter 3, which portrays these as formative experiences that continued to inform the minds and political projects of the isthmus in later times. In it I assert that as separate states were constructed, they were not able to completely disengage from one another, thus projecting a peculiar trans-state and transnational dynamics through generations. The process of breaking apart is further analyzed in chapters 4 to 7, which trace how the separate states of the region attempted to consolidate their control and construct a sense of distinct collective identity through their policies, visions, and practices, wrangling at the same time with persisting transnational pressures and the memory of their common origins, the protracted involvement in neighboring states, and recurring projects of reconstruction of political unity.

These chapters stress the process of growing divergence of state institutionalization while pointing out that the countries emerging as the result of fragmentation continued to affect each other across their porous borders in various ways. Chapter 5 discusses the creative process of construction of national identities that was delayed in the isthmus, with important consequences for the institutional and social development of these societies. Chapter 6 analyzes the political and economic foundations of distinct state development in the region. Together, these chapters provide hindsight on the process led by the balkanized states to develop as discrete nations.

Complementing the analysis, chapter 7 looks at the parameters of inclusion and exclusion predicated by the states in the region toward internal groups, both localized and particularly those with transnational links such as the Miskitu or the Garinagu.

Chapter 8 focuses on the persistent attempts of reconstitution of political unity or at least regional coordination carried out from the 1840s to the 1920s and points out the tension-ridden existence of broader regional and more secluded state-related perceptions of nationhood leading to the multilayered ebbs and flows of regional unification and dismemberment. Chapter 9 analyzes how the isthmian states fully developed their institutional distinctiveness and distanced from one another by the twentieth century, indicating how this process of divergence was reversed under the impact of the cold war, which led once again to war across borders, international intervention, and transnational involvement, an involvement projected also onto the peace efforts and the transition to democracy starting in the 1990s, as analyzed in chapter 10.

Several long-lasting transnational trends initiated in this period are analyzed in chapters 11 and 12, namely, the flow of refugees searching for asylum, followed later on by equally massive movements of transnational migrants gaining momentum in the 1990s and 2000s, under a series of challenges facing the region; and the phenomenon of transnational criminality and illicit networks, their roots, manifestations, and impact.

The following chapters move analysis to the interplay of economic, political, and sociological factors operating in the region in the late twentieth century and early twenty-first century. Chapter 13 traces the impact of globalization and transnational trends in the form of capital transfers and investment, intraregional trade, the growing relevance of remittances, and tourism. While indicating some improvements in macro-economic performance, analysis also points out the mixed sociological implications in terms of lopsided human development, persisting poverty and socioeconomic gaps, social exclusion, and violence.

The proliferation of interstate regional institutions in the late twentieth century is the focus of chapter 14. These institutions, launched with only partial success in the 1960s, gained momentum in the 1990s after the successful completion of the peace process initiated in the 1980s. The chapter singles out the major institutional developments while discussing whether such institutions reflect regional identity or contribute to it. The conclusions carry this study forward into analyzing the prospects of regional transnationalism in the isthmus under the growing impact of globalizing processes in the region. It suggests the need to consolidate coordination in economic domains but also to make interstate institutions accountable and relevant to rank-and-file citizens, reinvigorating public trust and social participation, crucial components of institutional success.

1

Nation-States and Transnational Theories

The State of the Art

The study of transnational processes has burgeoned in recent years, mostly driven by the parallel interest in several processes that gained momentum and public attention in the late twentieth century and early twenty-first century. These processes include the heralded decline of the nation-state;[1] the globalization of production processes and capital transference; the spread of neoliberal policies of economic restructuring and privatization, favoring corporate capital and the correlated emergence of countervailing transnational networks opposing the policy prescriptions emanating from the Washington consensus;[2] the massive movement of migrants, refugees, and sojourners that reinforced the multicultural and hybrid and translocal character of societies;[3] and the emergence of cross-national movements and networks supporting universal discourses of human rights and environmental issues.[4]

In connection with this heightened relevance and in tandem with the overused and abused notion of globalization, the concept of transnationalism has become a focus of interest and often intense debate for many scholars around the world. Indeed, certain kinds of relationships have been globally intensified, involving multiple ties and interactions linking people or institutions across the borders of nation-states. Research has increasingly identified "transnational" communities, capital flows, trade, citizenship, corporations, intergovernmental agencies, nongovernmental organizations, politics, services, social movements, social networks, families, migration circuits, identities, public spaces, and cosmopolitan cultures. In a review of the state of the art published in the late 1990s, Steven Vertovec stressed that globalization and transnationalism are obviously phenomena of very different natures, requiring research and theorization on different scales and levels of abstraction.[5] As too many processes and aspects are often conflated and subsumed under these notions, we need to make the perspective followed here explicit.

The concept of transnationalism, as considered in this work, addresses the interconnectivity across nations that is often triggered by, and in turn conditions, those social processes, political movements, and cultural networks extending beyond nation-state borders. Such interconnectivity can develop—although does not necessarily unfold—along organizational lines. Yet, often, it becomes equally visible in cultural bonds, historical memories, cross-border networks, and unstructured migration flows.

The meaning of "transnationalism" as used here should be distinguished from globalization. "Globalization"—or in its French wording, "mondialisation"—is usually defined as the reorganization of production across state borders and the removal of barriers to free trade, finance, and investment, with the consequently greater integration of national economies and supposed convergence of consumer patterns. Correlated are phenomena not confined to the economic realm—such as the growth of communication and mass movements of labor migrants across national borders—but attention is mainly drawn to the economic foundations contributing to these developments. In turn, transnationalism is often defined as covering those human activities, social networks, and movements that extend across national boundaries.[6] These two processes mutually impact one another yet should be differentiated, with the latter identifying a far broader range of phenomena, beyond economics, and stressing the development of transnational communities and political, economic, and cultural networks and movements driven but not completely subsumed by the logic of capitalism.

It is my claim that transnational actions transcending national borders have taken place not only in the form of economic processes and a recent "globalization from below," Peter Evans' term that aptly identifies the "counter-hegemonic" movements reacting to the spread of global capitalism,[7] but also in the form of political dynamics that can be traced back for generations. At least in Central America, a transnational dynamic has been rooted in political terms already by the early nineteenth century as the countries of the region emerged as the result of fragmentation but were not able to disengage completely from one another, continuing to affect each other across national borders in various ways that this book aims to identify.

As the term becomes fashionable, some observers have interpreted "transnationalism" in terms of an almost universal commitment to humankind. For instance, in the *International Encyclopedia of the Behavioral and Social Sciences*, Claus Leggewie identifies it with a paradigm shift that, moving away from the paradigm of international relations, will allow a new form of world politics, already on the rise: governance and citizenship beyond the nation-state. Leggewie explains the importance of this paradigmatic shift in terms of cross-boundary connections, life experiences, and visions:

> [The term] is used especially in connection with international organizations and the "multis" (transnational corporations, or TNCs). According to the original meaning of the Latin prefix "trans," it points beyond the usual diplomatic dealings among sovereign nation-states and the customary division of labor among "national economies"; the unit of analysis, not only in international relations, has become *Weltgesellschaft* (world society . . .). This does not intend to announce an "end of nation-states"; but state sovereignty as we knew it has become "anachronistic." . . . From the accustomed macro-perspective or bird's-eye view of the world economy, the glance drifts to the microlevel of *Lebenswelt* (life world), where we can trace the cross-boundary paths on which people and objects, metaphors and symbols, individual life histories and collective biographies are transferred. It is time for social science and political actors to acknowledge this "paradigm shift" from international relations to transnational that also allows that a new form of world politics is arising: governance and citizenship beyond the nation-state.[8]

While basically correct in identifying the importance of the transnational dimension, this approach fails to recognize that transnationalism needs not be necessarily conducive to or coterminous with global citizenship. Its range may turn global under specific circumstances, for instance, as the contemporary world faces increasing problems of energy, ecology, and sustainable development. Yet, transnationalism can be at work at other levels and may also be effective at macro-regional and micro-regional levels. Likewise, it may be linked to different historical horizons and varied civilizational premises, operating differently in various areas and periods and adopting a multilevel character.

More specifically, transnationalism can be—and, I would stress, has been—in operation also in a region such as Central America, due to the specific background of the formation of its societies and the forms of state development following political independence. By choosing to focus on regional transnational processes, I am focusing on a macro-region that at any point in time since the early nineteenth century consisted of at least five sociopolitical entities that have been involved in ebbs and flows of separation and fragmentation, of unification and coordination.

I should emphasize that it is the human dynamics implied in the lack of convergence or conflation of states and nations that creates such *transna-tional* dynamics. While those involved in crossing political and social bor-ders—for example, elites, exiles, or migrants—could have been motivated by various goals and identities ranging from highly particularistic commit-ments to supranational goals, their frameworks of orientation have been multiple, with bounds of society and culture not confined to the borders and regulatory powers of the state of their residence.

The perspective adopted should be assessed within the lines of analysis de-veloped in the social sciences and humanities. As already alluded to, a major venue of research into transnational phenomena has prioritized economic factors and has tended to equate them with global processes of trade and finance, capitalist expansion, and contemporary "time-space compression," especially of production processes. Scholars following this line of inquiry have drawn attention to an important aspect of the current phase of capitalist development, namely, the growing importance of transnational corporations (TNCs) and transnational investment, the rise of a transnational capitalist class comprised of TNC executives and globalizing state bureaucrats, trans-national professionals and elites involved in commercial advertisement and the media, and wealthy transmigrants living in two or more locations and becoming "cosmopolitans" in the sense stressed years ago by anthropologist Ulf Hannerz and sociologist Ulrich Beck.[9]

Another major venue of research involves following the increased human mobility, the transnational journeys, and the continued crystallization of ethnic diasporas and newer migrant populations.[10] While the globalization of production processes has led to the increase of human mobility, the pro-cesses taking place are transnational in the sense that they link individuals whose life experience and lifestyles span various national spaces and territo-ries, as if they were "betwixt and between," in the terms that Victor Turner originally used to describe rites of passage. All these have created transna-tional networks spanning countries and involved in many types of activi-ties ranging from traditional solidarity to illegal and violent social networks, which also operate on a transnational scale.[11]

Structural approaches are complemented with attention to other, no less important aspects of transnationalism: the formation of new forms of aware-ness and decentered attachment and the correlated emergence of hybrid and multiple identities, as well as cultural spaces encompassing syncretism, bri-colage, and cultural translation.[12] In parallel, "planetary concerns"—such as ecology, air pollution, energy, health, and sustainable development—have become increasingly important, as evidenced in the rising number of international nongovernmental organizations, including the International Red Cross and various United Nations agencies. Participation of individuals and other non-state actors in these organizations is a reflection of a growing concern for humanity broader than ethnic or nation-nation attachments.

Bringing together these various aspects of transnational research is a growing awareness that collective identities and personal commitments as well as public spheres and political projects are reformulated as a result of the changing experience of human beings in space and time. Yet, the emphasis on current processes of transnationalism—especially in their structural and economicist versions—has been paralleled by the implicit suggestion that transnationalism is a phenomenon of contemporary times, downplaying the occurrence of transnational processes at work in earlier phases of development.

Contrastingly, this book claims that transnational trends—reflected in movements of people, capital, culture, and ideas across borders—operated in Central America even before the establishment of separate states in the nineteenth century and that their impact continued thereafter, especially concerning images of collective identity and political projects affecting or even remodeling state sovereignty.

As transnationalism touches upon so many aspects of human life, it is no wonder that different disciplines have played increasing attention to its various aspects. A line of research with relevance to the current inquiry is that of drawing attention to macro-regional analysis, stressed in parallel by human geographers, sociologists, historians, political scientists, and experts in international relations.

From the perspective of the various social sciences, and particularly of geography, the current stage of transnational studies is instrumental in overcoming what has been defined as the "nomothetic" or functionalist approach. This approach, which dominated studies for more than two decades since the 1950s, colored research with ideas of convergence, of a Marshall McLuhan–like "global village" taking over locality, and of structural imperatives (for example, after Niklas Luhmann's ideas) overriding culture and regional identity. If focusing on regions, attention was given to territorial functionality, even though many researchers—especially in the Anglo-Saxon tradition—tended to exalt the economic components of geographical reality.[13] During the late 1970s and the 1980s there was a strong reaction to such functionalist approaches, leading geographers and others to consider other relevant but nonquantifiable aspects affecting territorial organization. The new theories, often defined as "systemic," have considered regions as open spatial systems consisting of linked physical and human elements oriented at attaining superior and mutable levels of territorial organization without normally changing their fundamental structure.[14] These recent perspectives have given increasing attention to transnationalism as recreating space-time relations,[15] as well as to regions as historical constructions with far-reaching consequences for societies, and carrying a variable yet persistent weight in the shape of material forms of localized collective identity.

Similarly, sociological studies have elaborated the notion of multiple modernities as going against classical theories of modernization predicating the convergence of industrial societies.[16] The latter theories, prevalent in the 1950s and 1960s, assumed that the institutions that developed in western Europe and the United States would ultimately prevail throughout the world. These homogenizing and hegemonic assumptions have been challenged time and again in recent decades by new approaches in sociology and anthropology stressing the multiplicity of social and institutional experiences crystallizing in different societies worldwide and the hybridity and multicultural setup reinforced by transnational movements of people, products, and ideas.[17]

While nobody would contest the occurrence of processes of structural differentiation and globalization taking place across a wide range of institutions and across societies worldwide, the new approaches put emphasis on the fact that these trends—occurring in domains as varied as economics and politics, urbanization, family life, mass communication, and the growth of individualism—are greatly influenced by specific cultural and territorial traditions and by the different historical experiences of the various societies in which they develop.

These new perspectives open a wide range of possibilities of recognizing the existence of distinct institutional formations, self-conceptions, and patterns of collective consciousness in various societies and transnational arenas in the understanding that modernity (or for that matter, globalization as replacing earlier paradigms of modernization) and westernization are not identical and that research should look for the specific developmental processes and specific constellations of forces that crystallize in different societies and regions.

In history, too, in recent years the move to a world history that poses challenges to the understanding of the past in Eurocentric ways has opened the way for debates on the possibility of approaching the world from different historiography perspectives,[18] raising awareness of the possible redefinition of historical trajectories from common points of departure, a development going beyond "an open-minded accommodation of alternative histories," as stressed recently by Arif Dirlik.[19] These new perspectives, stemming from the move to this world history and the criticisms it has generated by supporters of historical distinctiveness, have opened the way for combining comparative analysis and transfer studies closer to the analysis of transnational interactions and what Sanjay Subrahmanyam has defined as connected histories,[20] or what Michael Werner and Bénédicte Zimmermann have called *histoire croisée*,[21] a turn to analyses not fully determined by the whims and primacy of developed countries' geopolitical priorities and visions. Thus, for instance, by following inquiries into intercrossings between societies, the perspective of *histoire croisée* suggests being aware of how processes and reflexivity about them are—to follow Pierre Bourdieu—socially structured, reflecting particular positions in competition or power struggles; it stresses mutual impacts, resistances, inertias, new combinations, and transformations "that can both result from and develop themselves in the process of crossing" and conceives the transnational level as

> a level that exists in interaction with the others, producing its own logics with feedback effects upon other space-structuring logics. Far from being limited to a macroscopic reduction, the study of the transnational level reveals a network of dynamic interrelations whose components are in part defined through the links they maintain among themselves and the articulations structuring their positions.[22]

This transnational turn has been also informed by anticolonial and postcolonial scholarship, contributing to the analysis of "units that spill over and seep through national borders, units both greater and smaller than the nation-state."[23]

In political science and communication as well, there are increasing calls to recognize democratic regionalism, which implies the expansion of civil solidarity, the participation of non-state actors, and democratic network governance, for instance through electronic interaction and virtual voting. Such perspective suggests going beyond both the search for democratic legitimacy in the framework of the nation-state and beyond the search for cosmopolitan legitimacy as pushed through international institutions, primarily the United Nations.[24] Thus, these new approaches go beyond the traditional state-centered view of international relations and global politics,[25] thus opening ground for studies that recognize both multiple forms of interaction between individuals and societies as well as the transnational character of that interplay.

Scholars of international relations like Robert O'Brien and his coauthors have defined these multiple forms of interaction involving also non-state actors as a complex multilateralism,[26] moving away from the tradition of interstate or "club multilateralism," to borrow the term from Andrew Cooper and Thomas Legler's work on the soft forms of intervention by the Organization of American States (OAS) in safeguarding democracy in the Americas.[27] Likewise, international relations scholars have emphasized the growing impact of transnational advocacy networks in international relations, in what Margaret Keck and Kathryn Sikkink call the "boomerang effect" of these networks on the transformation of international norms such as human rights.[28] Another major departure has been the growing consciousness about regions and the construction of regional norms.[29]

Finally, international political economy has moved from analyses emphasizing state-led regional integration according to the European Union model toward analyses stressing the historical, multilevel, and multidimensional processes, partly led by states but also and increasingly by transnational corporations and networks and organizations of civil society resisting globalization. Marchand, Boas, and Shaw contend that the new approaches represent a clear break with conventional theories about regional integration and cooperation that focused attention on states and formal regional organizations, as if regions were intended to become closed systems, even if affected by globalization.[30] According to these authors, globalization and regionalization are not necessarily contradictory processes, and globalization is at least in part articulated through regionalization. Moreover, the new approaches that emerged in the 1990s have shifted emphasis toward regionalization as an open, complex process of change taking place simultaneously at various levels including the structure of the world system as a whole, the level of interregional relations, and the internal pattern of the single region.[31] These affect not only the level of formal institutions but also civil societies, associations, and networks, including small or larger and better-organized criminal networks. As Björn Hettne and Fredrik Soderbaum indicate:

> The NRT [new regional theory] seeks to describe this process of regionalization in terms of levels of "regionness," i.e. the process whereby a geographical area is transformed from a passive object to an active subject capable of articulating the transnational interests of the emerging region. Regionness thus implies that a region can be a region "more or less." The level of regionness can both increase and decrease. Mostly when we speak of regions we actually mean regions in the making.[32]

Departing from the new approaches that can be identified in these various disciplines, we should be aware that regions evolve and change form and may generate specific social and institutional dynamics, determining boundaries of self-identification and shaping personal and collective visions while at the same time being open to cross-national interactions and impact. Thus, on the one hand, regardless of their origins and size, which may vary from one region to another, regions may increasingly be recognized as real in their consequences. On the other hand, regions are not closed to global trends and influences. Accordingly, these dynamics call for attention to the intentional construction of regions taking place through a dual process of struggle for dominance and resistance, of inclusion and exclusion, in which discourse and culture play a crucial rule in the construction, maintenance, and decline of regions as ideas and structures affecting institutions and personal lives.[33]

From this perspective, we can identify several key processes implied in the notion of transnationalism that will be important in this inquiry. First is the awareness that despite the logic of fragmentation into separate nation-states—such as occurred in the territories once colonized by the Spaniards and included as part of their empire—there are historical experiences, collective memories, and structural trends that keep some societies closer rather than isolated from one another. Thus, the societies of Central America have undergone a tension-ridden separation and a series of attempted reunifications that embedded a vision of being sister republics (or "sections" of one fatherland) while often differing in their understanding of tradition and the paths they pursued into modernity.

Second, the notion of transnationalism may allow us to increasingly overcome futile debates among various schools of thought on international regimes, namely, those supporting neoliberalism, realism, or cognitivism. While supporters of neoliberalism have interpreted constellations of interests as the driving force of transnationalism, realists claim that power relationships among nations are the precipitating dimension, and cognitivism presupposes causal beliefs and social knowledge as the crucial factors. According to these categorizations, scholars in the neoliberal school stress that states are motivated to pursue their own interests; realists argue that power is the central component in states' cooperation or lack thereof; and cognitivists would rather stress values as embodied in practices and agency toward norm formation in international regimes.[34] Analyzing the transnational dynamics in Central America, one cannot fail to notice that interests, power, and imagination have come together in fragmenting the isthmus into states, which while separate, have mostly remained connected to one another as part of one imagined "divided nation." Accordingly, social and political actors have mobilized time and again toward or against the redrafting of state boundaries and the remodeling of the lost unity, embedding their actions with symbolic significance.

Third, while many studies of transnationalism place attention on the globalization of production and consumption, with both positive and negative consequences for the well-being and lifestyles of growing numbers of human beings, and on the correlated massive move of migrants and refugees across the globe, the study of transnationalism in Central America requires equal attention to be paid to other dimensions. Foremost, it must be noted that transnational processes have also had a strong political component in the isthmus and, moreover, that this component can be traced back to colonial times and was reinforced very early on, after political independence in the nineteenth century, and last but not least, that this political dimension has involved the crystallization of constellations of interests and power struggles strongly embedded in cultural understandings and meaning that historical and social research should reconstruct and make intelligible.

Fourth, to study transnationalism does not involve supporting premature forecasts about the decline of the nation-state. Indeed, in recent years, there is growing recognition that despite talks about the decline of the nation-state in an era of globalization pushing to erase borders, states remain powerful players, both in a descriptive way of their continuing role and in a prescriptive manner, in terms of the important functions they may fulfill in regulation.[35] The state is "a key site through which globalization must operate and the object for which national elites, minority (or ethnic or indigenous) groups, and global entities (even international terrorists, as Geertz suggests) struggle and compete."[36] This also implies that the state as a site of institutions and power now has evolving networks of very new kinds of actors around it, including international agencies and transnational NGOs, and that transnational actors have influence on its institutional setting. Thus, in contrast to a closed nation-state reading, a transnational approach implies following a multilayered perspective, discarding any one-dimensional reading of processes and developments in any region.

The above lines of analysis allow identifying several arenas as crucial for transnational research on Central America. One is that regional horizons have pervaded the political projects of individuals and social movements in the isthmus, irrespective of state membership and citizenship. It may not be superfluous to stress once again that this has been the case not only in the era of contemporary globalization driven by corporate capital, labor migration, and international organizations but also in earlier times due to the structural and normative factors that led to the dismemberment of the provinces of the former colonial Kingdom of Guatemala and to a dynamics of regional intervention and recurring attempts of reunification.

Another crucial aspect for transnational research is the study of the fluid mobilizing mechanisms and transnational connections that were generated time and again in Central America. Analysis should identify these transnational trends operating in the form of cross-national links of kinship and friendship, networks of exiles, and movements geared to the reunification of the isthmus, as well as in commercial and corporate movements of capital, waves of migration, and transference of remittances. These structures, which can be condensed in the concept of transnational network or "inter-network," have been present in the area for centuries, albeit in changing forms that need to be traced in detail.

Connected to the above, especially in recent decades, is the rising importance of specific transnational networks. Some of them are motivated by a new sense and idioms of cooperation and respect for human rights and are driven by international organizations, while others are motivated by the profit- and power-seeking drives of transnational illicit networks of narcotraffickers and gangs.

Finally, there are the ebbs and flows of regional institutionalization that have recovered momentum following the end of the cold war but that have been present in earlier periods, driven both by the will of regional power holders to dominate the region and by transnational networks of political and social activists, students and professionals, and exiled intellectuals who tried time and again to recreate trans-isthmian identity and solidarity and often filtered many external influences and experiences into their home societies.

These domains are crucial for understanding past developments and envisioning the future of the region. In transnational terms, Central America stands out comparatively since most of the states in the region were born out of a shared colonial administrative jurisdiction and a short-lived attempt at unification following independence, with long-lasting effects on the ways these societies have strived to construct their national identities and idiosyncrasy, to develop their distinctiveness, while at the same time being unable to completely disengage themselves from the sister republics of the isthmus.

2

Central America as a Region

One of the defining traits of Central America as a region is its location between North and South America and between the Caribbean Sea and the Pacific Ocean. This strategic location in terms of transportation and transit routes has constituted a core factor in regional development or lack thereof since colonial times. Whether serving the Spanish delivery of silver and trade in colonial times or reflecting the drives of smugglers, pirates, and European powers willing to take hold of land to build a trans-isthmian corridor to the Pacific, whether facilitating the move of individuals from the U.S. east coast to California during the gold rush or the U.S. initiative to build a fluvial canal—the region fell victim or capitalized on its strategic location as a hub of international transportation.

Geographically, the region is structured by the chain of mountains, hills, and valleys that runs parallel to the Pacific coast. The mountains and hills are interspersed with deep ravines, posing severe barriers to transportation and communication and leading to the formation of distinct ecosystems and human societies. Due to their location and configuration, with rapids and sandbars, most rivers have not been navigable but rather posed barriers to land transportation. Heavy rains further have made road transportation impossible for months in many places. From southern Mexico to northern Costa Rica, the continental watershed separates the dry Pacific fringe and its valleys and plateaus from the humid lowlands of tropical vegetation and swamps stretched far to the Caribbean coast. The former have been the most densely populated areas and traditional seat of major urban centers, while the latter developed much later, in the twentieth century, due to the growth of export-oriented agricultural enclave economies. In southern Costa Rica and in Panama, the watershed shifts to the Caribbean side. In central Panama, the land narrows to less than sixty-five miles separating the Caribbean coast from the Pacific Ocean. Rising only about eighty feet above sea level, this area became the principal trans-isthmian route of Spanish imperial trade already in the sixteenth century and the site of the Panama Canal in the twentieth century.

Geologically, the region is seismically active, with volcanoes erupting from time to time, as in the earthquakes that devastated the Nicaraguan capital in 1931 and 1972 and brought destruction and loss of life to El Salvador in 1986 and 2001. On the bright side, weathered volcanic lavas have created fertile soils that have served to sustain dense populations in the agriculturally productive highland areas close to the Pacific coast and in the fertile Piedmont valleys, as in Costa Rica. Vulnerability to natural disasters, however, has often affected the course of events, especially when dealing with such disasters has emphasized the administrative inefficacy and corruption of public administrations. A well-known case is that of the Somozas following the 1972 earthquake. Their handling of external aid in a way that benefited them personally through illegal appropriations served the opposition by eroding their legitimacy, leading in the late 1970s to their loss of power after four decades in Nicaragua.

Next among defining traits is the comparatively small size of these territories and population. As a region, the size of Central America—including Belize and Panama—is about 202,200 square miles, or 523,700 square kilometers, about the size of France and smaller than Texas by 66,000 square miles. In theory, the political union of these territories could constitute a springboard to larger internal markets and complementary economics, greater security and coordination, and the calibrated combination of specific advantages. In spite of these possibilities, the relatively small societies of the isthmus failed to pool together resources and skills, moving instead to internal strife and political fragmentation.

During colonial times, the Audiencia de los Confines, later renamed the Captaincy General of Guatemala, was a minor part of the Spanish empire in the Americas and was administered by New Spain (Mexico). Panama was more important strategically due to the use of its ports to transfer Peruvian gold and silver across the isthmus. In relation to its functionality, the *audiencia* of Panama was administratively made part of the Viceroyalty of Peru in 1567; later on, in the eighteenth century, it was made part of the newly formed Viceroyalty of New Granada that also included Colombia, Venezuela, and great part of contemporary Ecuador.

Panama thus became separated in its own vision from the isthmus and linked to South America as part of territories soon to become Greater Colombia (1819–31) and subsequently Colombia. Moreover, the initial charisma of Simón Bolívar and the distance from Peru further reinforced this

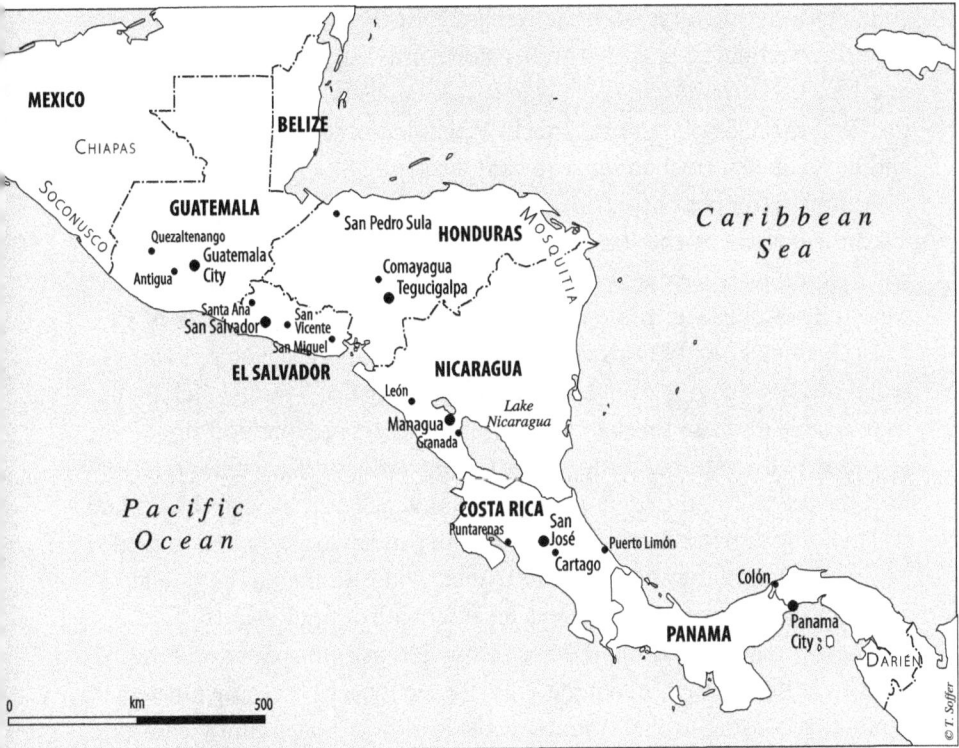

Map 2.1. Central America.

connection. It was only following its independence in 1903 and the construction of the interoceanic canal that Panama's position in the isthmus was increasingly and naturally recognized, becoming in the 1990s part of the Central American System of Integration, or SICA, a forum of membership for the countries of the region and the Dominican Republic.

Central America did not offer the advantages other territories offered the conquerors and colonial settlers. It lacked both mineral riches (with the partial exception of Honduras) and a dense indigenous population (with the partial exception of Guatemala and El Salvador) whom the settlers could dominate and coerce to provide work and tribute. This explains the somewhat dispersed character of Spanish colonial settlement, the tendency toward an economy of subsistence interspersed by short cycles of export-oriented commodities of limited territorial expansion, and the weak cross-cutting routes of land communication that in turn reinforced the centrifugal trends in the region well into modern times.

Also contributing to low levels of integration is the fact that in the comparatively small region there were at least three major pre-Columbian cultural traditions, themselves broken down into many other languages and/ or ethnic backgrounds: the pipil Nahuatl influence in the southern plains by the Pacific, the Maya cultural area in Petén and other parts of Guatemala, and the Chibcha tribal presence toward the south.

Although this plurality of social and cultural experiences may have facili- tated the control by the Iberian settlers, it created a background of spatial and cultural distance that would only be deepened once colonial structures were fully established in the isthmus. Thus, the western provinces of Chi- apas, Guatemala, and El Salvador maintained commercial relations with the realm of New Spain, particularly through the port of Veracruz, while they were unable to do so through the Caribbean coast of Honduras due to the lack of road infrastructure and security. Contrastingly, Nicaragua and Costa Rica moved within the orbit of Panama and Peru both through the sea and by land. Unsurprisingly, shortly before independence Costa Rica intended to become part of the audiencia of Panama, while Nicaragua imagined itself as an autonomous seat of audiencia together with Costa Rica.[1]

Another major trend was the sparse population of the region and the im- balance in its distribution among different sections. In the early nineteenth century, according to the "Apuntamientos sobre la agricultura y comercio del Reyno de Guatemala" (1811), the entire region of Greater Guatemala had around one million inhabitants. Of them 646,666 were Indians, 313,334 "pardos [mixed blood of African with Spanish and indigenous descent] and some Blacks" (and according to another source, also *castas* or all sorts of mixed blood), and 40,000 Spaniards or "white" inhabitants. Some of the provinces had particularly sparse populations and even narrower elite cir- cles. Toward the end of colonial rule, the population of Costa Rica numbered only about 70,000. According to a 1776 census, Nicaragua had a population of 103,943 inhabitants, composed of 45 percent Indians and 50 percent *ladi- nos*, a category involving two-thirds mulattoes and one-third mestizos. Only 5 percent were Spaniards, part of the elite.[2] Similarly, Costa Rica was sparsely populated, with 29,000 inhabitants in the seventeenth century and 63,000 in the early nineteenth century. Contrastingly, the areas of Guatemala and somehow also El Salvador, already more populated before the crystallization of colonial societies, turned into important commercial and administrative centers of political and cultural control in colonial times, with a numerical weight that persisted through the late twentieth century (table 2.1).

Being sparsely populated, the area attracted the attention of outsiders will- ing to use the "empty" territories for their own designs. For instance, in April

Table 2.1. Population of Central America 1820–2009

State	1820	1900	1950	1990	2009
Costa Rica	63,000	288,000	862,000	3,200,000	4,253,877
El Salvador	248,000	943,000	1,940,000	5,400,000	7,185,218
Guatemala	595,000	1,430,000	2,969,000	9,700,000	13,276,517
Honduras	135,000	500,000	1,401,000	5,500,000	7,833,696
Nicaragua	186,000	429,000	1,098,000	4,000,000	5,891,199
Panama	87,000	227,000	893,000	2,500,000	3,360,474
Belize	...	37,500	69,000	250,000	307,899
Central America	1,314,000	3,854,000	9,232,000	30,550,000	42,108,880

Sources: United Nations, *World Population Prospects 1988,* Population Studies no. 106, ST/ESA/SER.A/ 106 (UNO: 1989); Pérez Brignoli, *De la ilustración al liberalismo* (1993); Demyk, "Los territorios" in Taracena and Piel, eds. *Identidades nacionales* (1995), 30; *Internet World Stats,* http://www.internetworldstats.com/ stats12.htm (accessed June 10, 2010).

1861 and with his country heading to civil war, President Abraham Lincoln met with a representative of the Chiriqui Improvement Company, an enterprise founded in 1855 with the idea of colonization in Central America, in order to discuss the feasibility of sending freed slaves to Panama to settle and develop coal and farmland there. In President Lincoln's and in U.S. Postmaster General Montgomery Blair's opinion at that time, an exodus of blacks to "Intertropical America" (Central America) was the best means to end slavery and remove African Americans from the United States while extending the nation's influence in the Western Hemisphere. Foreseeing that the conflict between the Union and the Confederacy would bring about emancipation in one form or another, the Republican administration in Washington, D.C., thought this would be the best solution for the white and the black populations to remain "separated." As they tried unsuccessfully to promote this project, they promoted the idea that in Central America, African Americans could escape being a "degraded caste," would neither threaten nor compete with whites over land and work in the United States, and perhaps could also establish a "new empire . . . in Central America," as Blair said, supporting an idea first launched by Senator Samuel Pomeroy of Kansas. The plan was eventually abandoned due to the objections of Central American nations, which were fully cognizant of the structural weakness their lack of population implied.[3]

As late as 1910, the International Central American Office, charged with the promotion of regional solidarity and unity, identified the sparse population of the region as a major issue to be tackled if these societies wanted to develop. The problem was described as follows:

> In the poorly populated regions of Central America, we see also the decline of the spirit and energies of the diverse autochthonous races. The vast and solitary plains of Nicaragua, the immense deserts of Honduras, the unexplored woods of Guatemala, bordering both coasts, and the very extensive ones by the Atlantic coast of Costa Rica. . . . Like Bolivia and the other sparsely populated countries of the continent, Central America needs to populate the desert: bring immense regions until now unexplored or not cultivated within the orbit of active production and civility; connect these regions with one another, giving them good and easy ways of communication. But, over everything else, increase the number of inhabitants, since today the population [of the entire region] stands at four and a half million inhabitants, living in an area that could support twenty million inhabitants, if one adopts the population density of El Salvador as criteria.[4]

A sparse population was combined with densely knitted and compact elite circles, shaped in the framework of extractive colonial systems. What is singular, however, is that the compact nature of the elite circles did not deter them from engaging in intestine struggle. In Nicaragua the competition between the conservative city of Granada and the liberal city of León led to armed confrontations that tore apart the country and were only muted in the mid-nineteenth century, after they joined forces in evicting William Walker out of the region. At that point, conservatives and liberals took stock of the devastation they brought upon themselves by their deep division. This understanding was however short-lived, since in the early 1890s a new wave of factionalism erupted that was reminiscent of the situation in the 1820s and 1830s.

Such inner divisiveness was not absent in other parts of the isthmus, being evident also in the confrontation in El Salvador between competing urban centers such as Santa Ana, San Miguel, and San Vicente or between Comayagua and Tegucigalpa in what now is Honduras.

Yet, in parallel, there was recognition of distinct territorial domains within the region, and even the above struggles suggest mutual—although antagonistic—recognition of being part of a circumscribed area, the control of which various cities strove to attain. When delegates of Central America were nominated to the constitutional assembly of the entire Spanish realm, known as the Cortes de Cádiz in the early 1810s, the nominees came from

Guatemala, Chiapas, Honduras, El Salvador, Nicaragua, and Costa Rica, thus reflecting the distinctiveness of these "provinces" in the minds of contemporaries.[5] Even as the National Constitutional Assembly, which was convened in the isthmus in June 1823, approved the establishment of the Federation of the Center of America, uniting the provinces, the flag and shield of the new nation had as its centerpiece, in addition to republican symbols, the image of five volcanoes rising in a territory set between two oceans, thus representing the five provinces soon to split ranks as five independent and separate states of the isthmus.[6]

3

Balkanization as Formative Experience

The early nineteenth century witnessed developments of long-lasting effects in the region: the short-lived attempt of political unification followed by balkanization. These developments would turn into a formative experience, continuing to affect the historical memory and political projects of the region in later times as these societies developed their distinctiveness while at the same time were unable to completely disengage themselves from the sister republics of the isthmus.

The roots of these developments can be traced to colonial times. The Spanish colonial cities structured and divided space into territorial units within which justice and municipal jurisdiction regulated economic and social relations, attempting to construct well-defined territorial units, even if in practice there were overlapping domains and conflicting authority prerogatives.[1] Research has emphasized that at the colonial stage, cities were the materialization of spatial suzerainty, as they established the physical presence of the conquerors and settlers and created a spatial order that projected domination and was linked with social, religious, and sexual practices.[2] The construction of urban communities, epitomized in the urban grid, was geared to a hierarchical model of order that conceived cities as centers of an ever-expanding appropriation of space and control of human and material resources. Moreover, residence and membership in local communities had become a main criterion of being a native (as against a foreigner) and thus the avenue for inclusion into the broader realm, with implications for citizen control over positions of office holding, trade permits, and in general access to resources, rights, and privileges.[3]

The replication of this model with each new urban foundation and the parallel expectation of corporate supremacy prevailing in different urban centers contained the seeds of competition for recognition and control of human and material resources. Potentially, tensions could lead to open conflict whenever changes in actual supremacy or administrative jurisdictions transformed the balance of power and territorial hierarchies.

The reforms of the Spanish Bourbons in the late eighteenth century provided such trigger as they created, or at least reinforced, the centrifugal drive that would fragment Central America after independence.[4] These reforms, implemented throughout the Americas between 1759 and 1788, shifted the balance of power in the isthmus, creating new administrative jurisdictions and new criteria of spatial hegemony, which bolstered the will of secondary cities to attain autonomy from major cities and the capital of the kingdom. We should realize, however, that historical contingency and accidents of history were also at work here, as the regional capital had to be moved to a new location—la Nueva Guatemala de la Asunción—in 1775, after the old capital of Santiago de los Caballeros (Antigua) was destroyed by a series of earthquakes in the early 1770s. This transfer of spatial hegemony occurring rather late in colonial times further complicated the transition from colonial to postcolonial patterns of hegemony.

Following these reforms and the relocation of the capital, some cities gained assets and others diminished in power. The principle of urban predominance changed, shifting from a city's contribution to conquest and original status (translated in the size of territorial administrative jurisdiction) to new criteria of territorial primacy, according to which cities were ranked by population, including also non-Spaniards. This created a situation of conflicting old and new claims to urban supremacy. Moreover, only a generation later, Napoleon's invasion provided the cities a new window of opportunity to redefine their role within the administrative-political system. The principle of royal legitimacy was shattered, and authority devolved to the municipal bodies representing the localized political communities or *pueblos*, a force that had persisted underground and was recognized by Spanish political theory since the sixteenth century. An oath of allegiance to the imprisoned king also implied an opportunity to assert the claims of representation of sovereign communities unwilling to be under the jurisdiction of other urban centers, while facing the attempts by the important cities to prevent territorial fragmentation.[5]

Independence was initially attained in Central America under apparently propitious circumstances, coinciding with an economic recovery from the crisis that started in the 1790s and with the linguistic affinity of Spanish shared by all elites and without the struggle and bloodshed associated with the dissolution of the empire elsewhere throughout South America. However, the latter conditions, which seemed to be an advantage, turned into an impending factor in the development of national identity. Indeed, the lack of wars of independence from Spain, only punctuated by urban insurrections and plots, seems to have retarded a process of self-determination and definition of a common sense of collective destiny.

In the conservative strongholds of Central America and Mexico, the revolt of the Spanish brigadier Rafael del Riego in January 1820, demanding the restoration of the liberal constitution of 1812, triggered the movement to independence. King Ferdinand VII, who had abolished that constitution when he regained full power in the metropolis in 1814, was forced in 1820 to comply and swore to uphold it, ordering that it be sworn to again in all of Spain and the Spanish possessions. In the Americas, the most conservative strongholds that had resisted secession then moved to declare independence from the Spanish crown. In New Spain, Agustín Cosme Damián de Iturbide proclaimed independence in February 1821, followed by Central America's declaration of independence on September 15, 1821, issued jointly by royal representatives and the local authorities of Guatemala City. This started a process of "devolution" of sovereignty to the *pueblos* throughout the region and subsequent moves toward the reconstitution of administrative hierarchies and perhaps of unity, but in new ways. The contingent and open-ended character of the situation reveals itself in the lack of a "national" drive behind the decisions taken by the elites of the various urban settlements, which soon embarked in a move toward independence, albeit in ways that created an inbuilt and shifting tension between a de facto fragmentation and hoped-for reconstituted regional unity. As historian Jordana Dym indicates,

> Provincial capitals and villages throughout Central America responded in multiple ways to Guatemala City's declaration, which included an invitation to participate in a constituent assembly. Later in the fall, Comayagua (Honduras), Quetzaltenango (Guatemala), and León (Nicaragua) declared independence from both Spain and Guatemala, seeking separately to join Mexico. León also expressed a wish to "wait until the clouds pass" to determine its next steps. Tegucigalpa (Honduras) and Granada (Nicaragua) sought union with Guatemala and independence from Spain. Costa Rica's principal cities issued a joint declaration of independence in late October. Thus, the date recognized by all Central American nation-states as that of their independence reflects the constant tension between unity and division that prevented Central America from remaining a single political territory.[6]

In January 1822 the isthmus joined the short-lived Mexican empire of Iturbide, crowned as Emperor Agustín I. He was forced to abdicate on June 19, 1823. Five days later, a Constitutional National Assembly convened in the city of Guatemala and declared the final and "absolute" independence of the provinces of the Center of America, "recovering their rights, which have been encroached upon (*usurpados*) by their forceful union to Mexico."

The assembly decided that Central America should form a federal pact and become one nation composed of various states. For a decade and a half, between 1823 and 1838, most Central American territories constituted parts of a single state—the United Provinces of Central America, which became the Federal Republic of Central America in 1824. Simón Bolívar had envisioned such a development, as he expressed great hopes for the isthmus in his famous "Jamaica letter" (1815), in which he wrote:

> The states of the Isthmus from Panama to Guatemala will perhaps form a confederation [*una asociación*]. This magnificent location between the two great seas [oceans] could in time become the emporium of the world. Its canals will shorten the distances throughout the world, strengthen commercial ties between Europe, America, and Asia, and bring that happy region tribute from the four quarters of the globe. Perhaps someday the capital of the world will be located there, just as Constantine claimed Byzantium as the capital of the ancient world.[7]

Stretching from Chiapas in contemporary Mexico to Costa Rica, these territories were thus brought together into a single political entity by the region's liberals after a failed attempt by the conservatives to be part of Iturbide's short-lived Mexican empire. Leaders tried to consolidate the state. Yet, the United Provinces failed to construct a sense of nationhood as social and political forces wrangled with one another over the definition of the state. In the federal institutional structure, member states retained a high degree of autonomy, according to which each state would raise its own army and reproduce the union's institutional format, including electoral politics and a division of powers.

The liberals supported a federalist framework of government that would accommodate the various local networks, but they were unable to promote unity. And, once facing opposition from conservatives, they resorted to authoritarian, repressive measures rather than accommodating dissent and promoting consensus as a dynamic process evolving over time. According to Manuel Montúfar y Coronado (1791–1844), an insightful political witness and historian, the problem was the poor institutional framework, a framework built upon "political constitutions [that] have not been founded on customs or traditions, but on general theories accepted without examination and by the force of the prevailing interests of the moment." Interestingly enough, Montúfar adumbrated arguments that would remain valid for a very long time, even projected into discussions over institutional transfer of democracy in the late twentieth and early twenty-first centuries.

Writing in 1832, Montúfar foresaw that the partisanship and vindictiveness of those in power would generate a dynamic of retaliation that, creating abuse and impoverishment, would threaten the survival of the Central American Federation. His foresight is worth quoting at large:

> The results of the manner in which Central America ended its Civil War have not produced any advantage except the temporary suspension of hostilities that sooner or later will be renewed. The victors believed themselves secure with the expulsion and impoverishment of all who could oppose them; but they can't protect themselves from each other; they don't consider the opinion of the people of the State of Guatemala, who, say what you may, find themselves in a violent situation, recognize what they have lost, and do not see the happiness which they have been promised. . . . The people can eat neither theories nor beautiful principles; they remember other times, they cry for them, and when they see a banner of opposition being raised they run to it hoping it will bring back to them what they have lost.[8]

Attempting to develop their societies in the spirit of the Enlightenment, the liberals of the 1820s and 1830s enacted a series of reforms that galvanized a broad coalition of countervailing social and political forces that were to destroy the federal state. Opposition to the liberal reforms included small farmers, merchants, weavers, and artisans who suffered economic blows due to the liberal policies of opening their markets to British products, primarily manufactured textiles; Indian peasants who reacted with violence to the liberal policies threatening to change their traditional lifestyles and agreed-upon collective arrangements; village priests opposing the educational initiatives of the federal government, seen as anticlerical; and a myriad of individuals and groups resisting the abolition of the old regime's special judicial rights, or *fueros*. The enforcement of the liberal policies—with punitive measures ranging from exile to confiscation of property—backfired and led to the rise of political figures such as Rafael Carrera spearheading a conservative backlash throughout the entire isthmus. In their assessment of this process, historians tend to agree that the implementation of liberal reforms in the 1820s–1830s proved too radical a change for societies emerging from three centuries of conservative colonial rule and too intolerant of the indigenous population, providing a strong incentive for the formation of a conservative-indigenous coalition in Guatemala that would eventually unravel the union.[9]

In a context of poor communications, an economic structure of competing commodities, and the relative lack of complementary trading interests, a dynamic of increased disengagement led to the disintegration of the union. It all started in Guatemala, the richest and most densely populated state, which had been the seat of administrative and judicial authorities since colonial times. The rebellion in Guatemala was not stifled initially, as Francisco Morazán, a Honduran-born federal leader, failed to support the Guatemalan governor Mariano Gálvez, who for some time had tried to appease the local conservatives. Once Morazán reacted, it was forcefully, in an escalation of repression supported by troops of El Salvador, the liberal stronghold of the federation.

The federation then broke at one of its weakest points in terms of internal cohesion: Nicaragua seceded in 1838. The defection of Nicaragua was followed by a decision of the federal congress to allow the states to go separate ways. Morazán was forced to return to El Salvador to take the reins of power. Conservatives held power in Guatemala, Honduras, and Costa Rica, and these states also seceded. Morazán controlled only El Salvador, where he had been elected head of state. After a failed invasion of Guatemala City and facing forces opposing him in Guatemala, Honduras, and Nicaragua, Morazán was forced eventually to escape by sea into exile in Peru and Panama. In 1840 he led a renewed yet failing attempt to land forces by sea and regain power, hopeful that the British taking control of the Caribbean Mosquitia region from Nicaragua would galvanize those willing to unify Central America. When he returned two years later, he attempted once more to regain power—briefly succeeding in Costa Rica in 1842—but following a popular uprising, he was executed by a firing squad the same year.

All over Central America, conservatives with strong provincial loyalties had replaced the liberals. Rafael Carrera, the leading political actor in the region, had no intention of reuniting the countries. The countries signed a defensive pact against the federal spirit of the 1820s, vowing to maintain their individual sovereignty. It would take several decades for liberals to regain power and carry out new attempts at reunification.

The state system of Central America was thus born of dissolution and the recomposition of sociopolitical interests in different parts of the isthmus, with a major rift between El Salvador and Guatemala and secondary divisions between and within republics. Unity was focused around interests in various cities. Chiapas was pulled into the sphere of Mexican power, with the exception of a subregion, Soconusco, which remained tied to Guatemala between 1824 and 1842. Costa Rica—then a sparsely populated and poor region—oscillated between its former dependence on Panama (then part of Colombia) and the Central American sister republics. Tensions and wars over regional hegemony ensued, most noticeably in the case of Nicaragua, where León and Granada engaged in a series of protracted civil wars. Historian Jordana Dym sums up the historical process of fragmentation and fracture that led eventually to the balkanization of the region:

> [A]fter what many describe as a "peaceable and bloodless" independence, the Central American Federation suffered notable disputes in every province that would suggest fracture of states rather than their construction. The cities of Tegucigalpa and Sonsonate both sought to head independent states in the federation before agreeing to join Honduras and El Salvador. The cities of Granada and León began the first of a series of civil wars that brutalized Nicaragua almost from the moment of the federation's creation. Costa Rica, often portrayed as an exceptionally harmonious province, experienced a civil war between its four district capitals that led to the permanent relocation of the state capital from Cartago, its colonial center, to San José. A decade later, Quetzaltenango, an important city in Guatemala's hinterlands, tried repeatedly to attract neighboring districts into a breakaway state, briefly succeeding in 1838–39. In the meantime, the federal capital moved from Guatemala City to Sonsonate, San Vicente, and finally San Salvador in search of an acceptable home. Overall, the period between 1821 and 1839 was characterized by unstable state and federal governments, peripatetic capitals, and numerous military conflicts. When in 1838 the federal congress decreed that each state could withdraw from the republic should it so desire, the federation was essentially a dead letter.[10]

Such processes of dismemberment and replication of claims to sovereignty were at work throughout Iberoamerica with its lack of legitimate sovereign rulers, rooted in the restitution of sovereignty to the empowered members of localized communities.[11] Thus, for instance, the United Provinces of the Rio de la Plata in the Southern Cone underwent a similar decades-long process of fragmentation and reconfiguration that led to the redrafting of provincial and national borders of Argentina, Uruguay, and Brazil on the one hand and Argentina, Bolivia, and Paraguay on the other.[12]

There is nothing natural in such processes of dismemberment, as a comparative look at the Brazilian experience indicates. Based on its historical background and size, Brazil had a greater risk to disintegrate into regional entities. Regional sentiments and local patriotism had developed since colonial times, especially in the more economically dynamic areas such as São Paulo, Pernambuco, Minas Gerais, and Bahia, which provided fertile ground for insurrections. Many such rebellions occurred as a result of grievances and a desire for greater autonomy, among them the proclamation of Amador Bueno in São Paulo in 1641, the Pernambuco insurrection of 1645–54 and "Revolution" of 1817, the Inconfidência Mineira of 1789, and the Revolta dos Alfaiates in 1798 in Bahia.[13] In times of crisis, the centrifugal forces threatened to destroy a sense of common destiny, similarly to what happened in Central America. Unlike Central America, however, Brazil remained united throughout the transition from colonial to postcolonial times.

Such comparative perspective suggests that the decisive factor at work is not the sparse and diverse population or the regional distances and poor communications, even though these are important conditioning factors.[14] Instead, the most critical factor is the development or lack of development of a political center capable of overcoming the divisiveness of localized elites and linking them by institutional means, charisma, and coalitional structures, reinforcing the drive of those political forces working to support unity, and abiding by the political system adopted there in early independence. In Central America, it was the failure of the early liberal state to shape such drive among the localized elites that explains why, in sharp contrast with the Brazilian experience, the isthmus fragmented into separate nation-states, a process taking place in a territory more than sixteen times smaller.

In the process of fragmentation and reconstruction of commitments, even regional boundaries changed. Chiapas and later on Soconusco fell under the influence of Mexico, becoming parts of that state and ceasing to be seen and considered as parts of a isthmian identity, while Belize and Panama came to be perceived as part of the isthmus.

Being connected to South America during colonial times and the nineteenth century, Panama developed an isthmian identity as the "southernmost country of Central America" belatedly, following its independence via dissociation from Colombia in November 1903. Panama had experienced a short period of independence before, in 1840–42, and since the 1880s major sectors of the population seemed to support secession from Colombia. These feelings were exacerbated after Panama suffered by being drawn into the Colombian War of a Thousand Days (1899–1902) and after rebels from Nicaragua tried to take over Panama City in 1900.[15] Yet, as is well known, the formal independence of 1903 resulted from the U.S. wish to circumvent the

Colombian parliament's refusal to ratify the U.S. project of a trans-isthmus canal that would provide a passage for ships transiting between the Pacific and Atlantic Oceans. Since then, however, Panama has identified only partially with the rest of Central America and until recently did not join various regional bodies. Its position as an international trading center caused Panamanians to interact more with foreign powers than with most of the other countries of Central America.

The case of Belize is even more complex. The control of Belize was taken by the British from the Spaniards in late colonial times. With the immigration of settlers from the Mosquito Coast after 1787, Belize became a thriving center for Central American trading and smuggling for about three generations. The Spaniards failed to reclaim it in 1798, and their heir, the state of Guatemala, continued to demand its reincorporation into the national territory. In the mid-nineteenth century, Guatemala agreed to recognize British sovereignty over the area in return for the construction of a road from Guatemala City to the Caribbean Sea. Disagreements over where the road would end, as well as shifting British priorities, caused the project to fail. This in turn led to the Guatemalan abrogation of the treaty and to a persisting international dispute settled only in the last quarter of the twentieth century.

With the shift in economic importance from the Caribbean shore to the Pacific coast, following the emergence of trans-isthmus transportation, thinly populated Belize became more a liability for the British than a source of permanent influence in the region. Accordingly, a process of steep decline started that turned Belize City into an undeveloped and rather poor hybrid Caribbean outpost: "Belize City remained an unsavory, tropical village, with unpainted wooden houses, dirty streets, and open sewers."[16] Made a crown colony in 1862 and attaining self-government in 1870, Belize became an independent country in 1981. Even though it had threatened to attack Belize, Guatemala entered negotiations and eventually recognized Belize's autonomy, being aware that the United Kingdom guaranteed its territorial integrity. Guatemala officially recognized Belize's independence in 1991 and—after renewed disputes—finally achieved an agreement on their borders in 2002 through the mediation of the Organization of American States. With only around 300,000 inhabitants, a multicultural society, and English as an official language, this former English colony—known once as British Honduras—has joined SICA, the so-called System of Central American Integration, in addition to its membership in the Caribbean Community (CARICOM) and the British Commonwealth of Nations.

The failed project of political unification left the region balkanized, fragmented, and headed toward a process of incipient state formation. Being a very elite-based move and having failed to construct a common sense of nationhood, the project of a Central American nation was relegated to the realm of a discarded yet not completely forgotten collective experience, to be replaced by the logic of construction of distinct state boundaries, institutions, and nation building.

Photo 1. Tikal—witness of past Mayan grandeur.

Photo 2. Living traditions and cultural hybridity: a procession in Chichicastenango, Guatemala.

PALACIO
DE LOS
CAPITANES GENERALES
DEL
REYNO DE COATHEMALA
DURANTE 231 AÑOS
ESTA CIUDAD FUE LA METROPOLI
DE
CENTRO AMERICA

Photo 3. Colonial memories—Antigua (then known as Santiago de los Caballeros), capital of the kingdom of Goathemala (Central America) for 231 years.

Photo 4. State logic and nation building.

4

State Logic and Nation Building

Once separate, the nineteenth-century republics faced the dual task of consolidating their territorial control and domination while constructing a sense of collective identity through their policies, practices, and ceremonies. They had to define and create national membership and boundaries, which implied recognizing certain categories of citizenship as paramount, while replacing, ignoring, or denying—without fully eradicating—earlier forms of identification, including the pan-isthmian identity, and subsuming more localized and ethnic identities.

In Central America, as elsewhere in Spanish America, most states emerged as a consequence of imperial disintegration, in the great majority of the cases structured initially on the basis of previous colonial administrative jurisdictions. As such, states were destined to eventually create nations, attempting to "render them real" through the use of official accounts and rituals, the elaboration of hegemonic views and symbolic practices, and the structuring of images of people-hood, connected to spatial and temporal boundaries. Such strategies of nation building involved the partitioning of territories that once belonged to the same political entity, the formation of confined membership, and the delineation of borders, organized according to principles of national sovereignty.[1] The creation of nations also implicated systems of cultural representation that legitimized or delegitimized different sectors' and people's access to the resources of the nation-state.[2]

Different societies have undergone the process of nation building through different historical paths and a variety of concrete developments.[3] This process of nation building, shared in its generic traits by many states worldwide, became convoluted and protracted in Central America as the new states could hardly elicit in the population a sense of being part of an "imagined community."[4]

The complex and prolonged process of nation building in Central America was a result of many factors, with the following as most prominent: the shared colonial and early postcolonial identity; a strategy stressing the political structuring of the countries for lack of distinctive primordial identities to build separate nationalities; the improvisational character of the states representing cities interested in dominating other urban centers and enlarging the hinterland they controlled; and, as stressed by Robert Holden, the contested nature of personalistic, factional, and clientelistic politics that fueled public violence and did not allow the early consolidation of political centers with authority over the inhabitants of each state.[5]

For decades after their separation, the states of Central America could not consolidate their boundaries and seclude themselves from a dynamic of regional intervention. The interference came from factional armies and clientelistic entourages, driven by the prospects of taking power in their own home region or another region, disregarding borders and state jurisdictions. Rebels in one area were supported by allies in the neighboring states, willing to topple those in power and facilitate the rise to power of political forces sympathetic to their own designs.

What in contemporary views could be interpreted as "invasions" were at that time considered mere advances of forces willing to change constellations of power and, in some cases, define state boundaries anew. The wars that ensued were not seen as "national" wars or "anti-imperialist" wars. All political forces shared the understanding that these were internal, fratricidal wars. It will take external threats and interventions to generate a "national" interpretation of the struggle for independence. Yet, as we shall see, initially even the sense of national struggle was in fact embedded in the transnational resistance to external intervention and threats.

Moreover, overshadowing the construction of sovereign realms and separate identities were the common origins that left a legacy of cross-national networks of kinship, economic, social, and political ties and an image of an alternative project of regional nation building. Individuals could rely on such images when relocating to sister countries or challenging current institutional arrangements and political divisions. From the perspective of the symbolic enactment of separate national identities, primordiality—in the form of ethnicity or race—was secondary to the political and civic strategies adopted while constructing nationhood. From early on, elites were fully aware that local identifications existed but that at the same time there were no strong lines separating republics from one another or portraying the others as unalterably different in an incommensurable manner. Moreover, the way in which these states declared independence implied that they could not envision their collective identity as naturally given but rather as a civic accomplishment.

The construction of nation-states had to embody institutional arrangements resulting from the promulgation of agreed-upon documents representing the will of the communities or *pueblos* of the isthmus. Once established, the institutional arrangements depended on the continued will of the members of these communities and particularly on the will of leading elites to respect the promulgated charters and civic rules. Once routinized, these could be endowed gradually with transcendental meaning through the use of myths of historical origins, the cult of founding fathers and heroes, commemorative rituals, school textbooks, and recurrent practices and symbols aimed at stressing the distinctive virtues of those belonging to the national core.

In the case of the republics of the isthmus, this process of nation building was complicated due to their shared origins, the complex process of promulgation of independence, and the protracted mutual involvement of each state in the affairs of its neighbors. This set of factors made it hard to even promulgate clear-cut joint or separate independence dates. Accordingly, even establishing the date of independence has often been a source of dissent in the isthmus, as illustrated by debates in El Salvador. The September 15 (1821) act contained an invitation to the provinces of Central America to declare their independence from Spain, joining Guatemala, which the provinces did at various dates during the following months, including the swift decision by San Salvador, expressed on September 21, 1821. After the temporary annexation of the Central American territories to the Mexican empire, a new declaration of independence was promulgated on July 1, 1823, raising the question of whether the 1821 decision had been a move to independence. In the 1920s the government of El Salvador declared the date of July 1 a national fiesta, in remembrance of the declaration of 1823, a relatively late recognition. Likewise, debate continued on the identification of September 15 as the day of independence, involving various contentious issues such as the limited involvement of inhabitants beyond the city of Guatemala and the existence or nonexistence of the federation as a living reality.[6]

Similarly, the shared origins precluded the total erasure of common symbols, as reflected in the national shields of several of these countries, which even today reflect their common origins in the image of the five mountains, symbolically representing the founding sections of the failed Central American federation. I should stress, however, that recognition of the origin of the symbols has been lost to many in contemporary society. In December

2006, in the city of Antigua, Guatemala, I entered a municipal office close to the central square of the town and saw a wooden shield of the Central American federation hung on the wall. To test the current recognition of the history behind the symbol, I inquired of the two employees occupying that office about the significance, origin, or character of the shield. They looked surprised and, to my own dismay, were unable to articulate a single explanation about what this shield, with the five volcanoes symbolizing the five original countries of the nineteenth-century federation, represented. By the late twentieth century, the process of separation had crystallized and become part of popular representations. However, this was a long and protracted process that needs to be reconstructed along with countervailing yet failing attempts to reshape the Central American union (photos 5 and 6).

Once separate, states moved to consolidate their control over territories and populations and construct a distinct sense of collective identity through their narratives, policies, and practices. Following their separation, each

Photo 5. Nation building and beyond: traces of transnationalism in a Guatemalan shield.

Photo 6. Nation building and beyond: traces of transnationalism in a Nicaraguan shield.

country had to develop strategies of state control, institutional consolidation, and nation building that while conditioned by material resources and oriented by certain political visions, had to be articulated symbolically into constructing collective, national identities. The next two chapters will trace some of these strategies in detail, showing how they developed along transnational counter-currents. I start with a discussion of the creative process of construction of national identities, which was delayed in the isthmus, with important consequences for the institutional and social development of these societies. This assessment is complemented subsequently by an analysis of the political and economic foundations of state development in the region. Together, the two chapters provide hindsight on the process led by the balkanized states to develop as discrete nations. Such inquiry is guided by the conviction that research should pay equal attention to the political and economic foundations of these states *and* to their strategies of constructing collective identities. According to the approach followed in this work, research should not gloss over the creative process of nation building within a material or merely political reading of interests, while certainly recognizing the crucial importance of the material and political capabilities conditioning the legitimacy of the states' narrative constructions and symbolic articulation.

5

Breaking Apart and Constructing Collective Identities

Societies construct collective identities in diverse ways, involving a process of symbolic creation and reconstruction crafted to denote the shared experience and orientations that may unite the members and set them apart from others. The images societies construct and the stories they tell about themselves are crucial in representing who they are and in catalyzing feelings and emotions. They are equally crucial in crystallizing the group's consciousness and motivating individuals to identify with collective visions and aims. Condensed in key symbols and artifacts—such as flags, shields, and national anthems—these images acquire a presence of their own and a representational power that can be projected across time, shaping the visions and collective memory of future generations, albeit with an enormous variability among and within nations and groups.[1]

In Germany since the eighteenth century, the nation was represented as a *kulturnation*, the locus of a transcendental realm of sublime essences and forces of history, or as a sublime operator of historical action, in romantic ways that predated the process of state construction and nation building undertaken by Otto von Bismarck in the late nineteenth century. By then, the romantic idealization had led to a blood-and-soil-related nationality discourse that later on, under Nazism, assumed extreme primordial overtones leading to genocide and the Holocaust.[2] Contrastingly, in Japan, primordiality was given priority and was considered almost divine although not in the terms of a transcendental or universal mission, as was the case in the monotheistic religions and civilizations.[3] The case of Central America, however, differs from either of these.

The political and intellectual elites of the isthmus—with the possible exception of Costa Rica—could not easily romanticize their historical origins, in which power competition, domination, and fragmentation were typical developments. The elites could not assume primordiality as central for the construction of their collective identity, since their hierarchical social visions predicated cultural subjugation of internal ethnic and cultural groups that were bearers of distinctive primordial identities. Unsurprisingly, the new states gave priority to civil-political principles, which superseded and often even neglected the ethnic diversity of their populations. Furthermore, independence was attained without major heroic sacrifices and "hallowed grounds" that could be celebrated in poetry, ballads, holidays, monuments, or pantheons for fallen martyrs. Relying on civic markers, elites were entangled halfway between a pure factionalist contest for power and the need to construct a commitment to new nations with no distinctive origins, primordiality, or historical transcendence. Moreover, the states had to develop a sense of their distinctiveness by projecting idiosyncratic narratives, practices, and images as the legitimating basis for their claims.

The systematic analysis of how the various polities of the isthmus managed to construct and reshape the collective identities of their "imagined nations" is still much before us, even though research has provided illuminating guidelines.[4] The politics of identity and structuring of collective memory is central to the analysis of Consuelo Cruz contrasting the experience of Nicaragua and Costa Rica in this domain. In her work, Cruz draws attention to the distinct processes of these two isthmus societies through the analysis of the rhetorical frames that were constructed, a process that started in colonial times and fully unfolded after independence. These frames are those that—in the anthropological sense—these societies "told themselves about themselves," projecting them as credible stories of collective character upon which their citizens could rely as they envisioned their present actions and future endeavors.[5]

These frames constituted, in Clifford Geertz' terms, a model of and a model for society. That is, the images projected constituted concomitantly a description of behavioral patterns and status symbols as well as a blueprint for action, an organizing model on which functional roles and institutions could be modeled.[6] Cruz shows that the narratives shaped in colonial times pervaded the historiographies and the sense of self-representation and collective memory of these societies, which in turn affected subsequent policy options, allowing or disallowing strategies of persuasion on the basis of their presumptive realism and normative sway. In this manner,

> [t]he Costa Ricans' frame upheld as truth the claim that they were, both
> by reputation and in fact, an inherently peaceable and diligent people.
> This frame, in turn, restricted the intensity and scope of political debate

and struggle, creating in the process sufficient space for intra-elite consensus building and, ultimately, the political stability necessary to craft and execute developmental policies. In the case of postcolonial Nicaragua, the argument is exactly the reverse. The rhetorical frame that triumphed there generated a set of negative expectations that created incentives among political rivals for *preemptive, particularist* bids, thus closing off space for effective developmental leadership. The upshot of all this was the emergence of distinct national identities and equally distinct collective fields of imaginable possibilities—one as "civic" and optimistic as the other was "anarchic" and fatalistic.[7]

Nicaraguan elites had been weakened in early colonial times following their rebellious defiance of the Laws of Burgos and the murder of the local bishop, which were incorporated into the official monarchical record as historical indication of their anarchical character. Such weakened position led to the absence of later political and cultural figures attempting to dislodge the memories of anarchy and tyranny associated with their society during conquest and incorporated as part of the official chronicles of the Conquest. Moreover, these images turned into part of the self-representation of Nicaraguan elites for generations to come, reinforcing their orientations toward choosing competition for power over mechanisms prioritizing the construction of consensus and compromise that could be instrumental for effective nation building.

Nicaraguans engaged in a locally driven contest for power that threatened to destroy the state time and again and failed to lead a shared process of nation building for decades, while Costa Rican political elites managed to forge out of conflict—also present there—a foundational compromise, known as the Pact of Harmony (1821). The pact provided for an itinerant national government in which high officials would reside in each of the country's four major cities for part of every year. By sharing prestige and state power among Cartago, San José, Heredia, and Alajuela and projecting the vision of harmony onto the collective imaginary, Costa Rica was able to avoid the destructive cycle of internal war that tore apart some of its neighbors. Even as San José became the capital in 1823 after a short confrontation with the forces of the old colonial capital Cartago, the pact remained the emblem of that country's exceptionally peaceful transition to the national era, "even taking on a numinous quality not unlike that of the U.S. Constitution."[8]

This will to compromise was both the result and the foundation of a collective vision promoted by elites that encompassed recognition of the country's peripheral status and their people's unique capabilities for future prosperity, provided they would follow the path led by their colonial ancestors:

> In 1822 the country's first governing junta declared peace to be "virtually innate" to Costa Ricans because their colonial ancestors had adhered to a "sacred religion" that consisted of a "characteristic unity of opinion and calm." The first chief of state (1824–33) helped bolster this assertion, as did the State Assembly. The legislature declared that while Costa Ricans were "poor," riches were in store for them because they were "industrious," "calm," and "patriotic." [And] the executive vowed to "draw" on the "virtues, morality, and good sense" of his compatriots.

Furthermore,

> while in the rest of Central America clashes between these two branches of government over institutional predominance often led to war, in Costa Rica the branches outdid each other in their praise of the Costa Rican "people." But they did more. In 1825, they set out to provide the country's "virtuous people" with land, via their first agrarian reform.[9]

Contrastingly, Nicaraguans became entangled in logics of mutual distrust and disbelief in themselves, which reinforced time and again vicious cycles of internal divisiveness, civil war, and mutual annihilation. This self-perception was projected well into the twentieth century, as illustrated by the writings of cultural critics and authors. Paradigmatic is perhaps the renowned nationalist essayist and poet Pablo Antonio Cuadra (1912–2002), who often lamented the deceitful "nature" of the Nicaraguan individuals.[10] With the passing of time, these internal theories were canonized and projected as explanatory factors for the lack of development of a country endowed with considerable resources, undermined by the fractured character of its political and economic elite. The effects of such distinct visions on the country's development did not go unnoticed in research, as can be seen in recent analyses:

> Nicaragua is potentially one of the richest countries in Central America, with abundant arable land, considerable hydroelectric, thermal and (possibly) fossil energy resources, and significant timber and mineral resources. It also has access to two oceans and a lake and river system that could make it an ideal site for an inter-oceanic waterway. Yet Nicaraguans today are among the poorest Central Americans and Latin Americans. . . . Nicaragua's perennially fractured political and economic elite continue to fail to advance the country's development.[11]

The process of construction of distinct collective ("national") identities gained momentum in the mid- to late nineteenth century, when the region witnessed external threats and interventions. A major external intervention triggering such development was the case of the entire region facing the rise of William Walker and his private army of North American *filibusteros* (freebooters) taking control of Nicaragua in the 1850s.

Walker's intervention led to a war that was fought by what today we would define as a "transnational" alliance of nationals of various isthmian countries against Walker, while paradoxically—or perhaps not, since it fit the logic of state claims, advanced in parallel by several of the isthmian states—such war became known in isthmian historiography as "the National War." The transnational dimension of the struggle was so evident that its symbolic appropriation in terms of the emerging images of nationhood was done in a plural fashion and could not completely obliterate the transnational angle as an underlying current of narrative and symbolic representation. In such manner, the fight against Walker only rekindled once again the tension-ridden process of disengagement of the states and embedded the history of these nations within the persisting transnational dimension of their existence in the isthmus.

Born in 1824 to a fundamentalist family in Tennessee, Walker had been educated in medicine and law and had practiced journalism in New Orleans. The untimely death of his fiancée led to a radical change in his life that would take him to California and then by 1853 bring him to participate in filibustering expeditions in Sonora and later on, Central America. After gaining independence, Nicaragua had been involved in endless fighting between liberals, with a stronghold in the city of León, and conservatives, with their center in Granada. Facing a rising tide of conservatism led by Rafael Carrera in Guatemala, Nicaraguan liberals called in North American adventurers to their cause, promising them generous land grants.

Under contract with the liberals, Walker and 57 Californians arrived in the region and were reinforced by 170 locals and about 100 Americans upon landing. Initially, he suffered defeat by forces led by a conservative commander from Honduras, but due to parallel defeats of other liberal commanders, he managed to rise as commanding officer, taking over the city of Granada. This opened the door to his recognition as chief of the armed forces under Patricio Rivas and eventually led to his becoming head of state of Nicaragua. By executing and exiling opponents, he controlled the country and was elected president in June 1856. Walker's agents recruited over a thousand American and European men to sail to the region and fight for the conquest of the other four Central American republics.[12]

This move would galvanize the resistance of Central American states. Moreover, by aligning himself with railroad and shipping capitalists Cornelius Garrison and Charles Morgan in their competition with Commodore Cornelius Vanderbilt for control of the company that secured the only major trade route from New York to San Francisco through Nicaragua, Walker made an enemy of Vanderbilt. Vanderbilt supported the military coalition of Central American states led by Costa Rica, prevented supplies and men from reaching Walker, pressured the U.S. government to withdraw Walker's recognition as the Nicaraguan power holder, and gave North American defectors free passage to the United States.

Walker managed to gain control of Nicaragua by the mid-1850s, but he was soon thrown from power in a struggle that would become immortalized also as the "War of Independence" in Nicaraguan and Central American historiography and served as a substitute for the war of independence that Central America never experienced.[13] By May 1857, Walker had surrendered to the U.S. Navy and was repatriated. Subsequent attempts by Walker to regain power in Central America failed and led to his imprisonment by the British, who controlled the Caribbean coast of Honduras. The British handed Walker over to the Honduran government, which executed him in September 1860.

The fight to oust Walker became a source of collective pride and was portrayed as a cornerstone of national identity in more than one country of the region. This struggle against Walker also carried transnational connotations that emphasized Central American solidarity and patriotism. The built-in tension between nation building and transnationalism was thus encoded symbolically in the re-creation and commemorations of this historical event, instrumental in the construction of collective identity.

In Costa Rica, April 11 became one of the key national holidays, commemorating the battle of Rivas in 1856 in which a makeshift army of Costa Rican peasants chasing Walker defeated him at the locality of Rivas, Nicaragua, thus beginning the decline of Walker's power that culminated in his eventual surrender to the U.S. navy. Juan Santamaría, a young drummer from Alajuela, Costa Rica, volunteered to burn the wooden fort of Rivas, thereby forcing Walker and his men outside the fort where they had taken refuge. Santamaría, who immolated himself to burn the fort, was an overlooked hero at the time. Yet, beginning in the late 1880s and continuing officially in 1891, this illegitimate mulatto son was made into a national hero. A statue of Santamaría depicting a strong and handsome soldier carrying a torch was placed in Alajuela, and Rubén Darío, the great Nicaraguan writer, wrote a poem immortalizing his memory. Today, Santamaría's heroism is taught in schools, and his sacrifice is eulogized and celebrated by the children of Costa Rica in commemorative performances.

Unsurprisingly, the story of the opposition to Walker has been equally central to the construction of an "imagined national community" in Nicaragua. Promoted by historians and politicians, the struggle was portrayed in the country as a war fought by Nicaraguan patriots and joined by the armies of neighboring states, thus giving it a national interpretation without completely obliterating the themes of Central American solidarity and transnational patriotism.

There were many Central American leaders who were involved in the struggle against Walker. A look at one such leader, Nicaraguan General José Dolores Estrada, provides insight into how the conscious appropriation of symbols and creation of tradition in the service of national imagery occurred and how this glorified the state as the repository of the values of the Nation. On September 14, 1856, then Colonel Estrada commanded a force of 120 to 160 men that clashed with a force of "more than 200" led by Walker's friend Byron Cole at the Hacienda San Jacinto. Estrada's forces defeated them, which triggered a reversal in Walker's fortunes and—according to Nicaraguan historiography—diminished his chances of controlling Nicaragua.

Estrada was born to a respected family in a small Nicaraguan town, part of what could be defined as the oligarchy of the place, and grew up in Granada. He fought the Spaniards and then moved to Managua, where he became a well-known figure in social and political circles, participating in various rebellions. After the fight against Walker, he continued to be active in politics and was exiled to Costa Rica from 1863 to 1867. He returned to Nicaragua when an amnesty was declared but passed away in 1869 at the age of seventy-seven. While alive, Estrada organized private meetings of comrades and friends every September 14 to commemorate the battle of San Jacinto. After he died, his friends continued the tradition. A few years later, state authorities decided to officially adopt the September 14 commemoration and to make it a public celebration. The event was planned in all its details. After making a visit to the house of Estrada's sister, the dignitaries would continue to the Palacio Nacional to make a toast in the memory of the deceased hero, inviting all those men who had accompanied Estrada and were still alive to join the president, ministers, heads of the army, and notables for a toast and speeches to eulogize and pay honor to Estrada's memory.

A man of oligarchic origins, Estrada was thus officially appropriated by the state and transformed into a folk hero. In the process he was transformed into a public figure of popular background. Estrada became one of the people, full of humility and patriotism and ready to make sacrifices for *la patria*, the fatherland.

At the same time, Estrada's background as a son of Granada was downplayed. His home city, Granada, had been involved in the fratricidal wars that led to the involvement of foreign mercenaries like Walker in the internal affairs of Nicaragua. Instead, Estrada was increasingly portrayed as "the notable son of Managua," the city named as capital precisely to overcome the irreconcilable antagonism of Granada and León. This symbolic transformation of Estrada took place less than a generation after the war. After the promulgation of the constitution of 1858, a period of decline of intra-elite struggle was initiated, thus enabling the downplaying of a localized reading of Estrada's background.

Ceremonies commemorating September 14 began to be celebrated in all *pueblos*, cities, and towns on the eve of the declaration of independence of the Central American republic as a kind of second independence, this time of the Republic of Nicaragua.

The battle became a timely means of constructing collective—national—identity in a society that until Walker's invasion could not claim to have fought a war of independence and had no fallen heroes to mourn in order to claim a line of historical continuity connecting contemporary citizens to the sacrifices of its founding fathers, as in other lands that fought to gain their independence from the royalists. September 14 thus became the surrogate event for the war of independence lacking in 1821. According to a speech by the minister of foreign affairs of Nicaragua, Anselmo H. Rivas, delivered on September 15, 1873,

> Central America did not take part in that glorious war [of independence]. Here we don't have veterans of independence [wars] as in Colombia or Mexico, whom we could present to our youth in order to impregnate them with the selfless feelings that motivated the heroes' accomplishments. I wish the legacy of our fathers would have been some costly sacrifices! Then we could have spared our precious heritage with more sense than that which drove us to dilapidate it in fratricidal wars so harmful as unjustifiable! . . . The Fatherland has [finally] understood that the powerful weapon to fight these two enemies of its well-being is the patriotism of his sons; and to promote it, has established this civic occasion [the battle of San Jacinto] so that, while

remembering the heroic virtues of the American patriots, the youth should be encouraged to follow in their footsteps.[14]

Since then, September 14 (1856) and September 15 (1821) became linked to create a common historical past and to dilute the localisms still lingering at that time. Likewise, and as could be expected, this constructive process glossed over but could eradicate the tensions existing between national narratives and previous interpretations of the nation as anchored in a transnational realm. These different interpretations and narratives continued to coexist, albeit with changes in their relative saliency in different states and times. Thus, while analyzing the political lexicon of annual addresses by Costa Rican presidents between 1821 and 1949, Víctor Hugo Acuña Ortega found that until 1847–48 the terms of nation and republic were used to characterize Central America, with the use of province and state reserved for Costa Rica. Furthermore, the idea of the unity of Central America as needed and as the inevitable result of historical destiny continued to be promulgated repeatedly in presidential addresses from 1861 to 1921, along with the simile of the Central American family.[15] Contrastingly for Nicaragua, Patricia Fumero Vargas has found that during the early 1870s there was an increasing mention of independence in texts alluding to September 14, a similar rise in mentions of the independence of Nicaragua, and a less pronounced growth of mentions of Central American independence in speeches devoted to September 15.[16]

The experience of that war was highly important for the process of construction and reshaping of national and transnational identities in the region. Political centers promoted ceremonial traditions that served to commemorate the heroic deeds of the recent past as well as to recognize the vision and progress of the countries and in the case of Nicaragua, the military capacity of its armed forces. The Central American experience clearly fits in this regard within Eric Hobsbawn and Terence Ranger's analysis of invented traditions, Shmuel N. Eisenstadt and Bernhard Giesen's analysis of construction of collective identities, and Anthony Smith's studies of naturalization of historical events.[17]

That experience has the additional aspect of projecting a persistent tension between the redefinition of state boundaries and the reformulation of the meaning of the "national," thus re-creating the transnational dimension of politics, now from beyond the discrete state boundaries that crystallized by the late nineteenth century.

The war was rapidly appropriated symbolically as a "National War," but in spite of its name, it had been fought by armies from all over the region and across state borders, thus ensconcing persisting transnational threads, even as these nations entered new phases of state consolidation. The very character of the confrontation could not erase the transnational dimension that became projected into the next stages by the very fact that the war could be claimed in parallel by various states, so that its transnational character was projected into the rhetoric and memory of future generations, even in cases when this was officially discouraged.

6

Breaking Apart

Political and Economic Foundations

The ways in which states develop hinge in crucial ways on their institutional capacity to intervene in society, regulating political associational space and the flow of material and human resources, raising taxes, distributing benefits, regulating markets, and controlling the use of natural resources. High-capacity governments are effective in this regard, while low-capacity governments may try to carry out these functions, but they have little effect.[1] The political and economic foundations of state construction are thus crucial as we assess the capacity of the Central American states to establish viable strategies of institution building and governance in the region.

In the case of Central America, the existence of multiple independent centers of power within the same region, together with the consciousness of shared history and relations, added instability to the regional balance of power and political alliances. Reviewing the political and economic foundations of these states, we see persisting transnational pressures in political life and public spheres as well as waves of intervention of one state in the others, a process further rekindled by the emergence of transnational initiatives and movements in the early twentieth century. In other words, in tracing the paths of separation of the states in Central America, research traces also the intricate and subtle involvement of most states in the destinies of the other states and the recurrent though intermittent development of transnational networks and movements as trends that remained a major defining characteristic of Central American politics and society throughout the nineteenth-century and in different forms in the twentieth century as well.

Transnational connections remained salient in many domains long after the federal republic of Central America was torn apart. For several decades after independence, it was not uncommon for presidents and leading civil servants to have been born in neighboring states. For instance, Juan Lindo, president of El Salvador in 1841–42, was Honduran (he later served also as president of Honduras between 1847 and 1852). Likewise, Morazán, also a Honduran, was briefly head of state of Costa Rica in 1842, after being head of state of the Federation of Central America until 1839 and of the Republic of El Salvador from 1839 to 1840. Similarly, prominent public figures served almost concomitantly or subsequently as civil servants of several states of the isthmus.

Paradigmatic is the case of Lorenzo Montúfar, a liberal politician, attorney, teacher, historian, and drafter of the Guatemalan constitution commissioned by General Justo Rufino Barrios in 1879. Due to his intellectual stature and his vocal opposition to the Catholic Church, Montúfar became known as the Mirabeau and the Voltaire of Central America. Montúfar was born in Guatemala, but his career took him to many Central American countries. He served four times as minister of foreign affairs: twice of Guatemala and twice of Costa Rica. Montúfar was also the minister of public instruction as well as the Guatemalan diplomatic representative in Spain and Washington. He served as diplomatic representative of Costa Rica in El Salvador and representative of El Salvador in Peru.[2] Interestingly, another leading member of the Barrios cabinet was Ramón Rosa, who was also a Honduran. As Steven Palmer notes, "Leading liberals in the Barrios cabinets came from neighboring Central American countries, though, like their predecessors of the independence period, they had called Guatemala City their home since arriving in the 1860s as young students at the University of San Carlos."[3]

In addition to the cross-border background of prominent leaders and intellectuals, a lack of clear-cut boundaries was long evinced by the spread of influence in the public affairs of neighboring republics, sometimes in sharp contradiction to the process of distinct state-building. Combined armies of regulars and insurgents were common throughout the isthmus, bringing governing factions, neighboring insurgent factions, and political exiles together into strategic alliances aimed to unsettle rivals and place sympathetic rulers in power. Militias and armies crossed formal borders frequently, either driven by self-interest or called into action by a neighboring leader.[4] For example, in 1825, when Manuel José Arce took office as president of the republic he closed congress and the rest of the Guatemalan liberals fled to El Salvador. Liberals in El Salvador and Honduras then took up arms against Arce, which forced him to resign in 1828.[5] Likewise, in the 1830s and 1840s it was not uncommon for cities in Honduras to place themselves under the protection of the governments of Guatemala and El Salvador.[6]

The counter-current of distinct state consolidation took increasing precedence with the passing of time. In the heyday of the liberal period, territorial control and nation building went hand in hand, gearing the projects of national development to institution building and structural differentiation. Carlos Sandoval-García has stressed these linked processes for the case of Costa Rica:

> Between 1883 and 1920, the number of provinces went from five to seven and counties increased from twenty-nine to fifty-six. The number of police stations rose from 61 in 1890 to 102 in 1900 and to 257 in 1920. The development of the telegraph and post offices also favored integration. Between 1885 and 1910, the number of communities linked by mail services rose from twenty-seven to forty-three. Meanwhile the number of locations connected by telegraph increased from 28 in 1887 to 102 in 1910. The reforms in the educational system, the increase in newspapers as well as the foundation of other public institutions and monuments . . . were other important processes of nation building.[7]

Similarly, Steven Palmer has pointed out that between 1881 and 1897 there was an impressive official effort to permeate society with institutions and images geared to the creation of the collective identity of Costa Rica as a nation. As Palmer shows, this was a significant transformation:

> San José saw the establishment of the National Archive, the National Library, the National Theater, the National Park and the National Monument. The latter consecrates the National War of 1856–57, recovered in the 1880s as a substitute war of independence. Out of those who died, the state relieves from oblivion Juan Santamaría, a day-worker and illegitimate son, rediscovered as national subject starting in 1885 and beatified in 1891 with a statue in Alajuela, his native city. This is the period of ethical or instructional functions of the Liberal state, with its administrative and educational reforms. The flourishing journalism of the decade witnesses [the development of] a national historiography in its pages and, a few years later, a national literature. We can add to this list the creation of an image of a National Race. . . . Starting in the 1880s, the Costa Rican Liberals denied emphatically any racial differentiation within the national population and they talked of . . . a "homogenous race." Stressing this homogeneity became one of the principal goals of the Liberal ideologues in the next twenty years.[8]

Sooner or later, this institutional process took place in all the states of the isthmus, mainly in the second half of the nineteenth century and early twentieth

Table 6.1. Institution building and development

Institution	Guatemala	El Salvador	Honduras	Nicaragua	Costa Rica
National archive	1846	1870	1880	1882	1881
National library	1859	1870	1880	1880	1888
National theater	1859	1875	1916	1882	1897
First postal stamp	1871	1869	1865	1862	1863
Statistical office	1873	1881	1880	n.a.	1864
First census	1880	1878	1881	1906	1864
Telegraph	1873	1870	1877	1875	1868
Electricity	1883	n.a.	1899	n.a.	1884
Telephone	1884	1888	1891	1887	1878
Railroads	1880	1876	1877	1876/84	1873
First high school	1875	1861	1878	1874	1874
Military academy	1872	1888	1878	1928	1886
National museum	1898	1883	1898	1896	1881

Source: Based with additions on Acuña Ortega, ed., *Las repúblicas agro-exportadoras (1870–1945)*, (1993), 403.

century, a process schematically shown in table 6.1. Nonetheless, even as this process of institution building contributed to the creation of a sense of convergence between the state and the idea of the nation, transnational politics did not disappear and remained as crucial as ever. To retain control of a government, ruling elites often had to shift the balance of power by intervening in the neighboring countries. Likewise, even if unwilling to intervene beyond their borders, only seldom were these states able to seclude themselves from developments in the other "sister nations," as any such development could have trans-state consequences and perhaps trigger an intervention in the realm and territory they considered theirs.

Accordingly, it was not uncommon that presidents were imposed by the stronger states on the weaker states of the isthmus. Guatemala, Nicaragua, and El Salvador intervened in Honduras, making and deposing presidents for seven decades. It seemed only natural that Guatemala's president Justo Rufino Barrios (1873–85), who dreamt of reuniting Central America under his leadership and the liberal banner, instated Marco Aurelio Soto—a Honduran who had served him as minister of foreign affairs—as president of Honduras (1876–83). Similarly, transnational involvement characterized the juncture of Honduras and Nicaragua in the 1890s. In 1893, Policarpio Bonilla had become president of Honduras (1893–99) through the combined use of his own militias and the support of the military forces that had placed General José Santos Zelaya in the presidency of Nicaragua. In 1896, as a coalition of Honduran émigrés and a former collaborator of Zelaya tried to overthrow the Nicaraguan president, Bonilla sent two thousand Honduran soldiers to Nicaragua to help Zelaya stay in power. The Honduran president was fully aware that, if successful, after deposing Zelaya, the Nicaraguan rebels would likely follow to help Honduran insurgents in overthrowing Bonilla's government.[9] In 1906 Nicaraguan president José Santos Zelaya sent once again armed forces to Honduras to join a liberal uprising, in order to install a government indebted to him and thus move closer to achieving his transnational political designs.

All these were most likely moves in a region with permeable frontiers in which state borders had little deterring significance. Political exiles often joined forces with the host country's factions to regain positions of power in their home countries. Power holders supporting them expected to redesign the balance of power in the region. Aspiring chieftains moved across borders to launch attacks in unison with neighboring factions, which eventually would be called to assist them in their own factional wars at home.

With the separate states' apparatus lacking governing capacity, efficacy, and often also charisma, a requisite of successful political centers and leaders, as analyzed by Max Weber, Edward Shils, and Shmuel Eisenstadt, political actors continued to rely on power calculations and traditional morality. While there was recognition of the centrality of power, usually it was not connected to voluntary recognition of the exceptional qualities of leaders, which could trigger "personal devotion, arising out of enthusiasm, or of despair and hope," to quote from the classic definition of Weber.[10] Rather, recognition of power domains arose out of personalized interests to build patron-client networks driven to fight competing clientelistic factions and gain access to resources and positions of power from which to master such access.[11] At any point in time, some of these clientelistic networks were more or less able to control the state and its resources through the use of public force. Most of them, however, were unable to institutionalize a political center that could generate long-lasting commitment around a basic set of values while reflecting the inhabitants' desire for meaning, consistency, and orderly social life.

Accordingly, the isthmus witnessed periods of prolonged unrest and civil strife interspersed with periods of repressive control by power holders deemed successful due to their ability to suppress actual and emergent contenders for power.

In the background of these power struggles was a principled awareness of the common origins and, for some sectors willing to rekindle it, the vision of the different nations as "brotherly peoples," part of one fatherland. This underlying symbolic and rhetorical thread can be clearly identified in the lyrics to the "Anthem to Centro America," written by the Guatemalan poet Rafael Arévalo Martínez. The lyrics of this anthem, which was sung until the late twentieth century along with the Guatemalan national anthem in Guatemalan schools, are as follows:

> And that together the friendly hands
> And one Oh, Fatherland! your five nations
> Should have as emblem in your new legions
> The fertile olive alone . . .
> The sweet word of brother should resound,
> The flag of union should beat the air,
> Five fingers forming one hand
> Should highly wave a scepter of honor.[12]

On the institutional plane there persisted—with ups and downs—an openness in the criteria for membership and access to top administrative positions. Paradigmatic was the trend regarding citizenship and positions established under General Barrios as head of state of Guatemala. The constitution of Guatemala, commissioned and drafted by Lorenzo Montúfar in 1879, permitted to grant Guatemalan citizenship to any individual of the other four republics who resided in the country unless he wanted to retain a different nationality (article 6) as well as entitled any citizen of the five nations of Central America to accede to the presidency of Guatemala (article 65). Furthermore, professionals of the sister nations would have their titles recognized in Guatemala, provided they were approved by the proper authorities.[13]

The transnational trend and spillover effect described here was still in full evidence in the early twentieth century. Yet, by then, a sense of nation-state identity had been shaped, making it harder for cross-national access to power or transnational interventions to continue unabated. Illustrative is the case of Honduran President Francisco Bertrand (1913–19). As he tried to impose his brother-in-law Nazario Soriano as his successor, the political opposition was energized in fighting the decision—triggering a civil war—because Soriano was a resident of El Salvador.

The process of breaking apart implied certain economic foundations that conditioned the institutional sustainability of the different states. As subsistence agriculture remained the most important economic activity throughout the region, the independent states envisioned their inclusion in an international division of labor as providers of agricultural and primary products. The countries had neither the capital, technology, and entrepreneurship nor the skills needed to industrialize and wanted to take advantage of the demand for primary products in industrializing countries, providing them with agricultural and other primary commodities in exchange for manufactured goods.

By the mid-nineteenth century Central American states had started this pattern of development and were increasingly dependent on international, overseas trade. Consequently, links between neighboring countries weakened as states developed their economies in parallel to each other. In the *Historical Atlas of Central America*, Carolyn Hall and Héctor Pérez Brignoli indicate that starting in this period "political fragmentation was matched by economic separation as each state reoriented its international trade toward north-western Europe and North America" and "all the routes opened after independence either traversed the isthmus or linked the interior and coastal regions of individual states; none followed the old axis of the Camino Real [colonial Royal Road], linking neighboring states."[14] Some regional trade did still exist in 1850, significantly the sale of cattle from Nicaragua and Honduras to El Salvador and Guatemala, but this trade was only of secondary macro-economic importance when compared to international trade. In the case of Honduras, in addition to cattle sent to Cuba and other Caribbean islands and hardwoods sent to Belize, by the 1850s silver had replaced gold as the main mineral export sent to England and the United States.[15] Notably, Costa Rica and Panama developed new commercial ties independent of the other Central American states due to their relative isolation and secluded orientation.

Increasingly, Central American states relied on overseas trade, mostly with European countries, while the trade within the region remained minimal. This pattern of development did not necessarily energize state development on a countrywide ("national") level, especially where—as seen in Honduras—foreign investments were secured by concessions, tax exemptions and strongly reduced taxes on import-export duties. Overseas economic ties also went hand in hand with the foreign control of transportation and trade circuits. The foreign control of transportation and trade created economic enclaves that did not contribute to the integration of the countries and did not promote relations with each other.

The best roads ran from the capitals and producing areas to the ports, while interstate routes remained impassable. Instead of developing an interdependence which might have contributed to more sincere unionist sentiment, the states actually became more separatistic. . . .

Foreign control of internal transportation . . . was principally dedicated to convoying export commodities to deep-water ports. . . . Guatemala and El Salvador are the only Central American states connected to each other by rail. . . . Likewise, while steamer service connected all of the states with the United States and Europe . . . it was often difficult, if not impossible, to get service from one Central American country to another, or between ports along the coast. . . . [M]odern transportation improvements, which might have brought the states closer together, instead seemed to emphasize their separateness. Only in recent years has there been inexpensive bus service between the states.[16]

The process of separatism and widening the gap between the countries fit the goals of the British, who were not interested in a united federation but rather in gaining a hegemonic presence in the isthmus, specifically on the Caribbean coasts. After 1821 Britain, which already had an important trading presence through smuggling, replaced Spain as the major economic partner of the isthmus.

Unsurprisingly, the British had backed the conservative forces, opposing U.S. diplomacy, because the United States was more sympathetic to the early liberals who defended a federal union resembling the U.S. system of government. While the British and the North Americans were interested in promoting their economic and hemispheric interests in the isthmus, both meddling in the internal affairs of the various states, the British followed a policy of "divide and rule," while the United States usually backed more regional understandings.

Nonetheless, by 1850 the two countries signed an agreement aimed at joining forces in the construction of a future canal, while they agreed to guarantee together the neutrality and territorial integrity of Central America. This treaty, known as the Clayton-Bulwer Treaty, represented— as Gregory Weeks indicates—a diplomatic victory for the United States since it posed a legal block on British power, which at that time was considerable.[17] With the passing of time and as the United States increased its power, the treaty that remained in place for the rest of the nineteenth century curtailed the freedom of the United States to promote its own plans for the construction of an interoceanic canal under U.S. control. In the meantime, the enclave economies became sustained by treaties of friendship, navigation, and commerce that the countries signed with Britain and the major European states as well as by small numbers of English, French, German, Italian, and Belgian colonies of immigrants who settled in Central America, attracted by the prospects of trade, development of transportation, or military careers.

The configuration of nation-state boundaries and correlated citizenship confined to separate states was facilitated by the development of national economies, transportation networks, and state institutions gaining momentum in the second half of the nineteenth century and the first quarter of the twentieth century. The completion of the forty-eight-mile Panama Railway in 1855, financed and built mainly by private companies from the United States, led to a shift in commerce lines from the Caribbean to the Pacific coast, closer to the core centers of population and far away from lowland marshes and jungles. This shift changed the relative importance of different areas:[It] allowed El Salvador and Nicaragua, whose commerce had languished since the end of the Hispanic period, to return to the world economy. . . . Guatemala and Costa Rica also benefited greatly from the Pacific coast trade, as their freight costs dropped rapidly. Cart roads were built from the producing regions down to the ports, and beginnings were made on railroads. Regular steamship service connected these ports with Panama and opened the Atlantic to them. . . . Conversely, the Caribbean coast, now neglected, sank into a gloomy despair.[18]

The revolution of transportation made it possible for Central America to trade new crops abroad. During the nineteenth century, coffee replaced natural dyes (indigo and cochineal, a crimson or carmine dye derived from insects feeding on the nopal cactus) as Central America's main export, and toward the turn of the century bananas became a commodity with huge sales in North American markets.

In its relative isolation, Costa Rica was able to achieve relative political stability after independence. Starting in the 1830s it developed the coffee industry earlier than in other countries of the isthmus, contributing to the crystallization of a widespread landed class. In the early 1840s Guatemalan merchants and planters who noted this transformation in Costa Rica and the Guatemalan government started promoting coffee cultivation. The development of Pacific shipping led El Salvador to make the transition to coffee in the 1870s, to be followed by Nicaragua and then by Honduras in the 1880s. The volcanic soil of Central America proved particularly fit to produce high-quality coffee, and while the cultivation of other export commodities such as sugar, cotton, and cacao also expanded, none of the other crops could compete with coffee at that time.

This shift turned Central America into a bundle of "coffee republics," competing rather than cooperating with one another in the international markets and vis-à-vis foreign investors. The subsequent growth in banana production, which started in Costa Rica in the early 1870s and expanded fully throughout the Caribbean coast areas between 1890s and 1910s, reinforced the enclave and foreign-led character of Central American monocultural economic development. Companies like the United Fruit Company came to dominate not only the production operations but also the transportation and distribution system through the railroad and steamship networks they had developed as well as the radio communication they operated. The railroads were used mainly to serve the coffee and banana enclave economies, exacerbating the isolation of neighboring republics and reinforcing the deep internal imbalances that existed within each country between the enclave poles of dependent development and other sections.[19] Banana companies also began to influence and support political parties and affect state decision making to such extent that the popular imagery turned these countries into "banana republics." Honduras, which did not have a well-developed coffee industry or elite class, developed very influential banana companies that supported rival political parties and became involved in border disputes with Guatemala.

The economic transformation of the isthmus and its increasing neocolonial dependence on foreign capital and entrepreneurship was led by states that in most cases were interested in expanding their revenues, which were derived from customs, concessions, or duties in trade. The declining markets for natural dyes and their replacement by aniline dyes created a challenge for landed and commercial interests to find other exports. Small-scale mining of gold and silver was only important in Honduras and somewhat in Nicaragua, but the deposits were limited, and their importance merely reflected the lack of development of alternative exports. States learned from Costa Rica about the new opportunities that coffee and later bananas provided in the world markets. Other products such as tobacco and cacao would prove unable to compete on international markets.

States increasingly provided foreign companies, planters, and railroad builders with land grants and favorable conditions for expanding production while ignoring working-class interests. Tax relief, transportation development, and legislation providing available land and cheap labor were among the incentives states provided. These incentives were initially offered under conservative rulers but were intensified under the following liberal administrations.

The shifts in production were accompanied by changes in the ruling parties and a shift back to liberalism, which was fully accomplished by the early 1870s. The death of Guatemalan strongman Rafael Carrera in 1865 led to uprisings in Guatemala and Honduras. Failing at first in Guatemala, the rebels succeeded in Honduras, where Guatemalan exiles could find temporary asylum. In April 1871 the rebels joined Honduran forces that went to "liberate" El Salvador in a typical move of transnational intervention that would continue between the two countries. In June, liberal revolutionaries took hold of the Guatemalan government. Likewise, a liberal dictatorship was established in Costa Rica in 1870. In Nicaragua and Panama, the shift from conservatives to liberal leadership took longer. In Nicaragua, such delay was mainly due to the discredit of early liberalism, tainted by its alliance with William Walker. Yet, by 1893 Zelaya had established an iron-clad dictatorship allied with Honduran liberals. Panama remained part of conservative Colombia until it broke off with U.S. assistance and, by 1908, shifted to a government committed to the Positivist model of development.

As elites were structurally geared to defining themselves in relation to the western idioms of progress and reform, they were conceptually and discursively biased toward modernity, reflecting a universalistic outlook and global reflexivity that ensured reception to modern ideas and influences arriving from outside.[20] These ideas included a belief in evolutionism, liberalism, Positivism and later on, social Darwinism.

The emergence of these countries in the international division of labor as exporters of new raw commodities reinforced state consolidation. Elites supporting state consolidation were motivated by a full-fledged belief in, almost an obsession with material progress and scientific development. As the liberals took power across the region, coffee and later bananas became main exports throughout Central America. In some countries, notably Costa Rica, coffee predominated. In others, such as Honduras, bananas became the main export. In fact, Honduras became the major banana producer in the isthmus. According to the liberal and later on Positivist models, stable government and public security had to be the cornerstones of development. Under this model, allegiance would shift from religious to civilian authority. By curtailing the power of the Catholic Church, frozen lands and resources would be made available in markets, and the states would assume responsibility for public education and civil registry of births, marriages, and deaths. There emerged a desire to emulate northern European and U.S. models of development, along with a neglect of peasant and working-class interests. While the transition from conservatism to liberalism represented a reinforcement of Enlightenment ideals, it was translated into oligarchic, repressive, and undemocratic policies.

The Positivist motto of "order and progress" was endorsed enthusiastically as states tried to facilitate the development of urban infrastructure, transportation, postal services, telecommunication, and all other icons of modernity. The strong emphasis on material progress, modernization, and export-oriented economies implied a growing reliance on "law and order" as a code name for dictatorship, elite privilege, and a strong connection between economic interests and politics.

The process of structural differentiation accelerated in the late nineteenth century and early twentieth century. Costa Rica's coffee industry was unique in that it relied mainly on small farmers, typically owning only up to ten hectares of land, to cultivate the export commodity. In Guatemala and El Salvador most of the coffee was grown on large or medium-size farms that relied heavily on Indian and mestizo labor. As communal lands were abolished in El Salvador and the Indian labor force increased, wages on the larger farms decreased. Despite these differences, in Guatemala, El Salvador, and Costa Rica coffee growers were similarly dominant in society and politics until the mid-twentieth century.

The models of development adopted by the Central American republics created serious socioeconomic and social problems. Elites promoted the subdivision and privatization of communal lands. "Coffee cultivation in particular stimulated the privatization of land, since it was argued that few entrepreneurs would risk investing large sums of money in a crop that took five years to reach maturity unless they held legal title to clearly delimited properties."[21] In Costa Rica, where the Indian population stood at about 10 percent of the overall population, privatization of communal lands took place gradually and without drastic conflict. Thus, Indians were able to be incorporated into the larger society without too much conflict. Panama was similar to Costa Rica, with a myriad of ethnic groups—the Emberá, Wounaan, Kuna, Ngöbe, Buglé, Teribe or Naso, and Bribri—retaining their autonomy and cultures, principally due to the remoteness and disconnection of peripheral regions.

In Guatemala, El Salvador, and Nicaragua, however, privatization was much more abrupt and disputed. The worst case was El Salvador, where legislation was promulgated in 1881 and 1882 aimed at the extinction of communal and *ejidal* lands, which made up more than 25 percent of the national territory. Subsequently, conflict and repression proliferated for decades in areas where this legislation was implemented. This cycle reached a climax in

January 1932 when a peasant uprising in the western regions resulted in the murder of several landlords and the deaths of other residents. The state—run by the filo-fascist president Maximiliano Hernández Martínez, who had just been installed by a coup—retaliated brutally in the form of a massacre of thousands, including the Communist organizer Agustín Farabundo Martí.[22] In Honduras there was much less pressure to privatize lands, and communal lands persisted into the twentieth century.

Due to their increasing dependence on international markets, the countries became more vulnerable to fluctuations in the international prices of the few commodities they exported. Benefits went mostly to foreign companies and those connected to the enclave economies. The profits derived from the rise in custom revenues were channeled to the consolidation of the states' repressive capacity and to the conspicuous consumption of a tiny segment of the population, reinforcing the gap between rich and poor and the alienation of the latter. Economic growth did not lead to the enlargement of domestic markets or to any industrial revolution. Even on the economic domain, the states did not overcome such constraints as the inadequate deepwater ports, undercapitalization and capital flight, and slow development of communications.

The governmental structures of the modern states were consolidated by the liberal constitutions and legal codes that concentrated power in the national government, which mainly operated out of the capital cities. According to the institutional design adopted, heads of state were endowed with highly personalized political power that allowed them to subordinate the legislature and the judiciary, control provincial or departmental authorities, reward supporters with sinecures, and ostracize oppositions. Overall, heads of state could overrule any constitutional constraints and civil and political rights of citizens and even rule by decree whenever they declared a state of emergency due to states of external aggression or internal unrest.

Administratively, states expanded their bureaucracies, but the system of clientelistic rewards and personalized mobilization of political entourages reinforced the poorly organized and corrupt fiscal and state systems. Personnel lacked a civic ethic and did little to encourage the development of pluralistic public spheres. Foreign companies, which used bribes and unscrupulous practices to promote their interests, were partly to blame for reinforcing such corruption, reflected in the lack of trust of citizens in state institutions. A vicious cycle developed in which expectations of particularistic management reinforced the reliance on mediating mechanisms of access to state agencies and resources, used as personal assets by those controlling state positions and the resources derived thereof. Connections and clientelistic intercessions became the key for doing business with the state.

At the same time, most capital cities acquired a modern appearance through public buildings, theaters, monuments and parks, national libraries and museums, and professional schools and universities, reinforcing the gap with the hinterland. Such a gap was less remarkable in Belize and in Honduras, where Tegucigalpa replaced the colonial and immediate postcolonial city of Comayagua as capital of Honduras in 1880. In the first decades of the twentieth century, only 3 percent of the population of the isthmus could read and write. The isthmus received very little immigration, but foreign capitalists entered and were protected by governments. In Honduras in particular, foreign banana and railroad companies held more power than the local elite.

The armed forces saw expansion, but this was accompanied by a rise in the influx of arms, in crime and lawlessness, and in political instability that continued into the twentieth century.[23] Particularly damaging was the situation in Nicaragua, where elite factionalism and instability led to international interventions time and again, as in the U.S. Marines' deployment to that country between 1912 and 1925 and again in 1927–33. The exception to the expansion in armed forces was Costa Rica, where José Figueres abolished the army after the civil war in 1948.

The lopsided socioeconomic structures, the dictatorial bent of the political systems, and in some cases the affront to these countries' sovereignty generated protest, rebellion, and civil wars, affecting the isthmus until the last decade of the twentieth century. These scenarios of protest, rebellion, and civil wars once again recentralized the transnational dimension of intervention and conflict, as will be discussed in later chapters.

7

Citizenship and Subnational and Transnational Identities

A major aspect of these states' control over their populations and territories had to do with the attribution of citizenship along territorial boundaries, creating clusters of inclusion and exclusion of populations, and a dynamics of attempted state control over subaltern groups and ethnicities that otherwise could have prioritized localized, subnational identities or even projected transnational identities overriding the nation-state.

The crux of citizenship is the interaction of membership, public recognition, and politics. The character of such interaction varies according to the contextual and varied forms in which individuals and groups have connected to states and nations. By projecting specific forms of citizenship, shaping a certain balance and contents of inclusion and exclusion from the body politic, states have articulated certain visions of the nation. The cultural program embedded in citizenship has had political implications, reflected in the official recognition or denial of recognition of political, civil, socioeconomic, and cultural rights to different groups. In other words, citizenship was channeled through the construction of a national identity, subordinating or even neglecting some of the subnational identities (today we would call them subaltern), especially those that could potentially acquire transnational projection.

Inclusion and exclusion were an inherent part of the citizenship projects led by the states emerging at the end of colonial rule. While they may fight one another and disagree on policies, the elites in those states often developed deeper agreements about who would be represented and included as part of the nation and who would be excluded. Sharing the evolutionist vision of convergence to modernity, they adopted conservative liberalism and Positivism as policy guidelines, with important institutional implications for the differential access of groups and sectors to power and economic resources and for public recognition in society. This trend was present in the entire region, albeit with differences in the concrete character of the various groups and in the timing of the process.

This dynamics of constructed public recognition and denial was embedded in the collective representation of the nation and its heroes and can be followed in the case of Costa Rica. As we have seen, official historiography paid tribute to the figure of Juan Santamaría, the hero of the war against Walker, turning him into a national hero. Santamaría continued to be popularly known as El Erizo, the hedgehog, a clear allusion to his curly hair denoting his mulatto background. Official historiography could not obscure that popular memory of Santamaría, yet with the passing of time the official story as well as historiography in general overrode the realities of multi-ethnicity with a clearly homogenizing trend. This trend found its way into textbooks used in educating the new generations of citizens. Montero Barrantes' *Compendio de Historia de Costa Rica*, used as official history textbook in schools between 1892 and 1909, mentions only once the terms "Indian" and "mestizo" and not once the terms "mulatto," *pardo*, or "slave." The book *Cartilla histórica de Costa Rica* by Ricardo Fernández Guardia, which was used in schools beginning in 1909 and was still reprinted without changes in the 1960s, recognized the process of *mestizaje*, while stressing the prevalence of the white element. Imbued by Positivist and evolutionary ideas of European inspiration, this textbook indicated that the "weaker Indian race"—represented by Indian women—contributed to the process of miscegenation, but it disappeared quickly into the white race in a pattern that, according to the author, singled out Costa Rica, along with Argentina, Chile, and Uruguay, as the white nations of the Spanish-speaking Americas.[1]

The idea of the white nation was more credible in Costa Rica than elsewhere in the isthmus. The professed commitment to egalitarianism was combined there with the spatial marginalization of those enclaves containing "ethnicized" or "racialized" human conglomerates, such as the Guanacaste populations claiming descent from Chorotega natives and Spaniards or the Anglo-black populations of Limón on the Caribbean coast, whose increasingly important numerical presence in the 1890s was feared by the national elites and their supporters.

A major problem in the way of construction of an inclusive sense of citizenship has been the lopsided and polarized socioeconomic structure of most of these countries in the isthmus. Marked by histories of exploitation, rebellion, and violence, national official images disguised the national idea in shades that fit the interests of the ruling elites but could hardly win the hearts of the excluded masses.

Guatemala developed an early sense of identity as a hierarchical society that incorporated its indigenous population in a sort of "pact" dating back to colonial times through which the indigenous people maintained their autonomy in return for accepting the rules of the political and economic game, providing a cheap and docile workforce and serving in the armed forces. This arrangement included the maintenance of linguistic and cultural markers while precluding the formation of a pan-Maya or transnational indigenous identity until the late twentieth century. This pattern did not go unchallenged in the early nineteenth century. Between 1831 and 1838, liberals enacted a widespread agenda of citizenship that, if successful, would have changed Guatemala radically. The liberals endorsed free trade and attempted to simplify the complex taxation system. They aimed at making public and private lands available to widen the agrarian market. They invited foreign capital and immigrants into the country. Through the Livingston Codes (civil code and code of reform and prison discipline), the liberals abolished extraordinary privileges and distinctive judicial procedures (fueros) for special groups and instituted trial by peers. Additionally, the liberal agenda included legalization of divorce and separation of church and state. A growing sense of anticlericalism pervaded liberal ideology as liberals attempted to suppress religious orders, take over education from the Catholic Church, confiscate church properties, abolish tithes, and proclaim religious freedom in Guatemala. Secularization was also behind the attempt to reduce the number of fiesta days. According to this liberal view, public education and the establishment of a citizen militia would enhance the sense of citizenship in Guatemala.[2]

This project of accelerated transformation of Guatemalan identities through novel citizenship practices did not go unchallenged. Unlike liberals, conservative challengers emphasized law and order, the continuation of traditional relationships with the state, and a preservation of the Catholic Church. When Rafael Carrera became strongman and president from 1844 to 1848 and from 1851 until his death in 1865, he made Catholicism Guatemala's state religion, bringing back the clergy and permitting tithing. Thus, members of the clergy gained a prominent position in the creation of a national identity. Carrera sent clergy members into the areas that were most devastated by the revolutionary fights between liberals and conservatives that led to the breakdown of the United Provinces of Central America. The clergy took advantage of this opportunity to craft Guatemalan identity along traditional lines. Attempts were made to connect the independence of Guatemala with the liberation of Israel in biblical times, claiming that the people of Guatemala were chosen by God and would receive salvation by following the law. Rafael Carrera was heralded as the Guatemalan Moses, furthering the national theology and tying political figures to the religious community. The church teamed up with the conservatives in power to implement large anniversary ceremonies each year, celebrating the nation's independence from Spain. On these occasions, a large religious service was usually held, including a sermon on nation building, accompanied by a political speech across the plaza in the government offices.[3]

In such manner, Guatemala resumed the compartmentalized yet plural pattern of incorporation of indigenous groups it had maintained in colonial times. This unique pattern of incorporation assured the survival of particular traditions and languages to a greater extent than in neighboring countries.

Once the liberals regained power in the early 1870s, they instituted many reforms—such as placing the Catholic Church's property in control of the state, secularizing Guatemala's schools, and revitalizing Guatemalan farming and commerce[4]—but they did not completely undo the sense of group autonomy "by default." In addition to Spanish-speakers, twenty-three linguistic communities survived into the late twentieth and early twenty-first centuries, including Garifuna, Xinca (a non-Maya indigenous language), and twenty-one Maya languages, some of them mutually unintelligible.[5] In parallel, however, they fostered a strong bias in favor of the miscegenated yet hispanicized ladino sector, denying the recognition and symbolic representation of native (mostly Mayan) and Afro-Caribbean (Garifuna) sectors as more than a folkloric part of the nation.

Historians and social scientists have produced important works analyzing the exclusionary process of construction of citizenship as connected to the creation of a ladino identity, neglecting the multicultural setup of the country and relegating the indigenous populations to the category of ultimate "other," in a racial and racist duality. There is still debate among scholars whether such duality between ladinos and "indios" as part of the national citizenship regime was first articulated in the liberal discourse of the Reform period, by 1871, or whether the country adopted such policy of ladinization by the 1930s, yet there is agreement that this perspective promoted the national identity as a ladino identity that amalgamated Creole and acculturated mixed bloods, standing above the indigenous sectors, whose identities were marginalized.[6]

Contrasting with the development of a policy of mestizaje as a self-celebratory ideology of integration, which crystallized in Mexico after the revolution of the 1910s and projected a discourse of peasant corporatist incorporation, Guatemala eventually adopted cultural policies that did not enable indigenous groups—primarily Mayans—to be full citizens identified as part of the nation. Whether such policies reflected the substantial numerical weight of native populations, which precluded their foreseeable assimilation, as claimed by Steven Palmer, or whether the motivating factor was the racist attitude of the elites of the Generation of 1920, which attained hegemony a decade later, as sustained by Marta Casaús Arzú,[7] the results were the same. The Guatemalan elitist representation divided society in a dichotomous manner, separating the "decent people" from the lower sectors, which were defined in highly derogatory and racialized terms.

Alternative models of integration of subaltern groups had been promoted in the first three decades of the twentieth century in Guatemala and throughout the isthmus, by intellectuals willing to "regenerate" the Central American union on spiritual bases. In addition to their unionist positions, these intellectuals and men of action, among them Salvador Mendieta in Nicaragua, Flavio Guillén and Carlos Wyld Ospina in Guatemala, and Alberto Masferrer in El Salvador—and about whom more will be said in chapter 8—envisaged the creation of a model of society based on equal rights and social justice, the full integration of all inhabitants without any distinction of "race" (ethnicity), gender, or social status. Influenced by theosophy, modernism, and the ideas of Ernest Renan, they cooperated on a transnational basis to (re)create the union as a community of common purpose and vision, relying on the work, sacrifice, help, and solidarity of all the sectors of the population.[8]

Despite some initial success after the recreation of the Partido Unionista de Centro América (PUCA) in 1919 and the signing of a Unionist Pact in 1921, they lost ground in the late 1920s and 1930s, when other intellectuals—among them Federico Mora and Carlos Samayoa Chinchilla—reinforced stereotypical views of the indigenous population as a degraded sector. Probably influenced by Positivism, social evolutionism, and the racialist ideas gaining ground in western Europe, some of these intellectuals elaborated racially based ideas that promoted the "improvement of the race" by eugenics, the control of intermarriages, and immigration. According to these ideas, which turned hegemonic under the dictatorships of the 1930s, the state and the white, Creole, and ladino elites had to conduct the destinies of the nation, a nation in which the Indians at best were to remain marginal as docile workers and obedient peasants.[9]

Emboldened by their identification as representatives of the nation, the ladino sector deepened discriminatory and xenophobic attitudes toward the indigenous populations, attitudes that became associated with the construction of Guatemalan identity, permeating, until most recently, the views of many. Illustrative is the work of F. Hernández de León, who followed the example of Alejandro Marure in writing a popular book of famous dates. In the book *El libro de las efemérides* he openly expressed the attitudes of many in Guatemala toward the indigenous population. Clearly attacking the protective, paternalistic attitude that overlay the treatment of Indians ever since a 1582 Spanish royal decree defending them was handed down during colonial times, Hernández de León wrote:

> I have to confess, among the countless sins that weigh on my conscience is the sin of not accepting the Indian in any form. The Indian is repugnant to me [*me revienta*]. I see the Indian as obstructing the active life of society. The Indian has three aspects: a permanent lazy and spoilt brat; a rural worker; and a soldier. The first is the most generalized. The Indian is lazy by nature since society tolerates it. The Indian of the temperate zone cultivates his *milpa* . . . and the rest of the year he spends with his female companion, making her pregnant every nine months. Gladly enough, eight out of his ten sons usually die. The communal lands are the most comfortable protection fostering the existence of this class of Indians. . . . If all those Indians, who live in caverns, would till the fields, our agricultural situation would be less disastrous. . . . The work of ten Indians is equivalent to that of a single apt [rural] worker. . . . When time presses, the Indian obstructs work with his tardy and deficient performance. The third Indian, the Indian soldier, known also by the name of *cuque*, is the worst of all. At war he serves as cannon fodder and in peace, as the backing of tyrannies and agent of violence. . . . In the Americas, the strongest nationalities, the most dignified, democratic and advanced, are those in which there are no Indians. When Indians are the majority, as in Bolivia and Guatemala, the peoples have no redemption. . . . What feeble service did our Fray Bartolomé![10] How better we would be without defenders of Indians and without Indians in the countryside, without *cuques* at all! If the *encomenderos* finished the Indians, nowadays Guatemala would have been a free, sovereign and independent nation. Due to the Indians, up-to-now, we are certainly not [free and sovereign].[11]

These attitudes were very widespread in Guatemala and have died hard. In a study of elites' opinions conducted in 1980, Marta Casaús Arzú found that the ideas of racialist eugenics and "extermination of the Indians" were still exposed by approximately 15 percent of her sample.[12] In the 1980s and early 1990s, the wars waged under the framework and optic of the cold war provided a contingent scenario of civil war that led such exclusion to its ultimate consequence in the form of acts of genocide against indigenous groups, as in the case of massacres committed against residents in the regions of Ixil, Zacualpa, northern Huehuetenango, and Rabinal in 1981–82. These actions, committed in complete disregard for the lives, rights, and dignity of these populations is now widely known due to the work of anthropologists and human rights activists like 1992 Nobel Peace laureate Rigoberta Menchú Tum, whose activities and book promoted indigenous rights. They were also reflected in the findings of the Commission of Historical Clarification (CEH), which presented its findings publicly in February 1999. Equally important in disclosing the extent of such massive human rights violations in this period was the initiative of the Office of Human Rights of the Archbishopric, under the leadership of monsigneur Juan Gerardi Conedera, in organizing a project of "recuperation of historical memory," or REMHI, which resulted in the report *Guatemala nunca más*, made public in April 1998, ten months before the publication of the CEH's report, known as *Memoria del silencio*. Revelations such as these carried serious consequences for those implicated. Nonetheless, the resilience of these sectors was evident as Gerardi was assassinated in his parish, only two blocks from the presidential house in Guatemala City, forty-eight hours after his announcement of the REHMI's report.

Social, spatial, and cultural segregation was maintained, reinforced by the preservation of indigenous languages, which in the case of several of the more than twenty Mayan languages are not even intelligible to one another. Thus, in spite of the liberal discourse predicating the construction of a homogeneous nation, the state undermined the universalistic implications by legislating secondary laws that segregated native populations in domains as varied as the provision of forced labor, the appropriation of communal lands, the restriction of citizenship rights, and tutelary forms of education.

Only recently, mainly during the peace process leading to the accords of 1996 and the increasing empowerment of indigenous activists through their mobilization and their international connections and actions, state agencies have professed to be willing to relate differently to the multicultural setup of Guatemalan society. Thus, in addition to the peace accords (which addressed human rights, the resettlement of displaced populations, the establishment of a truth commission on human rights violations, and statements about constitutional and institutional reforms), a separate Accord on Identity and the Rights of Indigenous People was signed in March

1995 by the government, the military, and the high command of the guerrilla umbrella organization known as National Guatemalan Revolutionary
Unity (URNG). The accord recognized the legitimacy of using indigenous
languages in official communications and court proceedings as well as in
the school system and social services; it recommended the conservation of
indigenous ceremonial centers and archeological sites, involving Mayans in
their administration; it expressed a commitment to educational reform and
to indigenous representation in administrative bodies; and it recognized the
hold of localized customary law. Pan-Maya activists were very instrumental
in bringing about such development by mobilizing and advocating the issue of cultural rights and self-determination through a myriad of grassroots
popular groups, coordinating transcommunal associations like the Council
of Maya Organizations of Guatemala and their connections with international NGOs and intergovernmental organizations, or IGOs. Due to their
actions, Guatemala has become increasingly responsive to indigenous issues,
as Kay Warren and others have amply documented.[13]

In Nicaragua, El Salvador, and Honduras, the cultural program of citizenship promoted to a greater extent an ideology of mestizaje, which was
adopted as a means of symbolic appropriation or negation of the indigenous
representation, while the indigenous and Afro-American cultures were
deemed as destined to disappear. In El Salvador, since the late nineteenth
century, elites have tried to envision their country as entailing the complete
miscegenation of the indigenous and immigrant populations. State rhetoric
has stressed that the nation became racially homogeneous and had no significant Indian presence, being free of the backwardness attributed to the
Indians and seen as a cause of the lag of neighboring countries. They rather
represented Salvadoran identity as resulting from transnational processes of
mestizaje. Contrasting with these representations, the ethnic identification
of the Nahua in the southwest and the Lenca in the northeast continued to be
strong through the early decades of the twentieth century, with communities
retaining a cultural and political presence.[14] It was following the massacre of
1932, when a largely indigenous revolt allied with the communist movement
was brutally repressed, that ethnopolitics largely disappeared from the public eye. Following the repression, many indigenous communities disguised
being Indian, and many discarded specific dress and languages. The fact
that distinct dress and language became rare among the Nahua and disappeared among the Lenca conferred credibility to ladino Salvadoran views
that theirs was a homogeneous nation, not recognizing the persisting presence of nearly a half-million inhabitants—especially in the rural southwest

and northeast—who continued to see themselves as indigenous. Since the late 1980s and particularly by the mid-1990s, ethnicity was reevaluated and became again visible. This change was part of the state-led efforts to redignify Salvadoran national identity and attract international tourism, in the post–civil war reconstruction. It all started in 1986, as El Salvador joined in a cooperative venture with Guatemala, Belize, Honduras, and the southern states of Mexico to form a regional tourism initiative called the Mayan World (Mundo Maya) aimed to attract some of the millions of visitors to the country. While granting novel respectability to the indigenous sectors, however, the change has had paradoxical implications for the indigenous peoples of the country, as analyzed by Virginia Tilley. Specifically, the Salvadoran indigenous peoples have witnessed a process of state-led Mayanization that has prompted the redefinition of their identities in terms that entail a misrepresentation of their origins and culture, putting pressure on them to become part of a transnational project that has projected markers of identity that are not their own. Even when adopting the parameters of that project for practical reasons, as they aim to capture funding and resources derived from international tourism, the Nahua and Lenca remain uncompetitive in the transnational Mayan world. Moreover, when compared to the models of being indigenous assumed by the transnational indigenous peoples' movement and international funding agencies, the Salvadoran indigenous population has appeared not as distinct peoples in a unique situation but rather as peoples who have lost their ethnicity. Accordingly, they are subject now to a new stigma, the "not truly Indian" stigma, which remains a political obstacle to their full recognition as part of the vision of nationhood in El Salvador.[15]

The cultural program of citizenship—with its ideology of mestizaje—has been politically instrumental in reinforcing the positions of the mestizos vis-à-vis other groups. This trend can be followed in various cases, for instance in the Caribbean economic enclaves of Honduras, where mestizo employers and middlemen confronted the politically active black workers with the backing of the state.

Similarly, in Nicaragua, the ideology of integration was used to displace race into the realm of foreignness.[16] On a symbolic plane, the image and the dance-theatrical performance of the Güegüence, in the vernacular Spanish dialect impregnated with Nahuatl terms, projected a mythical representation of a local integrated society feigning obedience while mocking authority and improvising evasive strategies that came to be seen as synonymous with being Nicaraguan, full of wit and imagination.[17] Yet, in fact, the ideology of mestizaje was increasingly used to reject the activism of native populations with some transnational links as the Miskitu (Miskitos) and Afro-Nicara-guans. However, throughout the isthmus, the resistance of groups that were marginalized from the national imagery (for example, the Garifuna in Honduras or the Miskitu in Nicaragua) would often acquire political—internal and transnational—relevance in the late twentieth century.[18]

The case of the Miskitu is paradigmatic of the difficulties of states adopting organic visions and nationalistic narratives of representation to accommodate groups with distinctive cultures and transnational identities. The Nicaraguan national identity was conceived as developing from its core in the Pacific region, where a Nahuatl lingua franca had already developed in colonial times, obliterating earlier distinct Native American languages and eventually merging with Spanish, the hegemonic language.

This conception was diametrically opposed to that of the Miskitu, who resided on the Atlantic coast from Cape Gracias a Dios to the San Juan River and claimed as theirs an area incorporated into the "national territory" of Nicaragua only in the 1890s, an area covering around half of that territory yet sparsely populated and by groups culturally distinct from the Güegüenses. Unlike the Pacific region, center of Spanish control of indigenous peoples, the Atlantic region had become a borderland open to the predatory actions of buccaneers and the informal British presence at the northern Nicaraguan and Honduran coast. With the passing of time, the Atlantic region became a multicultural and multiethnic area in which Protestant, Afro-American, and Amerindian religious elements and linguistic elements coexisted.

A Miskitu kingdom ruled the area for more than two hundred years, most of the time under an alliance and with trade connections to the British. The Miskitu intermingled with other populations and turned into a transnational border presence in the region. The following passage describes the complex demographic background of the Miskitu:

> Systematic slave raiding, the exaction of tributes from neighboring tribes, and the continuing intercourse with logwood cutters and outlaws pushed Miskito culture on a more translocal trajectory; that is, adopting an increasingly outward-looking sense of place and a more exogenous set of sexual relations with coastal sojourners, they acted as the brokers of a Caribbean borderland. Ephraim George Squier would later describe the Miskito as a "mixed race, combining the blood of Negroes, Indians, pirates, and Jamaica traders."[19]

Even though the Mosquito Coast was under Spanish rule only briefly between 1787 and 1800, Nicaragua claimed sovereignty over the coast. In 1860

Britain recognized the sovereignty of Nicaragua and Honduras over their coast, and yet the Miskitu kingdom managed to survive as an enclave, with a hereditary chief and limited autonomy, although in a more restricted area than before. In the 1870s attempts were made to "nationalize" the coast by promoting Catholicism, the Spanish language, and the rudiments of Nicaraguan institutional authority, policies that failed partly because of the dispersed character of settlements in the region.

As Justin Wolfe stresses, Nicaraguan nationality and citizenship were constructed through the transformation of ethnicity and its dichotomization in the late nineteenth century and early twentieth century. It was during this period that the region of the Mosquitia was constructed as the "other" against which to measure the "true" Nicaragua. The coast—seen as Afro-indigenous, Protestant, and English-speaking—remained distanced from the mainstream society, conceived as being mestiza, Catholic, and Spanish-speaking. From the colonial census of 1776 to the national ones of 1867 and 1883, Nicaragua was portrayed as multi-ethnic, composed of Indians, Africans, Europeans, and their mixed descendants. In the census of 1776, 37 percent were categorized as mulattoes and 13 percent as mestizos, in addition to 46 percent Indians and 5 percent whites. In the census of 1867, Indians constituted 50 percent, mestizos 26 percent, and 24 percent were of mulatto, black, or zambo phenotypes. In 1883 these proportions were 32, 18, and 43 percent, respectively, in addition to 7 percent white. Nonetheless, toward the end of the nineteenth century, the complex racial-ethnic composition was increasingly described as dichotomous. Underpinned by the drive to abandon the old caste system, categories were abridged into two broad divisions—Indian and ladino—thought of as occupying polar positions in a hierarchical civilizational structure and geared toward the modernizing drive of the elites. In parallel, the "marked" racial category of the Afro-indigenous on the Atlantic coast was displaced in the national imagery, where it was associated with foreignness.[20]

In December 1893 Nicaraguans occupied militarily the Mosquitia and forced its incorporation into Nicaragua. The last Miskitu king, Robert Henry Clarence, fled to exile in Jamaica. Despite protests and requests of intervention forwarded by the Miskitu to Britain, the area was turned into a Nicaraguan territorial department named the Zelaya Department after the president who had ordered the military occupation.

By the early twentieth century, the political center demanded the full incorporation of the Atlantic coast residents (in their full heterogeneity, predominantly Miskitu, but also including Sumu, marginalized mestizos, and indigenous displaced peoples) into Nicaraguan society, overcoming their singularity. The following statement of 1925 by a Nicaraguan state official is illustrative of the prevailing discourse and thought of Nicaraguans about the peoples of the Caribbean coast at the time:

> Those tribes, so heterogeneous, little cultured and reduced in numbers, far from being able to rule the Coast, need that the civilized peoples of Nicaragua reach their lands, mix with them and improve the race, and impose the Nicaraguan civilization and language, so that the emerging peoples should be affine and not antagonist, and should share the Hispanic-Nicaraguan blood, language, customs and culture. As I assume that we don't want barbarity to prevail, we should agree that the Hispanic-Nicaraguan civilization must follow the legacy of Spanish Empire and colonize the Coast with the Hispanic-Nicaraguan blood, language, customs and culture. Nicaragua must tilt to the Atlantic until it brings the disappearance of those alien elements into the waters of Nicaraguan nationalism.[21]

Without sharing such a racist attitude, Augusto César Sandino, the legendary resistance leader of the late 1920s and early 1930s, supported indigenous rural peoples as a counterweight to American imperialism. Yet, he too shared the liberal belief in progress and civilization and its translation into a call for unity of the "Indo-Hispanic race." Sandino's heirs, the Sandinistas, shared these organic expectations, rejecting a more pluralistic and multicultural understanding, and they too adopted a narrative that contrasted the modernizing Sandinistas and the backward and yet to be modernized ethnic minorities. After their revolutionary victory over the Somoza dynasty, the Sandinista officials attempted to force their vision on the inhabitants of the coast. The Sandinista policies projected a vision that excluded that of the Miskitu. On the one hand, the revolutionary government considered Miskitus as "backward" people and claimed that their problems would be resolved through economic development programs, literacy campaigns, birth control, rural development projects, and land reform. They envisioned extending education and health care to all workers, peasants, and women. On the other hand, they viewed the Miskitu as a foreign presence, linked to British colonialism and U.S. imperialism, and tried to incorporate them forcefully into the nation-state and its mestizo identity while attempting to repress any resistance.

The Miskitu had not participated in the struggle against the Somozas, and they endorsed the idea of a Miskitu nation with "aboriginal rights" to about one-third of Nicaragua's national territory, which challenged the sovereignty of the revolutionary state. In August 1981 the government responded to the demands of the Miskitu—organized in the framework of an organization, the MISURASATA—by issuing a Declaration of Principles that promised to protect and promote indigenous peoples' rights but made it explicit that the government would not grant any special rights to the Miskitu. In their own vision, the Sandinistas thought that only the state had the exclusive right to exploit natural resources while being willing to recognize autonomy only to communal lands, waters, and forests that had traditionally belonged to the communities. As the government feared Miskitu's cooperation with the Contras, they adopted policies of forced relocation in the Río Coco region. Miskitu leaders accused the Sandinistas of human rights violations that they claimed were aimed at suppressing Miskitu resistance. They lodged a complaint with the Inter-American Commission on Human Rights (IACHR) that included charges of detentions, trials, imprisonment, disappearances, and forced relocation. Contrastingly, the government claimed it had evacuated Miskitu from the region as a protective measure because of the Contra attacks. In fact, the Sandinistas suspected the Miskitu to be conspiring with both the FDN, the anti-Sandinista National Democratic Front that—supported by the CIA—operated in Honduras near the Nicaraguan border, and the ARDE, the Democratic Revolutionary Alliance, which operated from Costa Rica against the Sandinistas. The Miskitu, among the most organized and belligerent of the coast residents, led armed uprisings against what they considered a new form of coercion. Supported by the Moravian Church, the largest denomination in the region, the Miskitu resisted and reasserted their collective identity and memory as part of an oppressed transnational minority fighting against the "Sandinista oppressors."[22]

The Miskitu became an embarrassment to the popular revolution of 1979–90, which claimed to be representing the people of Nicaragua and yet found itself forced to recognize the existence of groups challenging its homogenizing narrative and rhetoric of revolutionary nationalism. The confrontation was almost unavoidable. Mande explains:

> Sandinistas and Miskitu presented conflicting definitions of land rights, which rested on two irreconcilable historical narratives. On the one hand, MISURASATA leaders claimed that Indian "nations" had existed "from time immemorial" and that Miskitus had maintained enduring spiritual and economic ties to their land. On the other hand, Sandinista narratives revolved around a sovereign nation-state.[23]

The rift between the Miskitu and the Sandinistas turned into confrontation, repression, and the displacement of more than 35,000 Miskitu and Sumu refugees fleeing into Honduran territory. Only in 1987, after negotiations with the MISURASATA organization representing the indigenous peoples, the legislature passed Law No. 28, Autonomy Statute for the Regions of the Atlantic Coast of Nicaragua. The law recognized the rights of indigenous peoples to the lands they historically occupied and opened the door for the repatriation of the refugees by the United Nations High Commissioner for Refugees (UNHCR). In theory, since then, the autonomous Atlantic regions would be able to deliberate with the Nicaraguan government in ruling their economic, cultural, and environmental affairs and establishing regional control over lands and natural resources. However, autonomy plans were not fully supported by the central government. The representatives of the indigenous people—now led by a succeeding organization, YATAMA (an acronym for Yapti Tasba Masraka Nanih Aslatakanka—Descendants of Mother Earth) have continued to protest—sometimes violently—asserting their autonomy and protection of Indian cultural and land rights and challenging corruption within their regional councils and administrations.[24]

The 1987 constitution, revised in 1995, recognized the multi-ethnicity of Nicaragua, which in addition to the mestizo core population, is comprised of the Garifuna, Sumos, Miskitu, and Ramas. In Article 5, the constitution acknowledges the presence of indigenous people in Nicaragua, their right to develop their people's identity, promote their indigenous culture, and the official status of their languages, prevalent on the Caribbean coast of Nicaragua. Article 121 also recognizes the right of minority groups to an intercultural education in their own language. Article 89 recognizes collective forms of landownership, which are common among some indigenous communities.[25] Law 28, passed in parliament in 2003, and the constitutional amendments that are associated with it, were set forth to protect such cultural diversity. Law 28 provided for many of these same guarantees. Significantly, it granted autonomy to the Atlantic coast of Nicaragua. The law also stated that the autonomy of the Atlantic coast was a process "that enriches the national culture, and recognizes and strengthens ethnic identity groups; it respects the specificities of the cultures of the communities of the Atlantic Coast; it redeems the history of the same; it recognizes property rights on communal land and repudiates any type of discrimination; it recognizes religious freedom and, without deepening differences, recognizes distinct identities as coming together to build national unity."[26] Nonetheless, Nicaraguan legislation still maintains some contradictory threads. While the legislation

recognizes the land rights of the communities, it also states that natural resources are owned by the state and that the state may use these whenever it
chooses. Similarly, the Forest Law states that indigenous Nicaraguans may
not use the forest resources without a management plan drafted by an expert,
which most indigenous communities cannot afford.[27]

Beyond the different forms and tempos of nation-state building, citizenship in all these countries involved highly hierarchical criteria and a selective
process of inclusion and exclusion from access to membership and national
representation and narratives. Even Costa Rica, in spite of its self-congratu-
latory image of being a racial democracy and promoter of equality, idealized
"whiteness" to the point that the state did not recognize the black population
of workers who had arrived to work at the United Fruit Company and their
descendants as national citizens until 1949. And neither did its Constitutional
Court recognize the indigenous people as citizens until 1993. Only then they
were granted national identity cards, even though the newly gained citizenship did not improve their deprived living conditions and limited access to
public services. Moreover, Costa Ricans constructed their national image in
opposition, conflict, and narrative contrast with those projected onto Nicaraguans, who until recently have been "racialized" and "criminalized" as the
internal "others" and to those rejected as "undesired immigrants" such as the
Chinese, Arab, Jewish, Turkish, Armenian, and other groups.[28] This exclu-
sivist attitude had terrible human consequences during World War II, when
Costa Rica created all sorts of formal impediments for Jews who were looking desperately for sites of refuge to escape extermination and the Holocaust.

Among the countries emerging from the fracture of the Central American federation, particularly Honduras failed to produce a sense of collective identification among its citizens until rather late in its development as
an independent state. As one historian noted, "Everyone knew there was
an entity called Honduras, but no one knew what it was."[29] For nearly one
hundred years after the fall of the Central American federation, Honduras'
political fate was dictated as much by Nicaraguan and Guatemalan forces as
by its own nationals, and at times its political elites joined those forces who
strived to reunite the region of the isthmus into one political entity. At the
core of Honduran identity were the mestizos, yet along the coast were two
Afro-American groups, the Garinagu and the Afro-Antillans, in addition to
the elites and Salvadoran immigrants.

As elites and intellectuals alike feared the Afro component, they emphasized the notion of Honduras as a mestizo nation, which incorporated
a noble image of the Indian but until recently marginalized the Garinagu

or black Caribs. The Garinagu people trace their descent from the meeting of Amerindians and west Africans and are popularly known as black Caribs or—due to the name of their language—as Garifuna.[30] Their Honduran communities originated in a transfer in the late eighteenth century of rebellious Caribbean populations from the island of St. Vincent to Roatán, Honduras. Arriving first in Honduras in 1796–97, by the early nineteenth century they had moved from Honduras to Belize, especially following an 1832 massacre that occurred during the Honduran civil war.[31] They later moved also to Nicaragua, specifically during the 1890s and the first decade of the 1900s,[32] and to Guatemala, creating a transnational presence. A sickle cell genetic adaptation to malaria enabled them to survive where Europeans succumbed. Accordingly, the Garifuna population grew to more than 500,000, with as many as 250,000 in Honduras alone at one point.[33] By the 1970s younger populations of Garifuna no longer conversed in the traditional Garifuna language, but their identity as a people was projected through strong ritual and music-dance practices that supported their folkloric inclusion within the nation-state identities of Honduras and the other countries where they lived.[34]

Traditionally, indigenous groups dominated municipal governments longer in Honduras than in El Salvador or Nicaragua, so that even though there were local conflicts over land, they generated only localized, mild repression. Beginning in the nineteenth century, "Indians" were seen as part of the armies supporting military caudillos, and therefore the state conceived them as allies, supporting their education and providing some help. This started a process of increasing recognition. Discursively since the 1920s the indigenous sector was symbolically incorporated—as symbolized in the reverence shown to the figure of Lempira, the Indian cacique who, according to tradition, fought heroically against the Spanish conquerors. Illustrative of such symbolic incorporation was the fact that starting in 1931 the Honduran national currency was renamed after this leader of the Lenca people.

Nonetheless, the late development of education, of transportation and communications, and of the professionalization of the army also contributed to a late process of inclusion and only partial decline of separate particular identities. It was very recently, in the mid-twentieth century and especially in the late 1960s and during the short war of 1969 with El Salvador known as the Soccer War, that Honduran citizens rose together as one people fighting for the same cause, and a sense of nationalism was promoted.[35]

Likewise, until not long ago, the state claimed that the Garinagu were just mestizos like any other inhabitants of the country. More recently, a partial shift could be traced toward recognition of minority rights, as signaled by the country being one of the twenty two signatories worldwide of the 1989 convention adopted by the International Labor Organization concerning the Indigenous and Tribal Peoples in Independent Countries (ILO Convention 169). As of early 2010, the only other Central American countries to do so were Guatemala and Costa Rica. ILO Convention 169 was conceived as a means of protecting the identities and rights of these peoples while supporting their contacts beyond state borders. Article 4 says that all states that ratify the convention must "adopt special measures for safeguarding the persons, institutions, property, labor, cultures and environment of indigenous and tribal peoples," while Article 32 establishes that "governments shall take appropriate measures, including by means of international agreements, to facilitate contacts and co-operation between indigenous and tribal peoples across borders, including activities in the economic, social, cultural, spiritual, and environmental fields."[36] In the late 1990s Honduran officials started supporting transnational bicentennial-plus celebrations of the arrival of the Garinagu people to Central America.

However, such a commitment has only partially reduced the tension between the Afro-Caribbean and indigenous groups that have continued to protest the usurpation of lands and accused the government of failing to implement a full safeguard of their rights, demanding among other things a full investigation of the murders of several leaders in recent years and that indigenous organizations be legally recognized by the government. The University of Maryland's Minorities at Risk research project describes the tension as follows:

In 1997, after a month of nationwide protests by indigenous organizations that included a hunger strike, the government signed a 22-point agreement with representatives of various groups that made available 9 initial land grants of about 22,000 acres each to different tribes, granted some contested land titles outright to indigenous petitioners, and set aside government funds for indigenous housing. The Congress also created a commission to study indigenous land claims, which often conflict with the claims of small farmers, but the commission was largely inactive. Since 1997 the government has distributed tens of thousands of legal titles encompassing hundreds of thousands of acres of land to indigenous persons. During the year, the National Agrarian Reform Institute transferred 40,000 hectares (98,840 acres) of land to Afro-Caribbean and indigenous groups who had ancestral rights to a large share of disputed land. However, indigenous groups continue to charge that the government had failed to fulfill its commitments under the 1997 agreement. . . . The 1998 repeal of Constitutional Article 107 (which had prevented the sale of coastal lands to foreigners) generated strong protest from coastal groups (though it was seen as a more direct threat to Garifuna interests). Much of the persecution facing Honduran indigenous peoples is directly tied to their land claims and most of the threats against them have come from wealthy Hondurans and private companies, though the government appears reluctant to investigate claims too carefully. In the absence of clear land titles and unequal access to legal recourse, indigenous groups also are vulnerable to frequent usurpation of their property rights by non-indigenous farmers and cattle ranchers.[37]

Another case of late construction of nation-state identity and correlated universal citizenship that merits special attention is that of Panama. Shortly after it gained independence in November 1903, intellectuals drafted works that were geared toward strengthening the sense of national identity. A nationalist poetry emerged, with creations such as "Al cerro Ancón" by Amelia Denis de Icaza and "Canto a la bandera" by Gaspar Octavio Hernández, still cherished today as emblematic of national pride. Works of historiography were oriented in the same line, starting with the *Compendio de historia de Panamá* published in 1911 by Juan Bautista Sosa and Enrique J. Arce.[38] Yet, as Steve Ropp has indicated, from 1903 to 1931 the United States supported a "politics of suppressed identity" in Panama. Constrained by its own self-representation as a white society, the United States supported those social white sectors that declined to recognize the multiple ethnic character of Panamanian society, preferring instead to support the vision of Panama as a globalized city ruling over an almost deserted hinterland. This was further complicated by the presence of the Zonians, that is, the people who lived in and around the Canal Zone and were employed by the U.S. government to work at the Panama Canal. Lacking an institutional voice of their own, the mestizo, black, mulatto, and indigenous populations living mostly beyond the zone were largely ignored in discourses of self-representation, at least until the 1920s.[39] In the early 1940s Arnulfo Arias drafted a nationalistic discourse based on exclusion of minorities. The 1946 constitution still established in Article 12 as its ideal the spiritual assimilation of all inhabitants in order to enable their intellectual, moral, and political incorporation into the nation. Yet, following the 1964 violent clashes over the hanging of a

Panamanian flag in the Canal Zone and more fully the arrival of Colonel Omar Torrijos to power in 1968, nationalistic feelings were bolstered in the public domain, energizing the identity of Panamanians with strong feelings of amalgamated anti-imperialism, which lent credence and support to the government's policies leading to the renegotiation of the canal terms and its return to Panamanian sovereignty by 1999. More recently, Panama has moved to praise its multicultural composition, stressing its relevance for global integration and downplaying its connection to the other isthmian countries. In spite of colorful images of self-representation,[40] Panama has remained strongly divided socially into communities with their own associational life and rather secluded from one another, similar to the relative seclusion of the country from the other countries of the isthmus. In this latter respect, even today it is cheaper to make a phone call from Panama to Europe, Canada, or even Pakistan or India than to make that call to a neighboring Central American country. What enables the image of harmony to linger and be accepted by many is the relative prosperity of the country as part of globalized financial, trade, and commercial services and tourism, which even if not shared by all has definitely provided a horizon of optimism reinforcing the celebration of multicultural diversity. What remains to be accomplished, similarly to other countries in the region, is the development of participatory citizenship and bridging mechanisms bringing together the different groups and sectors in the country. In connection with the other countries of the region, it can be expected that historical and contemporary factors will continue to work to retain the local sense of distinctiveness and lack of strong political will to engage in tighter transnational relationships in the entire region.

The preceding analysis has singled out the rather protracted, late, and selective construction of a generalized sense of inclusive citizenship as the result of the development of separate statehood in most of the countries of the isthmus. As states moved to consolidate their control over territories and population, they engaged in a continuous process of construction of citizenship and collective identities that projected a cultural program involving key dimensions of disengagement from alternative transnational images and connections reflected in parameters of inclusion and exclusion predicated for the populations they conceived as their own. A major finding of the preceding analysis is that as citizenship included the symbolic appropriation of collective representation by the states, such representation was accompanied by mechanisms of exclusion, marginalization, and repression of certain groups, both localized groups as in Guatemala and particularly groups with transnational links and a transnational presence such as the Miskitu and the Garinagu.

Likewise, the mobilization of these groups has already contributed to posing substantial challenges to prevailing citizenship regimes, that is, to the combination of citizens' rights and duties and the modes of interest mediation and representation that in Deborah Yashar's characterization determine "*who* has political membership, *which* rights they possess, and *how* interest intermediation with the state is structured . . . *formally* defining the intersection between national politics, political membership, and public identities."[41] Some of the localized and transnational movements we discussed have demanded the implementation of equal rights but also aimed at recognition of their special status and rights as native peoples, opening to various degrees the debate on what citizenship entails in these societies. Insofar as they have fought for autonomous representation and for multicultural recognition and linked these demands to claims over collective resources, these groups and movements have triggered fundamental debates on the nature of citizenship and made a difference, albeit still partial, in some of these countries.[42] If their impact has been somehow more restricted than that of parallel movements in Bolivia or Mexico, it is mainly due to the central role that class issues and issues of regional hegemony have played in the configuration of the shifting political maps of the isthmus for most of the twentieth century.

8

Ebbs and Flows of Regional Dismemberment and Unification

Ever since the end of the federal pact and the disintegration into separate states, there were attempts of regional reunification. Some of these attempts were motivated by the will of leaders to establish their regional hegemony, as indicated earlier. Others were triggered as a reaction to the attempts of centralization, and still others were prompted by the reaction to external threats and foreign interventions.

Sustaining these attempts at reunification and beyond the specifics of each attempt was an underlying feeling of disappointment with the current achievements of the separate republics, often seen as "sections" of a more substantive fatherland. Motivating the supporters of these initiatives was sometimes the conviction that a golden age awaited to the strategically located isthmus, provided the countries managed to overcome past divisiveness.

Paradigmatic are the arguments brought by the general of division Justo Rufino Barrios, president of Guatemala, as a basis for the decree that attempted to launch a Central American union, issued on February 28, 1885:

> That in the current state of fragmentation, in vain [these countries] could attain among civilized nations the importance and respect suited to their autonomy, and which they certainly would enjoy if they left behind the seclusion dictated by their smallness and together they reconstruct a strong Republic. . . . Their strength could only derive from union, from which respectability, strongly established peace, material progress, enlightenment and republican morality will result.
>
> . . . That in the current situation, every State must care for its own security and the security of the other States, since the unrest and disorder in any of them spillovers shortly into the territory of the others; and the resources at the discretion of governments—that should be invested in public advancement, improvement and prosperity—must be

consumed in an unproductive and pitiable manner, in mutual spying, in safeguarding from each other, in preparing for war, and in maintaining armed forces living in a constant state of war, in weakness, suspicion and distrust . . . all of which turns into impossible any policy of truthful, cordial and mutual fraternity; shaping in contrast a fearful, jealous, mean policy, full of mistrust, jealousy and rivalries; maintaining anxiety, feeding fights and local hatred, opening an abyss of separation that—even if covered by friendly appearance—time will turn into irreversible, with harmony and union beyond achievement. . . .

. . . That with the states joined in a single Republic . . . the mutual surveillance, so expensive and hateful, would disappear . . . the government would be surrounded by the most eminent and distinguished individuals from all the different states, using their illustration, science, patriotism and knowledge of business . . . to sustain at last the peace in all sections of Central America.[1]

These arguments resonated of earlier visions expressed since the early 1830s on the direction the region had to follow. The path was the one moving toward modernization, as evident in the following characterization by Manuel Montúfar of the accomplishments of the first Constitutional Assembly of Central America:

With the decree of July 1, 1823, the foundation of a popular, representative form of government was established; legal equality, separation of powers, and unlimited freedom of the press; religious tolerance established through private worship; the abolition of slavery and the manumission of slaves; liberal immigration laws; commercial tariffs and mercantilist franchises to strengthen and protect them; the regulation of national finance; the designation of federal income and the separation of that of the states; experimentation with a poll tax and a just foreign loan; the Nicaraguan canal project; open and formal diplomatic relations with the European nations and many of those of America; the initiative for the American Congress in Panama; setting the foundations for the establishment of public credit and arranging many of the branches of the administration under the provisional government and the Constitution; all this resulted from the first experience of the Central Americans in the difficult enterprise of constituting a nation and giving it laws.[2]

While in the 1830s there were strong disagreements around the federal format of the union being reflected in political and historical controversies,[3] balkanization created even stronger disappointment in some circles, especially as they witnessed the vulnerability of the new states vis-à-vis one another and in the international arena. The institutional deficit of the new states and their sense of fragility re-created time and again the attraction of the unfulfilled dream of the reunification of Central America for political elites and non-state actors alike.

The following is a partial list of such attempts at reunification. This list portrays the intricate interstate ties and transnational perceptions that remained latent and at times were explicitly voiced to attempt reunification by diplomacy or by force. Among the most salient initiatives in the nineteenth century one should mention the following instances:

A series of attempts by El Salvador, Honduras, and Nicaragua to create a single "national government" occurred in the 1840s to counter the increasingly aggressive presence of the British, who had set foot in Belize, the Mosquitia Coast, and the Bay Islands and exerted pressure on El Salvador, blockading its only access to the Pacific Ocean, and in Nicaragua, where they blockaded Greytown in 1842–44 and later occupied it. The British presence on the Honduran coast dated back to their logging colony in 1622.[4] Accordingly, the countries signed pacts, entered discussions about constitutional confederate arrangements, and formed the Representación Nacional de Centroamérica. The confederation pact was signed in 1842, another in October 1848 with the provision that Guatemala and Costa Rica could join, and a third one in November 1849 stating the establishment of a three-partite "national" representation in Chinandega.

Subsequently, in October 1852, the República de Centro América (Republic of Central America) was declared in Tegucigalpa. These efforts spearheaded by Trinidad Cabañas, then president of Honduras, did not bear effective fruits beyond the drafting of a "national" charter.

A renewed call for union among the above three republics was made in 1862, this time opposed by the powerful ruler of Guatemala, Rafael Carrera, and paralleled by a project of union drafted by Francisco María Iglesias, a Costa Rican minister.

Attempts at forceful reunification occurred in the 1860s, with El Salvador and Honduras confronting Guatemala and Nicaragua.

In 1872 a meeting took place of all the republics except Nicaragua at La Unión (El Salvador), where they drafted a document aimed at establishing "the bases of a union of Central American states." A

border clash between Honduras and El Salvador followed by a coup
in Honduras frustrated the initiative.

In 1873 the Quadruplicate Alliance was conceived as a defensive pact
against the government of Costa Rica, which supported conservative
forces in Guatemala. The alliance was portrayed as a move toward
the union of the republics, yet due to its secluded offensive character, Honduras opted to remain neutral, and fearing the hegemony of
Guatemala, Nicaragua moved into the sphere of Costa Rican power.

In 1876 an attempt by Guatemala to launch the union by diplomatic
means was frustrated by internal conflict in Honduras and by war
between Guatemala and El Salvador, leading to heads of state agree-
able to Guatemala's president, General Justo Rufino Barrios, being
placed in power in El Salvador and Honduras.

In 1885 an attempt at reunification by force was launched by General
Barrios, perhaps dreaming of emulating Bismarck in Central America. It was preceded in 1882 by Barrios' renunciation of the territories
of Chiapas disputed with Mexico. This move was motivated by the
wish to avoid a second front as the general decided to push the union
before Nicaragua would achieve a U.S.-supported project of building
an interoceanic canal in its territory. The attempt at union launched
in late February 1885 failed when Barrios invaded El Salvador and
was killed in battle four weeks later, on April 2, 1885.

A meeting of representatives from the five countries took place in January 1887, a month later leading to the signing of a treaty of peace
and friendship, a consular convention, and a treaty of extradition of
criminals.

The Pact of Amapala, which was signed between Nicaragua, Honduras,
and El Salvador in June 1895, established the República Mayor de
Centro-América. The pact was made with the intention that Guatemala and Costa Rica would join. The project was led by President
Zelaya of Nicaragua and was mainly motivated by the wish to secure
Central American solidarity vis-à-vis the British, especially after Nicaragua took possession of the Mosquitia, as well as vis-à-vis the
increasing U.S. presence in the region.

The República Mayor de Centro-América assumed the symbols of the old
federation and contemplated the establishment of an itinerant assembly,
although this did not imply that the three states had to relinquish power
over internal affairs. A political constitution signed in Managua by the three
countries in August 1898 proclaimed that the sons of Guatemala and Costa

Rica willing to do so would be considered nationals of the United States of Central America. In November 1898 the República Mayor changed its name to the United States of Central America, but a few weeks later the project of union was impaired by a revolt in El Salvador against the government. When General Tomás Regalado seized power and withdrew his state from the union, the union collapsed.

As is well known, by the turn of the twentieth century, the star of the USA was on the rise in the region. The United States was on the road to hemispheric hegemony, sustained by policies aimed at controlling access to resources deemed important by the United States and by the protection of U.S. interests and investments in the Americas.[5] By the late 1890s the United States had also managed to curtail and contain German and French inroads in Central America and the Caribbean. Moreover, by 1901 Britain tacitly accepted—in the Hay-Pauncefote Treaty signed with the United States—that Central America was already within the U.S. sphere of influence. By 1903 the United States supported Panama's independence from Colombia in return for the exclusive right to build the Panama Canal and retain control over the Canal Zone.[6] Unlike the Monroe Doctrine itself, the Roosevelt Corollary of 1904 was no idle threat. The United States proceeded to assist in the "liberation" of Panama from Colombia and to establish control through treaties, customs receiverships, and/or military occupation over Panama, Cuba, Haiti, the Dominican Republic, and Nicaragua. Gunboat and dollar diplomacy helped to keep other Central American states submissive, and the owners of United Fruit and other companies openly boasted of buying and selling presidents.[7]

During this period a constellation of two powerful dictators, Manuel Estrada Cabrera in Guatemala (1898–1920) and José Santos Zelaya in Nicaragua (1893–1909), threatened to bring the isthmus to international war. This prompted the mediating efforts of U.S. President Theodore Roosevelt and Porfirio Díaz of Mexico to bring the countries of the isthmus into agreement on transnational cooperation and limit the potential of transnational destabilization. Carolyn Hall and Héctor Pérez Brignoli describe the process as follows:

> In 1906 Zelaya supported an insurrection led by José León Castillo to overthrow Estrada Cabrera. Insurgents invaded Guatemala from El Salvador and Mexico. The rebellion ended with Guatemalan victory in the brief War of Totoposte. Alarmed by the prospect of hostilities throughout the isthmus, the United States and Mexico convened the five northern states to a peace conference on board the USS *Marblehead*

and a subsequent meeting in San José attended by all presidents except Zelaya. The following year, Zelaya supported a rebellion against his Honduran adversary, President Manuel Bonilla. . . . With the isthmus on the verge of civil war, the United States and Mexico convened another Central American peace conference, held in Washington in 1907. The states agreed to end intervention in each other's affairs, repudiate regimes that came to power through revolutions or coups, and uphold the neutrality of Honduras. A Central American Court of Justice was established in Costa Rica, to resolve future disputes by peaceful means. Any violation of the Washington treaties might provoke non-recognition or intervention by the United States.[8]

A General Treaty of Peace and Friendship was signed in Washington, D.C., in December 1907 under the sponsorship of the United States. Efforts to revive a confederation failed, but the delegates signed eight conventions aimed at stopping transnational fighting, as countries agreed not to intervene in the affairs of their neighbors through the manipulation of political exiles and other measures. With the opening of the Panama Canal only years away, the United States was strongly interested in the political stability of the isthmus. Within the isthmus the position of El Salvador was crucial, since its policies of distrust of Guatemala's striving for regional hegemony assured the parallel projection of Nicaraguan influence until 1908. Likewise, Salvadoran opposition to the increasing dependence of Central America on U.S. financial support led to various early transnational initiatives such as the idea of creating a Central American bank in 1912.

An International Central American Office was created and located in Guatemala with the intention of supporting "the peaceful recreation of the Central American Fatherland." The office, in which delegates of the various states were represented, cooperated with the member governments in promoting the harmonization of constitutional charters, the unification of educational contents and custom tariffs, monies, weights and measures, the adoption of a single shield and flag, and so forth. The office published a quarterly journal that promoted the spirit of transnational unity through notes on the common history and national heroes and symbols, reports on regional treaties, and information on the member states. The spirit of transnational mission that pervaded its activities can be assessed by quoting the opening paragraph of its April–June 1920 issue:

> Central America, wake up. The feeling of nationality stands up boldly in each of the five Republics of the Isthmus. Our peoples, melted by

misfortune, diminished by animosity, increasingly sense the imperative need of transforming into optimal reality those spiritual ties that, albeit in weak form, have maintained the noble and fertile idea of Central American solidarity during the painful phase of our separation. Tying our fraternity within an indissoluble bond and enabling the emergence of a free, great and prosperous nation in the heart of the new world, constitutes the imperative mandate of our peoples. An intensive work of regeneration is needed. After so many years of exhausting experience, it is hard to imagine that the sacred fire of patriotism would still be impotent to melt the ice of indifference that controls minds and of egoism that makes hearts sick.[9]

Those committed to a Central American fatherland were encouraged by the experience of Italy and Germany, which were united after centuries of fragmentation. Writing about the Italian experience, they imagined the future of their own fatherland, choosing to stress the voluntary, spiritual commitment of those willing to work for "national unity" beyond "sectionalism." The following quote is representative of this line of thought:

Even before the current kingdom of Italy emerged, there existed an "Italian fatherland." On the basis of the identification of the old kingdoms, principalities and duchesses with memories, interests and aspirations, thinkers elaborated the notion of Young Italy, an ideal of the future fatherland, united, great and powerful. Young Italy became [then] a reality and its organization as a single nationality was due to the patriotic propaganda of Mazzini, more than to the political manipulation of Cavour and the military feats of Carlos Alberto, Victor Emmanuel and Garibaldi. The national unity was the crystallization of an audacious and illuminating thought that, already in the past, beat in the spirit of Italians, obsessed with the emergence of the Fatherland. . . . Central America stands in an analogous evolution now. . . . [In the last decade] such spirit moves calmly due to fraternity and what circumstances claim, toward the crystallization of the idea of national unity. . . . The re-emergence of the Central American Fatherland turns into the most elevated political aim of the sectional governments converging with the most pure desires of the peoples. . . . The Fatherland exists as a moral entity. . . . Its spirit—the spirit of a Young Central America—lives in the minds as a regenerating force . . . and searches for the material form that will become the active factor in the society of nations.[10]

In the 1910s and 1920s the institutional trend of treaties signed by delegates of the isthmus states was accompanied by renewed transnational activities led by the unionist movement, a non-state actor committed to the idea of a great Central American fatherland. The movement constituted a transnational network of idealistic activists who tried to recreate the project of a Central American nation.

The origins of this movement date back to the 1890s, spearheaded in Guatemala by a group of students led by Salvador Mendieta (1879–1958). Mendieta was a Nicaraguan youngster who arrived in Guatemala in 1892 to study in the Instituto Nacional de Varones, where he became acquainted with other Central Americans of means who were studying there. Expelled from the Guatemalan institute due to his student activism, he moved to complete to his secondary education in El Salvador, remaining active in student circles willing to promote a sense of Central American brotherhood. In late 1897 he was back in Guatemala, where he started his studies in law at the university, and in 1899—under the government of Manuel Estrada Cabrera—he founded a student association committed to promoting Central American bonds and fighting the dictatorships of the isthmus. Imprisoned and expelled from the country, he completed his studies in Honduras in 1902. Back in Nicaragua he continued to create unionist associations and afterward turned into a most prolific writer and speaker defending the regeneration of the Central American societies and the re-creation of the union.[11] In the early twentieth century, Mendieta founded the Partido Unionista Centro Americano and relocated serially to Costa Rica, El Salvador, Honduras and Nicaragua, driven by confrontations with those in power. Later on, as he and others launched again the Partido Unionista de Centro América (PUCA) in 1919, the movement achieved its full impact, benefiting particularly from the support of pro-unionist governments in 1920–21 led by those in Honduras and Guatemala.[12]

The spirit of unification was promulgated by unionists at the grassroots level. They were convinced that the union of early independence failed due to a combination of factors: the egoistic drive of reactionary elites, their manipulation of ignorant masses, and their cooptation of intellectuals who otherwise could have opposed the dissolution. Accordingly, they envisioned reunification as led by a new cohort of committed intellectuals who would spread the word and nourish the latent massive support for the unionist revival, which in their eyes was the "truth of the future," soon to turn into a reality with many benefits for the well-being and pride of Central Americans, living in liberty, democracy, justice, and the rule of law.[13]   The core of unionism was constituted by intellectuals, teachers, and students, most of upper-class background, who were disillusioned with liberal, Positivist, and materialist projects and refused to recognize the true republic of which they dreamt in the states in which they lived. According to the unionist creed, being a divided nation, Central America was prey to a new form of slavery—serving the whims and interests of foreigners and their internal allies who amassed fortunes at the expense of the blood and sweat of the peoples of the region. Mendieta and the activists envisioned that in order to prosper, Central America had to unite as a region open to all humankind. Moreover, once Central America was united, Mexico and South America would be in a stronger position to resist the onslaught of U.S. economic interests. The unionists wanted to regenerate the nation, promote the spiritual consciousness of a shared destiny among all the inhabitants of the isthmus, and create a just society in which individuals would not only be considered abstract citizens with duties. Rather, they envisioned individuals as concrete persons enjoying basic rights, irrespective of ethnic, gender, or status differences.[14]

Many of these ideas seem to have been elaborated in connection with theosophy, a spiritual doctrine preaching universal brotherhood, cultural understanding, and self-development that started in the USA in the late nineteenth century.[15] Yet, they connected such idealistic visions with concrete claims and positions dealing with political, social, and economic rights, addressing as well their contribution to the regeneration of society and the reconstruction of the Central American nation. In "El minimum vital," a civic catechism elaborated in the 1920s and published in 1929, Alberto Masferrer (1868–1932) singled out the need to recognize the right of the people to work and earn a living and the right of having access to the land, water, and products of the land as the bases of common good and justice.[16] In a statement published posthumously, Masferrer indicated the need to overcome previous divisions in order to attain the reconstruction of the Central American nation:

> You should not be Liberal nor be Conservative, but Unionist. The most pressing need is to build the union. Since, if we do not do it soon, others will control us and then there will be no Conservatives and no Liberals, but subjects of an alien power, enjoying at best the use of their own language. When we shall consolidate the union, time will come to see if we are Liberals or Conservatives.[17]

The unionists were fully aware of the failure of previous projects of Central American union, but they believed in the bottom-up regeneration of the Central American nation, to be attained by promoting a consciousness of common destiny and building a model of equality, social justice, and tolerance that would encourage the union while respecting the autonomy of the various states and regions. They did not exclude other projects such as continental Bolivarianism but thought these projects would have better chances of realization once the vision of a united isthmus was attained.[18]

They were more critical of pan-Americanism, due to its top-down agenda and its connection to imperialist and interventionist schemes, which some of them resisted with armed struggle, foremost in the case of Augusto César Sandino (1895–1934) resisting the U.S. military presence in Nicaragua from 1927 to his assassination in 1933. Starting in 1920 Sandino had experienced life in the economic enclaves of the Atlantic coast of Central America, first in Bluefields (Nicaragua), then in La Ceiba (Honduras), then briefly in Guiriguá (Guatemala), and finally in Tampico (Mexico). In these places he got to know the diversity of the circum-Caribbean area populated by "British West Indian Blacks," Garifunas, U.S. plantation and farm managers, and a multinational labor force that included foreign radicals and adventurers, many of whom led economic struggles and fought U.S. economic interests and imperialism.[19] Sandino developed his vision of resistance to international intervention and Bolivarian, transnational commitments as he wandered through the Americas. His key officers (and some of the rank-and-file soldiers) were drawn from all Central American territories and some from even Mexico and the Dominican Republic.[20] Donald Hodges has fully documented the ideological foundations of Sandino's ideas, pointing out that Sandino was strongly influenced by spiritualist and apocalyptic ideas predicating "the solidarity of all spirits" and revolutionary changes geared to establishing a society "without private property, parasites, autocrats, plutocrats, and religious, national, racial, and male supremacists." Hodges indicates that these ideals were combined with the use of violence as part of a Sorelian legacy transmitted into the Americas by Spanish anarcho-syndicalists that Sandino eventually incorporated while adopting a spiritualized vision of social justice.[21]

Imbued by the vision of Central American regeneration and especially in the years preceding the 100th anniversary of the end of Spanish rule in Central America, many of the unionists wandered through the sister nations of the region, either suffering the perils of exile or as expatriates, trying to promote enthusiasm for the unionist creed in their new environments. Years later, Joaquín Rodas, one of those activists working for the ideal of the great fatherland, reconstructed the sense of "pilgrimage" and "apostolic mission" that imbued their wanderings and their work for the cause of reunification. In a book of memoirs Rodas describes some of the practices that were used to energize the movement:

I recall that in one of the fraternal *fiestas* that we held, people printed thoughts on flags and signs decorating little gift baskets distributed among all guests to the dance and dinner [so that women and men] would not desert the unionist ideal ever. Let me recall a few of those delicately drafted thoughts:

"You should not marry a partisan of locality, who will only be a sterile and ungrateful plant for the home and the Fatherland." "You will add enchantment to your grace, oh, beautiful woman, if you can say: 'My Fatherland is united Central America.'" "Whoever is not a unionist does not deserve to have been born in this beautiful land, where the volcanoes, the lakes and the sky, everything speaks of union and harmony." "A separatist is a valueless number, a disharmonious note in the harmonic concert of all the peoples of the Isthmus."

If two persons who join by love have faith in the Unionist Ideal, what generation of patriots will grow in that home![22]

Central American activists moved hectically throughout the region in the 1920s, partly due to deportation by state authorities or motivated by their own transnational agendas. Paradigmatic though perhaps extreme is the case of Agustín Farabundo Martí (1893–1932). In 1920 he was deported from El Salvador to Guatemala, where he spent five years as a university student and worked in factories and among indigenous peasants. He then became active in the Central American Communist Party established in Guatemala City in 1925. In 1927 the Guatemalan authorities deported him to El Salvador, whence he was expelled to Nicaragua, to return shortly to work with the Salvadoran labor federation. In 1928 Martí traveled to New York and became connected to the Anti-Imperialist League of the Americas, an organization that sent him to Nicaragua to serve as its representative with Sandino. He joined Sandino in his exile in Mexico in 1929–30, to return to El Salvador, where he activated in the recently founded Salvadoran Communist Party. In December 1930 he was again deported from El Salvador and bounced back and forth between the United States and Central American countries, including El Salvador, Costa Rica, Panama, Nicaragua, and finally back to El Salvador, where he helped start a peasant uprising against the government of President Maximiliano Hernández Martínez in January 1932. In spite of initial occupation of a half-dozen towns in the western region of the country, the reoccupation of rebel-held towns led to state repression and a massacre of between 10,000 and 30,000 peasants and rural laborers, most of them indigenous or ladino laborers, many of whom were machine-gunned collectively while others were shot or hanged by local citizens and military reservists. The memory and legacy of this activism was projected in El Salvador for decades by the FMLN—the Farabundo Martí National Liberation Front, which fought U.S.-backed military rule during the cold war and remained a major political force also after democratization.[23]

From a transnational perspective, probably the most important long-term contribution of the unionists was the widening of the Central American public spheres through the creation in the 1920s–40s of many publications, spreading their ideas in the struggle for cultural hegemony,[24] along with the opening of spaces of sociability beyond distinctions of gender, nationality, and to a lesser extent class and race.

This work of diffusion of ideas and creation of spaces of sociability expanded public debate on issues such as the incorporation of indigenous and mestizo subaltern sectors and women to full citizenship and the regeneration of society from the bottom up. Through such activism and diffusion of ideas, they influenced ideational paradigms, impacting the thought of thousands of individuals across the isthmus, some of whom—Juan José Arévalo, for one— would later on take an active part in politics, and others—the daughters and granddaughters of the women participating in the female circles named after Gabriela Mistral—in 1946 would attain female rights to vote and run for office in Guatemala.

The spirit of reunification that the transnational movement kept alive also combined with the sincere attempts of the International Central American Office to work within the framework of pan-Americanism, publicizing efforts of regional coordination and promoting the sense of Central American solidarity.

The 1910s witnessed major efforts to develop transnational cooperation, including the development of a Central American corpus of international law supported by Washington as part of its policies of pan-Americanism. However, the entire transnational project coordinated by the International Central American Office constituted a sui generis case ridden with inner tensions.

These tensions were due to the fact that this set of nations was supposed to unify their legal and economic frameworks through regional treaties, "as their destinies are the same," while at the same time retaining their sovereignty intact. Thus, on the one hand, the office stressed time and again that Central American treaties were aimed "to translate the aspirations of the peoples and governments, which consider that the traditions of the past and the needs of the present are, at the same time, promise and guarantee of absolute unity in the future."[25]

Yet, on the other hand, there were almost contradictory expectations in the mission, since, as the quarterly publication recognized,

> this is not a political federation, but a confederation of interests: it is the Centro-Americanism within the Pan-Americanism itself; more intimate, more connected than the latter, since it is not an aspiration or a general behavioral line, but a reality concretized in imperative and binding principles.[26]

Unsurprisingly, the "confederation of interests" soon broke apart and once again came to nothing. The first major blow to the institutional mechanisms devised by the conventions resulted from the placement of Nicaragua under the protectorate of the United States in the 1910s. The United States stationed Marines in Nicaragua to protect commercial interests and investments and back a failing state that was facing increasing civil strife and banditry. In 1913 and 1916 formal treaties were signed, granting the United States exclusive and perpetual rights to build and operate an interoceanic canal through the San Juan River and Lake Nicaragua in return for a payment of three million dollars to be used to relieve Nicaragua's foreign debt. In addition, Nicaragua would grant the United States the long-term lease of the Maíz Islands and allow the construction of a military base on the Gulf of Fonseca on the Pacific coast. Costa Rica and El Salvador, Honduras, and Colombia protested, with Costa Rica bringing the case before the Central American Court of Justice. They claimed that the U.S.-Nicaraguan treaty constituted a violation of territorial rights and of Central American conventions, violating the neutrality of the region. As the court accepted their arguments, Nicaragua withdrew from the court, and it became evident that there was no way to enforce the ruling, as the United States ignored it as well. This led to the discredit of one of the key Central American institutions. When the court's convention came up for renewal in 1918, Central Americans rejected the opportunity to renew it, mainly due to this incident.[27] An attempt was made to revive the court in 1923, but states and citizens alike were skeptical, and the pan–Central American hopes of 1907 were gone.

Central American skepticism was sustained by recognizing the increasing binding of regional interests to those of the United States, both with what was later called the Big Stick interventionism and the U.S. presence in the Caribbean and Central America. Such interventionism, however, cannot be attributed exclusively to the expansionist drive of the United States. The weak institutionalization of states generated a situation in which domestic contenders called on the United States to serve as the transnational actor that could intervene, supporting them in their power struggles. As Robert H. Holden indicates, under situations of hollow legitimacy and fragmented authority that existed in the region, the United States easily became

> a kind of transnational *patrón* who distributed favors and bought clients by playing on divisions within and among the governments of Central America. As early as 1911, Adolfo Díaz, the U.S.-installed president of Nicaragua, offered the U.S. *chargé* in Managua a treaty that would permit Washington "to intervene in our internal affairs in order to maintain peace" . . . Díaz pointed out that politics in Nicaragua had for many years been nothing less than a "state of war" between political parties that drew inevitably on fighting forces elsewhere in the isthmus; only U.S. intervention held out any hope for lasting peace. When the *jefe máximo* of Guatemala, Manuel Estrada Cabrera, began to see night fall on this twenty-two years in power in 1920, he summoned the U.S. minister to his office and, in the latter's words, "placed the entire situation and the fate of the country in our hands and would agree to abide by any decision which we make."[28]

These complementary interests brought about the recurrent direct intervention of U.S. forces in Central America and the Caribbean in the early twentieth century.

The fall of the Guatemalan president Estrada Cabrera in 1920 created a short-lived window of opportunity for reunification. The unionists had the support of Carlos Herrera Luna, acting president and president of Guatemala between April 1920 and December 1921. A federal congress, with the participation of delegates of Guatemala, El Salvador, and Honduras, was convened and signed a union pact in January 1921. The pact was subsequently ratified by Guatemala, Honduras, and El Salvador. While Costa Rica was reluctant to accept a regional government, Nicaragua's situation was complex, as the state had signed the 1916 treaty with the United States—almost becoming a U.S. protectorate—and was under occupation by the U.S. Marines. In September 1921 a federal constitutional assembly was convened in Tegucigalpa that promulgated a constitution for the Centro-American Republic establishing a federal council of delegates as an executive body and declaring Tegucigalpa the capital of the newly created state. The constitution was issued by Guatemala, El Salvador, and Honduras, with an explicit recognition that Costa Rica and Nicaragua were expected to join as part of the "Central American family," a commonality the five countries supposedly shared on the basis of ethnic, geographic, and historical reasons.[29] The interstate initiative led, however, to nothing, as it was frustrated by a coup d'état operating to remove the pro-unionist government of Guatemala, which was the strongest institutional anchor for this initiative, in December 1921.

While it was asserted that the drive to Central American coordination was founded on the need to regulate coexistence and the impossibility of remaining isolated from international circuits, even the International Central American Office had to recognize that the international treaties signed by the countries of the isthmus were indeed "doctrines" more than "binding laws," therefore lacking the capacity of being implemented except through "moral recognition." In the following decades, such recognition was marginalized.

In 1923 a new treaty was signed by the Central American states that reiterated the principles of the 1907 agreements. Nonetheless, by then, the United States was clearly the sole arbiter of interstate tensions and the force behind the possible consolidation of separate nation-states in the isthmus. This became evident in 1927 when tensions almost led to a "banana war" between Guatemala and Honduras, beyond which stood the United Fruit Company and the Cuyamel Fruit Company, both looking for further land concessions. The United States intervened forcefully to put down the conflict, and two years later the source of tension ended as the Cuyamel Fruit Company was taken over by the United Fruit Company.[30]

Following three decades of interventionism, the United States elaborated a strategy for containing or controlling political change by leaving behind well-trained local forces to protect the claims of U.S. corporations and the governments and political leaders favored by U.S. policy makers.[31] From the mid-1920s to the early 1930s these developments would bring university students—especially many of those studying in Guatemala—to retain the pan-Central American perspective yet move beyond unionism, which, according to their understanding, was looking backward, into more radical positions, phrasing their goals in anti-imperialist terms. Inspired by the Mexican Revolution's new ideals, the rising star of Marxist ideas, and the potent surge of the university reform movement in Argentina, many became fervent supporters of anti-imperialist and pan-Iberoamerican positions (although a minority adopted conservative ideas). Some of them participated along with workers in trade union activities such as those generated by the establishment in 1924 of a Central American Worker Confederation (Confederación Obrera Centroamericana, or COCA), which was conceived as a regional umbrella organization for country federations (with the exception of Costa Rican workers, who declined to participate).

Increasingly, however, the transnational orientation of these sectors was diluted as it clashed with or was absorbed by the distinct institutional interests of the different states. Illustrative was the participation of many Salvadoran university and teacher seminary students along with their Guatemalan peers in the Holy Friday student strike of 1931. The brutal repression of Guatemalans and Salvadorans alike by president General Jorge Ubico (1931–44) raised diplomatic tensions between the governments of the two countries in sharp contrast to the rank-and-file transnational cooperation of their citizens in the framework of the student movement.[32]

The recurrent attempts to reconstruct political unity or at least regional coordination, carried out from the 1840s to the 1920s, failed. Their ebb-and-flow character is highly revealing of the tension-ridden existence of political and social forces supporting transnational projects alongside more secluded projects of nation-state building in the region. The transnational drive did not vanish, and yet, often it was suspected by some of the states as a mechanism geared to an expansionist project led by another isthmian state or coalition of states willing to expand its or their own influence and regional hegemony. Moreover, as time passed, the recurring transnational initiatives were increasingly superseded by the individual states' development of institutional distinctiveness and distance from one another, compounded by international interventions and hegemony over the isthmus. Nonetheless, it is worth stressing again that there were civil movements like the unionists that kept alive the dream of a united Central America. Likewise, there were certain historical moments, such as the period from 1900 to the early 1920s, in which the transnational project of these movements coalesced with a certain constellation of power in the isthmus and the strategy of the United States rising to geopolitical hegemony, thus creating favorable conditions for attempting to implement such a project. The ephemeral character of the project reflected, as we have seen, internal contradictions and the growing weight of the distinct paths of states' development as a major factor in the transnational equation. Increasingly, states consolidated their hold, and even though they could not disengage completely from each other, their involvement increasingly took more the form of facing an unwanted spillover, a kind of challenge to be confronted, rather than the result of ebbs and flows of initiatives of regional reunification or coordination. Such a dynamic was already visible in the early twentieth century yet reached its strongest impact when some of the countries in the isthmus turned into a battlefield of contrasting political and ideological forces in the cold war.

9

Distinct Paths of Development and the Cold War Transnational Spillover

While a central argument of this book is that the countries could not and did not completely disengage from one another's affairs and internal devel opments in any of these countries continued to affect circumstances in the others, by the twentieth century Central American state development was highly differentiated as states consolidated their hold and increasingly followed distinctive institutional paths.

State dissociation had led by then to the crystallization of distinct paths of institutional development and separate nation-state consciousness. This divergence was reflected in the failing attempts of reconstituting Central American unity or coordinating isthmian interests by the third decade of the twentieth century. Even if one finds nuanced differences and debates on the exact timing of this process, most historical, sociological, and political analyses support the view that the isthmian states had entered such a cycle of increasing institutional differentiation.[1]

A path-dependent analysis of Central America linking the formation of distinct institutional structures to the strategies chosen by state elites has been suggested to account for this development. Following a long-term analysis, James Mahoney has focused on the choices of key actors at critical junctures as vital to institutional differentiation.[2] According to this analysis, strategic choices led to the formation of institutions with self-perpetuating properties, shaping a series of reactions and counter-reactions that culminated in the creation of distinct political regimes. Specifically, as Mahoney looked at the late nineteenth and early twentieth centuries, he identified a major point of divergence under the liberals in power between countries in which the liberal rulers faced intense political threats and accordingly built powerful militaries while pursuing radical policy options (Guatemala, El Salvador, and Nicaragua) and those other countries in which none of this threat-and-reaction cycle occurred, namely, Honduras and Costa Rica. In turn, this led to the emergence of three types or models of liberal regime—a radical type in Guatemala and El Salvador, a reformist type of liberalism in Costa Rica, and an aborted type of liberalism in Honduras and Nicaragua. The latter two types lacked the polarized rural class structures and coercive military apparatuses of the first, while in addition the aborted liberal model lacked emergent agrarian elites with significant political power and a centralized state apparatus as was typical of the reformist type of liberalism.

Within this framework, the next critical juncture of divergence was shaped by whether major democratizing episodes occurred in the aftermath of the liberal reforms and whether these were successful. Military authoritarian regimes arose in Guatemala and El Salvador as major democratizing episodes failed. Liberal democracy was taking shape in Costa Rica, as the major democratizing moves in the country were successful, and traditional dictatorship arose in Honduras and Nicaragua because there were no major democratizing episodes during their twentieth-century development (figure 9.1).

This line of analysis should be supplemented with an analysis of the transnational linkages that remained at work and shaped what we could define as transnational contacts and spillover from time to time, as for instance during the cold war years. That is, we should be sensitive to the fact that the process of breaking apart institutionally did not obliterate a transnational dynamic, although it certainly redefined the terms of its impact.

A clear indication of the path-shaping or at least path-conditioning persistence of transnational linkages beneath and beyond the process of institutional and state divergence is provided by the persistent role of political exile and asylum in the region, along with its changing format.[3] Translocation of political dissidents across the isthmus soon turned into a transnational non-state mechanism of political reconstitution in neighboring countries from which the exiles could plot plans of return to power in the home country, from which they hoped to ostracize those who expelled them or forced them to escape, perhaps with the support of the host governments, thus being at once political agents and peons of transnational strategies.

As analyzed above, the crystallization of the new states did not preclude at first overlapping territorial claims, a trend evident in the high measures of influence that the political class of each state continued to exercise in the neighboring countries. Then elites in power intervened in the configuration of neighboring countries' political factions according to their own interests. When the faction they supported was defeated, they often hastily accepted the vanquished political actors in their territory, hosting them and

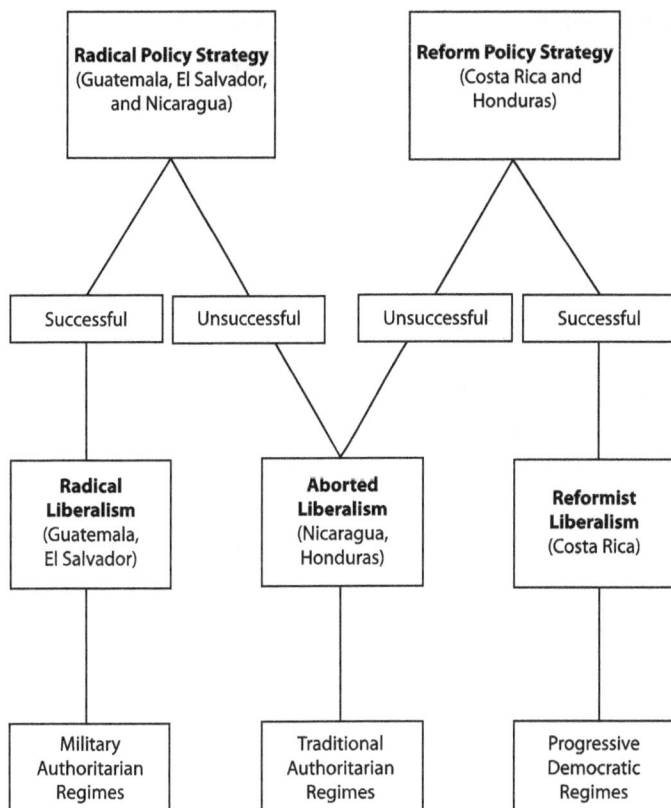

Figure 9.1. Policy strategies and path analysis following liberal reform. Source: James Mahoney, "Path-Dependent Explanation of Regime Change: Central America in Comparative Perspective," *Studies in Comparative International Development* 36, 1 (2001): 11141.

even supporting their plans of return. The political class of each state acted in such a manner in order to regain control of the neighboring political scene or at least exercise their influence by strengthening sympathetic political allies. When the defeated faction was inimical to their political script or design, they could still host the expelled individuals and control their freedom of action in order to curtail their possibilities of plotting against the ruling government in the neighboring country.[4]

Central American countries have used exiles as pawns in transnational games of power and in turn have been influenced by and benefited from these connections as they tried to regain power in the home countries or remained in the host countries. But exiles were also active players in these arenas pursuing their own agendas within transnational spaces and with a transnational impact in the region. Exiles conspired against their home governments from the asylum of other Central American states. Only through the mediation of the United States in 1906–7 did the Central American countries agree to stop using those who had taken refuge in their territories as part of their international strategies of power aggrandizement. With the United States as the broker, in 1906 the Central American states agreed "to bar political exiles from other states and from the border regions of their homelands and to refuse to allow their territories to be used as bases for revolutionary movements against their neighbors." While the agreement was soon broken by Nicaraguan aid to Honduran rebels and the Honduran invasion of Nicaragua in retaliation, new meetings in Washington led to conventions that, among other things, confirmed the barring of exiles from border regions and agreed that rebels be brought to trial in the country in which they staged their revolts.[5] Central American countries supported the non-intervention doctrines that would be fully endorsed at the inter-American conference in Buenos Aires in 1936. Yet, in spite of the conventions and agreements, exiles continued to be a persistent factor of third-party involvement by non-state actors in Central American politics in later decades.

The regional wanderings of activists and revolutionaries permeated these societies, whose borders remained porous. Illustrative were Farabundo Martí, Modesto Ramírez, Felipe Armando Amaya, and Gabriela García, who relocated from El Salvador to Guatemala and Honduras to continue their political activities. Likewise, Hondurans including Manuel Cáix Herrera and Juan Pablo Wainright did proselytizing journeys in the other isthmian countries. The wandering was facilitated by constitutional provisions that often allowed any Central American individual to nationalize ("naturalize"), reside, and work in the other countries. Not only activists crossed borders into neighboring states; it turned customary for agricultural workers to search for employment in other countries. For example, many Salvadorans came to work regularly on the Honduran plantations and the coffee estates of southwestern Guatemala.[6]

By the 1950s the exile activities were increasingly acquiring transnational momentum. In both the isthmus and the Caribbean region, a series of dictatorships were generating waves of exiles who spread all over the region. Consequently, there transpired intense activity of exile groups from the states in this region, particularly in Guatemala, Nicaragua, Cuba, Venezuela, and the Dominican Republic. By 1952 virtually the entire region was dominated by dictators persecuting and suppressing internal opponents, so that the political oppositions came almost exclusively from exiles and the networks they managed to create and sustain abroad. At that time, principal centers for exile activity were Mexico City, San José (Costa Rica), San Juan (Puerto Rico), Miami, and New York. Nicaraguan and Honduran exiles preferred Mexico and, depending upon circumstances, San José, Costa Rica.[7]

It should be stressed that not only dictators had been using—and abusing—political exile as a major mechanism of institutionalized exclusion. This can be clearly assessed as one reviews the policies of both the reforming government of President Rafael Angel Calderón Guardia in the 1940s and the revolutionary junta that acceded to power in Costa Rica after the civil war of 1948. José Figueres, a prominent politician and economic entrepreneur who criticized democratically elected President Calderón, found himself expelled to Mexico from 1942 to 1944. In Mexico, Figueres joined a group of Latin American politicians who formed the Caribbean Legion. The legion plotted against the ruling governments of the Dominican Republic, Venezuela, Nicaragua, and Costa Rica. The policies of Calderón, who expropriated German assets in the framework of World War II, alienated coffee growers and bankers of German descent and many conservatives who backed Figueres against the reformist government of President Calderón. In 1948 a situation of political polarization existed, and a short but bloody civil war resulted from contested electoral results. When Figueres took power at the head of a self-proclaimed revolutionary junta, Calderón was forced to flee into exile in Nicaragua and later in Mexico, where he stayed for nearly a decade.

In fleeing political persecution and relocating in exile, close proximity to one's home country was a preferable choice in the isthmus as elsewhere because displacement within a short distance allowed exiles to sustain the hope of a prompt return. Anastasio Somoza, the president of neighboring Nicaragua who had backed Calderón in the civil war, harbored exiles fleeing persecution by the government of Figueres. Exiles were primarily individuals associated with former President Calderón and his followers, activists of the labor movement associated with the communists, and parts of the oligarchy. Animosity between the two leaders reached a climax when in 1954 Figueres allowed Nicaraguan exiles in Costa Rica to launch an invasion of their home country in an attempt to overthrow Somoza. The Nicaraguan president retaliated by launching an invasion of Costa Rica in January 1955, integrating Costa Rican exiles in an attack that almost cost Figueres his presidency. Figueres' position was only saved by the intervention of the Organization of American States and the United States.[8]

The more militant exiles of all nationalities were in Costa Rica, where many exiles and university students from all Central America joined in the rebellion of 1948, hoping to trigger a regional movement of change. Also prominent, even though of all sorts of ideological convictions, were exiles residing in Jacobo Arbenz' Guatemala until the coup d'état that deposed him and forced him into exile in 1954. Some of these exiles were sympathetic to the Guatemalan government. Other exiles became involved in the operation that, under the leadership of Carlos Castillo Armas and Miguel Ydígoras, deposed Arbenz with arms received from the United States in Honduras and Nicaragua. From Tegucigalpa the exiles openly formed a Movement of National Liberation and announced their plans of ousting Arbenz, which they carried out as they invaded Guatemala in June 1954. Once in power and after disbanding political parties, Castillo Armas led a wave of repression that caused many of his conationals to flee into exile.[9]

In later years Guatemalan exiles continued to flow into El Salvador and Honduras to escape persecution by those in power and to try to rally forces to regain state power. For instance, most of those involved in a failed attempt to take power in mid-November 1960 fled to the "sister nations," where they were approached by leftist militants who managed to convince them to adopt thereafter a guerrilla strategy against the government of President Ydígoras (1958–63). The emergence of the guerrilla in Guatemala, particularly in the capital, can be traced directly to the influence of these transnational connections.[10]

Besides political activities and in many cases organizing for invasions and insurrections, many exiles engaged in writing, teaching, lecturing, and public speaking, partly because this was a way to make a living. These activities had a clear transnational impact, communicating their cause to the Caribbean, Central America, and North America. The activities of the exiled politicians were important enough to provoke the reaction of local dictators and engender transnational sympathy in rival countries and advocacy networks of solidarity, which in turn generated international pressure. Likewise, democratic dialogue and alliances cemented transnational cooperation among democratic leaders and exiles throughout the Americas.

Physical exclusion from domestic ("national") public spheres was increasingly not the equivalent of political exclusion, due to the transnational and international impact of the exiles. Through their transnational impact, exiled individuals could affect the equation of power in their home countries while abroad. The attempts to assassinate exiles abroad are a clear indication of the increasing importance of a transnational tier as part of the structure of exile in the region. The activities of the agents of Trujillo, Batista, Somoza, and other dictators, although largely uncoordinated, signaled a move to radicalizing tactics of dealing with important leaders of the exile oppositions, as would be typical of the Operation Condor in South America nearly two decades later and of the Central American transnational war in the 1980s. Although countries respected the right of asylum, they watched the activities of exiles carefully in order to avoid radicalizing influences in the domestic arena and at the same time diminish international friction and embarrassment with peer governments. Students in particular were a category not always welcome, as they tended to be politically active. While exiles were usually a minority of the population, existing communities of migrants, students, and sojourners were often politically activated and radicalized by incoming exiles. In 1956 the Honduran government was reported to be trying to persuade Guatemalan student exiles to depart for Costa Rica because it did not want them to stir up the local student body.[11]

In early times, exile politics was transnational by default, comprised by the three-tiered structure of the expelling countries, the exiles, and the host countries, in which there was always the possibility of exiles becoming a tool to further the agenda of the host country. By the mid-twentieth century, however, exile politics already involved an explicit transnational involvement. In the following decades, as the cold war fully impacted the region, the problem of exile became compounded by the massive waves of refugees escaping repression and the bloody confrontation of forces inspired by ideological drive of the 1980s.

The transnational dimensions were once more of crucial relevance under the impact of the cold war, as there was an intensification of transnational forces in the region. Following the Sandinistas' takeover in 1979, the isthmus entered a period of civil wars, compounded with international intervention and transnational involvement by third parties, an involvement that was projected also into the peace efforts of the late 1980s and during the democratic period that started in the 1990s. The purpose of the following pages is not to provide a detailed analysis of the region in the cold war years, something that has been comprehensively treated by previous research.[12] Rather, I aim at analyzing those transnational dimensions of the conflict in the proximate states of the region, which cannot be merely accounted for by the "domino theory" that was projected by the USA to advance its own hegemonic plan in the region.

The roots of the regional conflict can be traced in the growing socioeconomic imbalances and increasing political inefficacy that Central America experienced throughout the twentieth century that led to radical changes and a conflict of transnational impact. Beginning in the 1920s the decline in mortality rates along with sustained fertility rates led to an explosive population growth in Central America that was particularly salient in El Salvador. By 1930 the region had recuperated and grown to its estimated population size prior to the Spanish conquest, that is, roughly between five and six million inhabitants. After this recuperation, a geometrical growth started, which increased the regional population to more than thirty million by 1990. This trend put tremendous pressures on the structure of unreformed land ownership and control, existing resources, and models of development. This in turn created unrest, which was tied to pressures from social sectors demanding greater democratization, with such demands meeting repression and, in some cases, international intervention in the early twentieth century.

By the mid-twentieth century, developments seemed propitious. Central American economies had grown in the three decades since the Great Depression, although the growth was at the cost of a widening socioeconomic gap and under political systems increasingly dominated by dictators, who faced the rising political mobilization of democratic and nondemocratic forces committed to ousting them from power.

Following the military coups that started with the CIA-orchestrated removal of President Jacobo Arbenz in Guatemala in 1954, the Cuban Revolution of 1959, and Che Guevara's commitment to create as many Vietnams as possible, the United States moved to condone and often support authoritarian rule in the name of national security.[13] If Latin American countries were unfit to follow the U.S. model of development and in the context of the cold war were on the brink of political breakdown and the threat of revolution, perhaps it was time to make room for a renewed domestic model of "order and progress" resembling that which, in the late nineteenth and early twentieth centuries, had been successfully adopted by the followers of Positivism in Latin America. From a geopolitical perspective and in terms of resources, small countries depended heavily on U.S. decisions.

Political life had become polarized and fragmented at the same time. Against the backdrop of the cold war and the inability of ruling elites to lead their countries to peaceful coexistence and more equal development, a growing sense of support for radical change dominated intellectual circles and the younger generations. Youth were attracted to the option of the revolution to the detriment of the democratic left. Starting in the 1960s the impact of U.S. hemispheric policy combined with domestic trends, primarily the increasing socioeconomic mobilization and polarized political arenas. Having the supportive vision of being on the frontline of defense of western civilization, as led by the United States and encoded in doctrines of national security, the governments renewed the use of regimes of exception, military interventions in public life, and suspension of constitutional freedoms and guarantees, with severe consequences in the realm of human rights. By the 1960s and 1970s guerrilla movements had emerged in El Salvador, Guatemala, and Nicaragua. The region lived through increasing problems of governance rooted in the dual processes of polarization at both the left and right ends of the political spectrum, coupled with a severe fragmentation of political forces in both camps. In Guatemala, for instance, there were in the 1960s severe disagreements and fights between supporters of armed struggle and those willing to use nonviolent political participation; and yet, in parallel, pro-Moscow, Maoist, Trotskyite, and Cuban-related groups disagreed on strategies and tactics, creating contradictory moves. On directives from Moscow, mainstream communists tended to support a "peaceful coexistence" strategy, rejected by Trotskyites who supported internationalist struggle and at first by the Castrists who, still under the spell of their success in Cuba, supported a policy of *foquismo*, a small revolutionary vanguard that supposedly would serve as catalyst for a massive popular uprising, since the conditions for a socialist revolution were already in existence, according to their biased perception. In turn, Maoist supporters favored a prolonged popular war modeled after the bloody civil war in China, again misreading the Central American scenario and ignoring the huge difference in territorial size, which played such a fundamental role in Mao's rise to power. The potential for violence was imbued in the ideological polarization in public spheres and civil society. The messages contained in the elaborations of the left were rejected by others who held diametrically opposed visions of their society and who were no less passionate in their own views and positions.[14] The right-wing camp was equally fragmented and unable to offer a democratic alternative built on consensus, depleting the democratic center and leading to the rise of military officers who often took power hoping to create conditions for public life, reforming the administration and hopefully enabling a more orderly return to democracy. The very principled positions of these circles and the semi-sacredness with which they cognitively structured and evaluated the forces of society contributed to the clash that tore apart these societies in the period leading to the military takeovers. Increasingly men in arms take control of politics only to realize that the closure of electoral avenues to power embolden the armed resistance of what until then were relatively marginal groups. A mounting cycle of protest for change, followed by repression and violence, ensued. Even though only Nicaragua experienced popular uprising that brought about the demise of dictatorship and the rule of a revolutionary government, guerrillas had taken root in Guatemala by the 1960s and in El

Salvador and Nicaragua by the 1970s. This was compounded by the fact that, as A. Douglas Kincaid has stressed, at the outset of the authoritarian period, "Central America was already characterized by policies that prioritized the security of the national state over public security (or more accurately, that identified public security with the security of the state). . . . The subsequent rise of Cold War doctrines above all that of the 'national security state,' only served to strengthen a set of prejudices and practices already in place in the region."[15]

The struggle of the guerrillas and their insurgency tactics met policies of counter-insurgency supported by the only hegemonic power in the Western Hemisphere, the United States. The United States refused to let revolution spread through the isthmus, something both Republicans and Democrats feared, especially after the victory of the Sandinistas in Nicaragua. By the late 1970s and the 1980s civil wars became particularly entangled with international and transnational interventions.

Countries reached this stage of transnational spillover despite starting at very dissimilar points, and yet, the regional conflict in the context of the cold war eventually brought countries like Guatemala, El Salvador, and Nicaragua closer in terms of revolutionary struggle and counter-insurgency strategies, with clear transnational impacts. In Guatemala, as indicated, the military administrations that ruled the country after the coup that ousted Arbenz in 1954 failed to consolidate a stable government. Furthermore, with a divided oligarchy and split leadership in the armed forces, there were frequent coups d'état. By the early 1960s Guatemala was faced with guerrilla actions in the capital city and in remote rural areas that failed to trigger revolution on a countrywide level. After increasing repression, however, a decade later new organizations such as the EGP, or Guerrilla Army of the Poor, adopted novel strategies aimed at mobilizing the indigenous populations of the western and northern highlands. Cities were affected by strikes and guerrilla attacks, while the army adopted scorched-earth tactics, committing massive human rights violations, as part of their counter-insurgency strategy. Indigenous villages were caught "between two fires," and many were devastated, with thousands killed and many more displaced, forcibly conscripted into the guerrillas, while others were relocated to "model villages." Many others were enrolled in civilian patrols known as Patrullas de Acción Ciudadana, or PACs, in order to fight the guerrillas. Yet, by the early 1980s many in the countryside understood that while they distrusted both the guerrillas and the army, the latter at least would be able to protect them from the former. Peasants chose the side of order, partly because of their traditionalism and partly due to the fact that the guerrilla had acted in no less authoritarian and violent ways and that their promised revolutionary order disregarded the social perspective of the local inhabitants and had little chance of being achieved.[16] This added to the militarization of civilian life in the countryside. With the spread of violence there were many cases of human rights violations committed by neighbors for the purpose of personal profiteering or as retaliation for old enmities. The failure of the judicial system to instill a sense of accountability also enabled the establishment of special military tribunals that operated in the early 1980s in total secrecy and sentenced citizens to death with complete impunity. By the mid-1980s, and with a change in the approach of the army to the rural populations and a more offensive strategy of counter-insurrection, the guerrillas had been contained, at an enormous loss of human life, massive human rights violations, territorial displacement or annihilation of entire populations, and property destruction.[17]

In Nicaragua it was the erosion of the early populist model adopted by Somoza Senior and the magnified corruption of the Somoza dynastic regime, intensified by its cynical appropriation of funds originally raised to ease human suffering due to natural calamities and the 1972 earthquake, that brought many citizens and sectors of the society to reject the continuing rule of the Somozas. The increasing use of repression only exacerbated the determination to overthrow the Somozas on the part of those who eventually won power after leading a popular war in the late 1970s. In January 1978 Pedro Joaquín Chamorro, publisher and editor of an independent daily and leader of an opposition alliance campaigning for the removal of President Anastasio Somoza Debayle, was assassinated. His death galvanized violent demonstrations and demands for Somoza's resignation, marking the beginning of the end of the authoritarian regime, whose removal was ultimately brought about by the armed offensive of the Sandinista National Liberation Front (FSLN) in July 1979.

El Salvador's transition to civil war and insurrection was different from Nicaragua's and Guatemala's. The factors that operated such variance were diverse: a more entrenched social conflict in a society with a sharp concentration of economic power in the hands of a small class of coffee-producing and -exporting landed capitalists who for decades delegated power in the army and preferred democratic elections over dictatorships as long as they could; a high degree of mass mobilization on the part of a large working class, probably the most politicized of the isthmus and one in which peasants joined unions and radical organizations long before any plan of armed insurrection; and a more prominent role of an orthodox pro-Moscow communist party.[18] The memory of the 1932 massacre in the western part of the country, together with the efficacy of coercion led by the National Guard and vigilante networks in the countryside, caused many to refrain from supporting guerrilla tactics until the 1970s. In parallel, sectors of the military and civilian politicians hoped to reform the system by reaching positions of power without using violence. The reformist civilian politicians gained power through electoral methods. It was after 1972, when the electoral victory of José Napoleón Duarte and the PDC (Christian Democratic Party) was not recognized, and particularly after the 1979 crisis and coup that El Salvador entered into a more violent phase. Radical Catholics founded the ERP, or People's Revolutionary Army, while others founded the FPL (Popular Forces of Liberation) and the FARN (Armed Forces of National Resistance). In a densely populated environment and a country of smaller dimensions than its neighbors and not enough rearguard territory for guerrillas, activities were concentrated in cities, with bank robberies, kidnappings, and terrorist acts. By 1980, under the model and encouragement of the Sandinistas, the Salvadoran rebel groups joined a unified Farabundo Martí National Liberation Front (FMLN), but even then the fragmentation of the radical left continued. El Salvador then seemed to be on the verge of replicating Nicaragua's path. Nonetheless, there were constraints—such as a smaller territory and a dense population, the lack of inaccessible mountains or densely wooded areas, and borders less permeable than Nicaragua's—that forced the FMLN to adopt different strategies. The lack of large pockets of refuge and rearguard avenues of retreat, such as those available to the Nicaraguans in their country, forced them to engage in a strategy of socialization of supporters into class consciousness. However, their confidence in having reached such support when they launched their "final offensive" in January 1981 proved unfounded. The FMLN failed to secure a military victory, and repression mounted with the support of the U.S. administration, while the PDC retained significant popularity in the early 1980s. In spite of harsh policies of repression, those in power reached only a stalemate, recognized a decade later, when peace agreements were reached, acknowledging no winners but only the grim legacy of the massive human rights violations committed during the struggle.

While carrying out distinct institutional paths and a specific tempo of realignment of coalitions and armed confrontations, in the framework of the last phases of the cold war the isthmian countries were forced to confront transnational dynamics by the late 1970s and early 1980s. Once again, isthmian countries faced an intense recomposition of power due to the internal processes of institutional breakdown, revolutionary pressures, and the armed intervention promoted by the United States to prevent a spillover of the Nicaraguan revolution.

In this context, U.S. circles advanced a "domino theory" as both a descriptive and a prescriptive framework to contain the leftist threat and possibly topple the Sandinistas from power in Nicaragua. The domino theory was adopted by U.S. leaders and used to justify the U.S. military and political intervention and containment of communism in Southeast Asia and Central America. The domino theory, a cornerstone of U.S. foreign policy from the 1960s to the 1980s, stated that if one area in a region came under the influence of the communists, then additional democratic breakdowns could likely follow in a kind of domino effect, that is, as resulting from a spillover and linear sequence similar to a falling row of pieces.[19] When President Ronald Reagan came to office in 1981 this vision led him to engage in counter-insurgency support in Central America that would trigger unrestrained repression in the region. With communist Cuba just to the south and the recent triumph of the Sandinista revolution in Nicaragua in 1979, the new administration envisioned the threat of a Soviet-Cuban campaign aimed at generating a domino effect throughout Central America and the Caribbean. The Reagan administration began combating the perceived threat by developing interventionist policies by which it claimed to be promoting democracy in Central America. The primary focus of these policies was the destabilization of the Sandinista government in Nicaragua and the consolidation of anti-communist political forces in El Salvador, where entrenched elites had been unwilling to reach compromises with the moderate opposition and rebels had begun to seriously challenge the authoritarian regime. The Reagan administration swiftly resolved that it would stand firm in El Salvador against "Soviet expansion" by supporting a substantial military and economic assistance program that would prevent the communist rebels from seizing power as they had in Nicaragua. The second part of Reagan's plan involved removing the Sandinistas from power. He terminated all economic aid to Nicaragua and supported the formation of counterrevolutionary guerilla groups, the Contras, with a base of logistic support in neighboring Honduras. Moreover, to contain the enemy, Honduras became an "armed bastion."[20] Reagan initially rationalized the use of the Contras as a means of preventing arms shipments to El Salvador and later promoted their image as a pro-democracy force that sought to topple the Sandinista regime.

Often debate on the heuristic value of the domino theory has been conflated with opinions on its forecasting value for U.S. policy. During the cold war, supporters and critics of the domino theory argued in favor of or against it in terms of its predictive power in *realpolitik* terms. The theory was basically correct in pointing out the relevance of mutual impact in societies sharing regional closeness and facing similar challenges. Indeed, at least after 1979 it was possible to imagine revolution spreading through Central America. However, at the same time, the theory posited a major fallacy in assuming the mimetic reproduction of policies and developments from one country to the other. The Nicaraguan experience seemed to color the understanding of events elsewhere in the isthmus.[21] Moreover, while paying attention to the fact that intrastate conflicts tend to generate externalities in the international environment via spillover or contagion and the intervention by a strong international actor, as stressed in the literature on conflict resolution,[22] the theory paid less emphasis on other aspects of third-party involvement, such as multinational reciprocal effects and the differential willingness of various state and non-state actors to support different sides in a transnational conflict.

As we take distance in time, it is important to decouple the "domino theory" from the U.S. realpolitik and international strategy of hegemonic hemispheric control followed in the cold war. Rather, the theory reflected—and was defined to confront—the transnational dynamics at work in various forms for generations in the isthmus. In other words, it is my claim that these societies have been affected on a transnational scale not only by the United States and not only in times of crisis. As implied in the pioneer work of Laurence Whitehead on linkages to the international arena, these societies have also been affected by developments in the other societies of the region, deemed as reference points by parts of their internal constellation of social, political, and cultural forces, and affecting their own constellation of forces through their differential willingness to support different sides in the conflict.[23]

The transnational undercurrent has emerged time and again in the region, as these societies are close geopolitically, have shared a historical background, and have often faced similar challenges. The experience of sister nations in the region has influenced the strategies of political actors in the other countries. At times, there has been a public demonstration effect of neighboring countries' events and processes that should be entered into the equation of isthmian politics and development. Neighboring countries' policies and developments became an input for policy making on the part of those who held the reins of political power or wished to achieve power, that is, political and social actors with the capacity to shape the institutional paths of their country in ways that were attuned to international and transnational developments. Sharing borders and being in relatively close geopolitical distance, these countries and societies closely observed one another. In a sense, their histories were connected by historical experience, common background, and cultural affinity. And while their policies did not mimetically reproduce the others or lead to the same results as in the other countries—a major fallacy of the domino theory as envisaged by the U.S. administrations during the cold war—they were affected at specific moments by the proximate countries' preferences, their willingness to support different sides in a conflict, and the consistency of such policies along with the changing equation of forces in the sister nations.

The historical background and the spatial location of these countries in the isthmus created conditions for such intense mutual impingement, at least for political actors paying close attention to the developments in the other countries of the region. If the countries in the region faced similar policy challenges, it was even more likely that the decisions taken in one country were evaluated closely in the others, leading to third-party and transnational actions.

The scenario of transnational spillover posited by the domino theory, even if realized, could have been a very specific form of a wider spectrum of transnational dynamics taking place in the region intermittently for long periods. As analyzed earlier, a transnational dynamic can be clearly identified already in the nineteenth century, when paradigmatically the destinies of Honduras and El Salvador seemed to depend as much on the course of political events in Guatemala as on their own internal political development. Likewise, even in the period of state consolidation and increased institutional divergence that preceded the cold war there were transnational movements, connections, and mutual influences; these are important, as we need to remember that the transnational dynamics were not new or peculiar to the cold war. The likelihood of transnational organizational spillover was present also in labor, peasant, and student politics from the 1930s to the 1950s that involved workers from different nationalities employed and engaged in strikes in the enclave economies. For instance, in 1942 workers and university students demonstrated in Guatemala in solidarity with a revolt against Salvadoran president Maximiliano Hernández Martínez (1931–44), who was responsible for the repression of his country's opposition and the massacre of the peasant uprising of January 1932 known as La Matanza. When Hernández Martínez fled El Salvador in 1944 and sought asylum in Guatemala, the protest spread to Guatemala, shaping an incipient alliance of military officers, students, and workers that soon led to street fights and to the capitulation of their own country's supreme dictator, Jorge Ubico (1931–44). The fall of Ubico, who left for exile in New Orleans, opened the way for the rise of exiled university professor Juan José Arévalo to the presidency and to the return of political exiles, many of whom contributed to the renewed organization of trade unions and political forces.[24]

Likewise, during the 1960s and 1970s guerrillas emerged in several countries, learning from one another's strategic decisions. Starting in Guatemala, they soon organized in Nicaragua and El Salvador, engaging in armed confrontations that lasted until the 1990s. The early movements in Guatemala and Nicaragua had adopted a strategy of *foquismo*, based on the theory of small guerrilla cells leading a revolution. In most cases, this strategy, modeled after the Cuban revolution, failed to induce mass insurrection. The failure of Che Guevara and his death in Bolivia in 1967 led to its replacement by the strategy of sustained popular war that, at least in Vietnam, led to the victory of the Viet Cong over the U.S. and South Vietnamese forces. Guerrillas in Guatemala and El Salvador attempted to build peasant support in the countryside as a requisite for a future assault on power. Paradoxically, however, it was the Nicaraguan example of a small Sandinista commando taking control of the national assembly building in August 1978 when the parliamentarians were in session and Somoza Junior agreeing to release guerrilla prisoners that energized the mobilization of a broad political alliance and led to the eventual success of the FSLN less than a year later. The FSLN strategies of mass insurrection and construction of a wide political alliance were then attempted in El Salvador and Guatemala.

In El Salvador the Nicaraguan experience contributed to the unification of the various rebel groups in the FMLN. In parallel, however, subversion in El Salvador was mostly concentrated in urban areas due to the densely populated character of rural areas and their surveillance by the security forces and the paramilitary Democratic Nationalist Organization (ORDEN). Accordingly, it was in urban areas that those guerrillas conducted acts of economic sabotage, kidnappings, and bank robberies. In Guatemala the various guerrilla movements similarly united in 1982 to form the URNG, or National Guatemalan Revolutionary Unity, that sparked rebellion in the rural highlands. As the guerrillas seemed on the verge of taking power, the government conducted a brutal counter-insurgency policy, assassinating activists, supporting right-wing death squads, and soon adopting a strategy of scorched earth, mass killings, displacement, and forced enlisting of civilians to fight other civilians identified as guerrilla members or sympathizers.

There were several transnational dimensions to the conflict, according to which progress or recess on one front could enhance or reduce the power of maneuvering of a political movement in the neighboring countries. This was a dimension connected to the externalities that an intrastate conflict could generate in proximate states. Although each country was under a different scenario, the ups and downs of revolutionary uprisings in the neighboring countries clearly sustained or undermined the prospects of victory and defeat as envisioned by movements in the other countries. When by the mid-1980s the revolutionary euphoria in Nicaragua had given way to disillusionment and the war against the Contras had left the economy in ruins, leaving the population of that country exhausted, guerrilla activity in El Salvador also decreased, and the armed conflict entered a phase of stalemate similar to that in Nicaragua.

There were also transnational aspects related to the willingness of states to prolong the crisis or generate a change in the regional conflict due to their preferences over outcomes and their willingness to support different sides in the conflict. In an analysis of third-party involvement in the region, Kristian Skrede Gleditsch and Kyle Beardsley single out the consistency or inconsistency of policies as important factors in prolonging a conflict or bringing it to conclusion as they affected intrastate equations of power and interplay with the susceptibility of the different sides to the conflict to alter their strategies based on international and transnational influences. For instance, Gleditsch and Beardsley indicate that the changes of policies of Costa Rica had such an effect on the ways in which the Sandinista revolution and regional war unfolded.[25] Under Somoza that country had supported the FSLN. As the Sandinistas took power in 1979, Costa Rica moved to neutrality, a policy it shifted in the following years. As the conflict escalated and the Nicaraguan government targeted the opposition forcefully, the Costa Rican government threatened to impose sanctions and at other times was more willing to condone the crackdown on operations by the Contras in Costa Rica. In 1982–86 the Monge administration supported U.S. policies and thus prolonged the conflict. It was only when the new administration of President Oscar Arias, who assumed office in 1986, closed down operations that assisted the military activities of the Contras and consistently reinforced transnational efforts seeking a negotiated solution to the conflict in Nicaragua and the region, despite reservations about the Marxist orientation of the Sandinista regime, that the efforts turned critical for ending the conflict in Nicaragua.

10

Peace Making and the Challenges
of Democratization and Liberalization

The confrontation with communism and the vernacular forms of radical socialism generated policies that condoned genocidal practices whenever they could be justified in terms of "saving the soul" of these nations. This confrontational vision, supported by what came to be known as "doctrines of national security," led to the use of counter-insurgency methodologies involving repression and lack of respect for human rights. As a result, the conflict in Central America produced much suffering, social disruption, displacement, and attrition, with devastating impact on human life, infrastructure, and resources. It led to the killing of thousands of individuals, including many completely unrelated to any armed movement but only concerned with improving life conditions or attempting to promote social justice, agrarian reform, health care, education, or fair working conditions, or even bystanders.

The conflict also generated new transnational contacts, as many individuals crossed the permeable borders willingly or forced by violence. Some of these contacts were instrumental later on as diverse sectors of civil society formed transnational associations to defend or advance their interests in the postwar period.

By the 1980s countries in the region and throughout Latin America started looking for ways out of the regional crisis. The global economic crisis of the 1980s added disincentives to economic sustainability under conditions of war. During that time the world community faced substantial increases in interest rates and oil costs, decreases in exports, and partial stagflation. As a result of this and the destabilization brought about by war, trade among the Central American states fell approximately 50 percent from 1980 to 1985, while producers were left with very little to grasp onto.[1] While the war continued and internal violence did not disappear even in the 1990s, the region—troubled by combined political and economic crises—was about to engage in processes of peace negotiations and transition back to civilian rule.

The shift to civilian rule started in Honduras in March 1980 with elections to a constitutional assembly. First was the initiative of the Contadora group, named after the island where diplomats from Colombia, Mexico, Panama, and Venezuela started talks in January 1983 that aimed to promote dialogue and peace in the region while reducing foreign military intervention. The reactions to the Contadora group's initiative were mixed:

> Their proposals received lip service approval from the United States and Nicaragua, but the rising tension and U.S.-supported disinformation, destabilization, and counterrevolutionary activities against the Sandinista regime, as well as the heavy presence of Cuban and eastern European advisers within Nicaragua, precluded an agreement under Contadora auspices.... [In addition to economic sanctions on Nicaragua], the United States also engineered the resurrection of the Central American Defense Command (CONDECA) by Honduras, Guatemala, El Salvador, and Panama, with Nicaragua excluded and Costa Rica declining participation. . . . Costa Rica found itself walking a tightrope between the Contadora and U.S. positions on Nicaragua.[2]

The flow of assistance to the Contras, which continued through the use of CIA-approved illicit sales of arms to Iran, and the reluctance of the United States to agree to anything less that the ousting of the Sandinistas brought the Contadora plans to a halt by 1985. In 1986 Costa Rican President Oscar Arias and Guatemalan President Vinicio Cerezo launched a new peace plan, which was also geared to promoting the establishment of democracy in the isthmus. The 1986–87 initiative, known as the Esquipulas Plan after the Guatemalan town where talks began, was a follow-up response to the crisis, taking over where the previous initiative stopped. The Esquipulas I and II meetings brought together the heads of state of Central America, who agreed on a framework for peaceful conflict resolution and economic cooperation as means to end the regional military crisis and promote national reconciliation and democratization. Transnational measures included the termination of all assistance to irregular forces in adjoining nations, assistance to refugees, and the first steps toward international verification.

By the late 1980s the process was fully under way. The failed "final" attempt of the FMLN to take the government by force in November 1989 reflected the lack of popular support for a mass uprising, contrary to what the Salvadoran guerrillas expected. The support for the guerrillas in El Salvador, as elsewhere in the isthmus, was also affected by the collapse of communism in the Soviet Union and the electoral defeat of the Sandinistas in Nicaragua in 1990. Likewise, the demise and discredit of military governments in the Southern Cone also hastened the crisis of legitimacy of military rule in Central America, especially in those situations when internal dissent was perceived among the ranks of the armed forces. With the world about to move toward a monopolar environment, the prestige of western democracy and economic liberalization was on the rise.

The initiative of the peace plan signed by the presidents of the Central American countries in Esquipulas, Guatemala, in August 1987 contributed to a negotiated settlement of the war in El Salvador under the auspices of the UN and the OAS by 1992 and to peace agreements in Guatemala by 1996. Peace seemed to have finally been reached in the isthmus.

When the peace accords were signed, human rights laws were promulgated and more stable governments were established. These societies wanted to close the book on their past, and they did so with varied degrees of success. The details of the process have been clearly defined in the literature.[3] I shall trace only some of the main issues and dilemmas these countries faced as they confronted the legacies of human rights violations and the challenges of democratization and liberalization.

Any society emerging from fratricidal actions and violations of human rights must confront a series of difficult institutional and moral dilemmas. Among them are the following questions: in what ways and through which channels the society should ascertain and confront the knowledge of what happened and agree upon some version of past events, that is, how to attain a collective "truth"; how to make those involved in human rights violations accountable for their past deeds; whether to ask forgiveness from the victims and expect expiation from the perpetrators; along which lines to elaborate mechanisms of expiation and compensation; and how to shape collective memory, recreate a sense of collective identity, and prepare the grounds for reconciliation.[4]

The cold war confrontation in the isthmus resulted in massive violence and violations of human rights in both countries. In El Salvador, the United States had funneled hundreds of millions of dollars in military aid to fund a repressive military government's bloody war against communism, and in Nicaragua, the United States' Contra guerillas engaged the government in a war that cost thousands of lives while ruining the country's infrastructure. In El Salvador during the civil war, state forces were responsible for killing an estimated 75,000 civilians, or well over 1 percent of the total population.

The conflict spilled over to Guatemala as well, where guerrillas had been in existence for more than a generation. In that country the civil war lasted until 1996, with estimates of victims ranging from 32,000 to more than 250,000 persons killed, including up to 50,000 *desaparecidos*,[5] and hundreds of thousands of individuals displaced, either at the hands of the armed forces or of the militarized civilian units known as the PACs.[6] In Central America the treatment of these issues has been partial and minor. The countries mostly endorsed policies of lack of accountability for past gross human rights violations, particularly those that had been conducted within the legal framework of procedural laws that permitted arbitrary mass arrests, the suspension of constitutional guarantees, and the declaration of states of emergency. The transition to democracy, amnesty laws were issued as the Salvadoran Amnesty Law to Achieve National Reconciliation (1987), which provided a basis for ending the prison terms of the few military men convicted or accused of atrocities and for dropping ongoing inquiries against others. Moreover, the cooperation of the judiciary in sanctioning the legality of the policies of counter-insurgency conditioned the possibility of leaving the book open on past human rights violations. Salvadoran groups have been unsuccessful in appealing to the country's supreme court to declare the amnesty law unconstitutional. This failed effort reflects the need to reform the judiciary or leave an imprint of impunity and lack of accountability at the very core of the institutions charged with carrying out justice. Moreover, under such circumstances, very little was achieved in undertaking criminal prosecutions against perpetrators of gross human rights violations.

Connected to these institutional dilemmas and problems while providing a basis for them was the theme of attaining some sort of collective truth through official or public sanctions. The establishment of truth commissions and their timing are crucial for enabling an agreed-upon version of past events. In El Salvador after a 1979 coup by young officers against President Humberto Romero, the revolutionary junta established a special commission to investigate the whereabouts of *desaparecidos* and the existence of clandestine prisons, sites of torture, and cemeteries. Yet, it was met with a complete lack of cooperation by the security forces that still believed their mission was to destroy the opposition. Indeed, killings and disappearances actually increased after October 1979, with the involvement of death squads in assassinations, including that of San Salvador's Archbishop Oscar Arnulfo Romero in March 1980. With the institutional protection of authorities, the armed and paramilitary forces fought the FMLN while also committing serious violations of human rights and many massacres, often covered up, such as the slaughter of three hundred noncombatants attempting to flee into Honduras by crossing the Sumpul River in May 1980 or the massacre of hundreds of men, women, and children, often by decapitation, in El Mozote in December 1981 that was carried out by the U.S.-trained Atlacatl Battalion.[7] By the early 1990s a military stalemate between the warring sides and a loss of international legitimacy of the military rulers due to their repressive policies led to swift negotiations and a peace agreement by January 1992. When peace agreements were reached, with the mediation of the United Nations, the parties arranged to establish an ad hoc commission to purge the military of human rights violations. That commission reviewed the human rights record of military officers, suggesting the retirement of 130 on these grounds. It was decided that a National Civilian Police and a National Counsel for the Defense of Human Rights should be installed to lead the process of reform.

Likewise, it was agreed that a UN Truth Commission would begin an inquiry into the extent of past human rights violations. As the protracted polarization of Salvadoran society precluded establishing an agreed-upon national commission, the Salvadoran Truth Commission was constituted in March 1993 as an international commission. The commission focused its efforts on looking at "serious acts of violence" that had occurred since 1980. The commission heard 22,000 testimonies and identified the armed forces as responsible for 85 percent of the cases of human rights violations and the FMLN as responsible for another 5 percent. The commission strongly criticized the U.S. role in the conflict. Graduates of the School of the Americas (SOA), which trained Latin American officers in counter-intelligence practices, have been implicated in massive human rights violations. In El Salvador more than half of all officers cited for human rights violations in a major massacre, including 83 percent of those implicated in the massacre of El Mozote, were graduates of SOA. The UN Truth Commission report of March 1993 found that two of the three assassins of Archbishop Oscar Romero—men who also were implicated in other human rights abuses including the organization of death squads—had been graduates of the SOA.[8]

Due to time and other constraints, the Truth Commission focused on thirty-three notorious cases, selected for their expected paradigmatic impact on civil society. In parallel, the commission considered determining individual responsibility as part of its mandate, singling out the names of forty officers involved in gross human rights violations and recommending their dismissal from service. The choice of cases, weighted against official atrocities, was contested by some sectors that criticized, for instance, the biased selection or the lack of inquiry into atrocities committed by the FMLN against individuals in their own ranks. The commission had a strong impact internationally, but internally its findings were not embraced by the government. Aware of its institutional implications, President Alfredo Cristiani led a call to forget those memories and made no effort at implementing or disseminating the findings of the commission. The commanders of the armed forces, for their part, utterly rejected the report's findings and refused to recognize institutional responsibility either. Nevertheless, the government pushed for amnesty for the sake of national reconciliation. Contrastingly, in Honduras, which had less political polarization and a lower number of disappearances (174) of nationals and foreign residents, "the Commissioner for Human Rights named those he could identify and urged state institutions to carry out investigations and prosecutions in accordance with law."[9]

The magnitude of the problem was even more daunting in Guatemala in terms of loss of life, displacement, eradication of entire villages, militarization of the countryside, and the crystallization of a culture of violence and fear, resulting from massacres, disappearances, and acts of brutality by the armed forces and citizens enlisted in the PACs against neighbors and other peasants.

The transnational implications of the Salvadoran situation and its path to achieve closure did not go unnoticed in neighboring Guatemala. The Guatemalan government expected that a full-fledged search for accountability in El Salvador could impair its own efforts to achieve negotiated peace in the country, a process that was protracted for years until 1996 in spite of the comparative weakness of the guerrilla forces. While aware that Guatemalans could not avoid dealing with these issues, the lead taken by the Salvadoran truth commission convinced the Guatemalan civilian administration that it should opt to create a Guatemalan commission with a more restricted mandate, namely, historical clarification. Indeed, the mandate of the Guatemalan Historical Clarification Commission (CEH) established in 1997 was to inquire into violent acts related to the armed conflict without attributing individual responsibility for those acts.

Contrasting with the weakness of Salvadoran human rights groups, by the mid-1990s Guatemala had a strong and multifaceted network of human rights organizations and organizations of civil society concerned with the construction of the realm of human rights. Among these groups one may mention associations of victims and their relatives such as the Grupo de Apoyo Mutuo (GAM), Coordinadora Nacional de Viudas de Guatemala (CONAVIGUA), Comunidades Etnicas Runujel Junam (CERJ), Familiares de Detenidos Desaparacidos de Guatemala (FAMDEGUA), Comunidades de Población en Resistencia (CPR), Consejo Nacional de Desplazados de Guatemala (CONDEG), Comisiones Permanentes de Refugiados (CCPP), Asociación de Refugiados Dispersos de Guatemala (ARDIGUA), Asociación de Mujeres Refugiadas Mamá Maquí, and Asociación Ixmucané; numerous Maya organizations affiliated with CONAVIGUA or the Defensoría Maya, the Academy of Mayan Languages of Guatemala (ALMG), and the Council of Maya Organizations of Guatemala (COMG); foundations and centers of technical support such as the Foundation Myrna Mack, the Center for Legal Action in Human Rights (CALDH), the Institute of Comparative Penal Studies (ICCPG), the Forensic Anthropology Group (EAFG), the Foundation Rigoberta Menchú, and the Institute of Political, Economic, and Social Studies (IPES); religious supporting agencies such as the Office of Human Rights of the Archbishop (ODHA), the Pastoral Social Office (OPSA), and the Conference of Evangelical Churches (ICIEDEG); and coordinating associations such as the Coordinadora Nacional de Derechos Humanos de Guatemala (CONADEGUA), Convergencia por la Verdad, and Alianza contra la Impunidad.[10]

The crystallization of such dense networks explains why Guatemala did not enact an amnesty law but rather issued a reconciliation law in December 1996 that left the door open for criminal prosecution. The human rights organizations have also sustained the strong effort to attain a truthful account of past human rights violations. In this domain, the work of the Catholic Church was prominent. In 1995 the church launched a Commission of Recovery of Historical Memory (REMHI), which worked for years, finally releasing a 1,400-page report—*Guatemala nunca más*—in April 1998. As the leader of this effort, Bishop Juan Gerardi was assassinated two days after the release of the report, which became a powerful indictment of those responsible for human rights violations in Guatemala. Both the commission and the government made it clear that those responsible should ask for forgiveness, while the state committed itself to providing some form of reparations to the victims. In parallel, an UN-sponsored CEH truth commission of mixed composition—with one UN-designated member and two Guatemalans—started operating as well, releasing its own report, *Memoria del silencio*, in February 1999. In terms of concrete achievements, while the armed forces were reduced to two-thirds of their former size (albeit with full pensions) by 1999, little has been accomplished in the realm of justice or reparations due to the weakness of the judicial system and the sustained reluctance of the establishment.

One of the unintended consequences of the regional confrontation and civil wars of the 1970s and 1980s was the transnational flow of young people throughout the region and beyond. The confrontation brought activists from different countries into contact and enabled observation and learning from each other's experiences. For once, the internationalization of the Nicaraguan revolution provided room for frequent meetings of solidarity and the participation of individuals from the other countries of the isthmus. Marc Edelman has studied how a young generation of peasant leaders emerged as a result of the decades of upheaval, war, and crisis who years later led transnational organizational efforts to advance or protect sector interests on a macro-regional level. Leaders of agricultural cooperatives met in events sponsored by the Confederación de Cooperativas del Caribe y Centroamérica, while representatives of rural workers' unions attended meetings of the Coordinación Centroamericana de Trabajadores, founded following the 1987 Esquipulas Peace Accords. This organizational drive, supported by European governments at least since 1983–84, led by 1991 to the establishment of ASO-CODE (Asociación Centroamericana de Organizaciones Campesinas para la Cooperación y el Desarrollo), a very active transnational association of national peasant organizations that paralleled the regional business bodies and tried to defend *campesinos'* interests in the framework of the new policies of macro-regional integration. Not without inner tensions due to divergent experiences and styles, nonetheless, it established a presence for popular movements in the new supranational bodies that have increasingly led Central American integration, later superseded by other associations and coalitions of labor, peasant, and small-business organizations.[11]

In parallel, and in spite of some expanding impacts to be fully realized progressively once peace was attained and electoral democracy deepened, the countries of the region had to face two other major transnational processes that resulted from the years of war and deserve separate treatment, namely, the massive displacement of refugees shaping a strategy of successive migration by waves of Central Americans moving across the isthmus and into Mexico and the United States and the return of formerly displaced individuals to the home countries, with some of them affecting the countries with dysfunctional implications, foremost among these being transnational illicit networks and criminality. The next two chapters follow these two processes in detail, discussing some of their long-term consequences for the region.

Photo 7. Corporate presence in Orange Walk, Belize: customers enjoying a Coca-Cola.

Photo 8. McDonald's in Antigua, overlooking an impressive volcanic landscape.

ATENCION

ODOS LOS CENTROAMERICANOS QUE SOLICITEN LOS
ERVICIOS DE MIGRACION PARA ENTRAR O SALIR
DEL PAIS, SE LES RECUERDA QUE:

DEBEN CANCELAR IMPUESTOS MIGRATORIOS

ALVADOR ES RESPETUOSO DEL CONVENIO DE LIBRE TRANSITO
POR LOS PAISES DEL ISTMO CENTROAMERICANO.

Photo 9. On the Salvadoran border: free trade for Central American products; border fees to be paid by Central American people.

Photo 10. Drawing the future: a mural in the Nicaraguan National Palace. Here, in August 1978, a Sandinista commando force took the Nicaraguan congress hostage, attracting worldwide attention to the Sandinistas fighting Somoza.

Photo 11. A bridge to the world—the Panama Canal.

Photo 12. Panama's phone connections: cheaper calls to Turkey and Pakistan than to Honduras.

11

Transnational Displacement

The Refugee Crisis and Migration

The wave of armed conflicts that destabilized Central America in the late 1970s and early 1980s sparked a severe refugee crisis. International intervention and civil wars in Nicaragua and El Salvador and the major counterinsurgency operations by the Guatemalan military and the PACs created an unprecedented flow of refugees, generating a process of transnational migration whose unintended consequences are still felt today.

It was a transnational dislocation of populations far wider than anything the Central American states had experienced before. In a region from which relatively few inhabitants had emigrated in the first half of the twentieth century and the process of rural-urban migration occurred later than in other parts of Iberoamerica, the wars started massive dislocations of populations and waves of refugees searching for asylum, followed later on by equally massive movements of transnational migrants gaining momentum in the 1990s and 2000s.

Salvadorans made up the largest group of refugees, followed by Guatemalans and Nicaraguans. The case of Salvadorans was particularly acute as the number of refugees reached around 750,000, or 16 percent of that country's population in the mid-1980s; of them 175,000 were in Nicaragua, 120,000 in Mexico, 70,000 in Guatemala, 20,000 in Honduras, 10,000 in Costa Rica, 7,000 in Belize, and 1,000 in Panama. The number of political refugees was estimated to be 245,000 in 1984. In addition, there were internal refugees (*desplazados*) who had been forced to flee within El Salvador.[1] Hans Wollny's figures are even higher. According to his assessment, the total number of Central American refugees surpassed 1.3 million in the 1980s, and out of these, Salvadorans comprised more than 1 million, while the number of Guatemalans and Nicaraguans was estimated to be around 200,000 and 63,000, respectively.[2] The United Nations High Commissioner for Refugees

(UNHCR) estimated that at least 1 million people, perhaps twice as many, had been displaced by the generalized violence afflicting the region by May 1986. Of these, only 46,600 had received UNHCR assistance by the end of 1987, when the peace process began.

Mexico was particularly affected by the refugee crisis. To deal with the mass influx of refugees, in 1980 the Mexican government created a special interministerial body, the Mexican Commission for Aid to Refugees (Comisión Mexicana de Ayuda a Refugiados, or COMAR). At that time, COMAR proposed to recognize most Central American refugees as political refugees. However, that proposal was not implemented, as Mexican immigration authorities defined the mass of Central American refugees as economic migrants rather than victims of political persecution. The restrictive Mexican policies toward the Central American refugees was underpinned by several factors, among them the economic situation at that time, the complex relationship with the United States, and last but not least, Mexico's fear of a spillover of the Central American wars into its territory, which would put Mexico at risk of becoming an indirect victim of political turbulence in the region.

Between 1980 and 1982 at least 70,000 Salvadoran refugees were deported from Mexico to Guatemala or directly to El Salvador. Some estimates put the number of Central Americans deported annually to their home countries at more than 46,000.[3] Moreover, beginning in 1983 the Mexican government stopped recognizing Salvadorans as refugees. Mexican authorities claimed Salvadorans were economic immigrants and refused to grant them asylum status or otherwise legalize their presence in the country. Accordingly, the number of Salvadorans residing illegally in Mexico grew. In 1987 the Mexican coordinator for Salvadoran refugees estimated their number to be at least a half-million, far beyond the estimated 110,000 Guatemalans and few thousand Nicaraguans residing illegally there. If caught, Salvadorans had to provide documented proof of employment or face deportation. Although Salvadorans were, by and large, well-educated young people belonging to the urban middle classes, government officials portrayed them as a problematic and undesirable population.

Among those moving to Mexico in the early 1980s were many indigenous Mayans from Guatemala. Most of them entered Mexico as refugees, escaping counter-insurgent campaigns by the Guatemalan army and paramilitary groups. Comparatively, these Guatemalan refugees had to confront even harder obstacles than the Salvadorans since they were an indigenous rural population who had been the subject of discriminatory policies in their home country. These indigenous people were mostly illiterate and lacked economic means. Even though most of the displaced Guatemalans shared a common ethnic background with the inhabitants of southeastern Mexico, many of them did not speak Spanish but rather their own languages, a fact that greatly impaired Guatemalans' ability to integrate.[4] Most tended to settle in improvised camps near the border, mainly in Chiapas and to a lesser extent in the states of Campeche and Quintana Roo, where they shared cultural and linguistic ties with the local population. They hoped to return home when possible. In this case, Mexico was forced to confront a novel situation when in a relatively short time tens of thousands of Guatemalan peasants crossed the border. While in the earlier waves of exile—from the Southern Cone in the 1970s, for example—those seeking asylum or residence came from the middle and upper strata, the refugees from Guatemala were mainly peasants and of lower-class origins, adding pressures on access to land, already a problem in existence in southern Mexico. A change in foreign policy took place in this period as a result of the situation. Mexico pursued the pacification of Central America in order to both stop the flow of refugees and facilitate the return of those refugees already settled in Mexican territory. In parallel, as indicated above, the Mexican government attempted to expel illegal immigrants by the thousands while granting asylum to only a small number of individuals. In a 1984 survey of Guatemalans in Mexico City, 80 percent of the sample declared having left their country for political reasons, 73 percent did not possess any kind of document, and 13.6 percent had tourist visas, while only 3 percent had received political asylum. Within Chiapas, the government promoted a policy of resettlement into neighbouring states, but by 1987 it had only managed to convince an estimated 18,200 peasants to move on. Many others refused to abandon the state of Chiapas. The government granted documents to them as border visitors or agricultural workers, and the Catholic Dioceses of San Cristóbal de las Casas and UNCHR provided them with support and recognized many of them, thus precluding the possibility of expulsion.[5] Likewise, the United States attracted successive waves of refugees and migrants, becoming a major pole of attraction.[6]

The arrival of successive waves of refugees and exiles has often turned a host country into a pole of attraction for future immigrants. Once refugees settle and community bonds are re-created, a process of learning and accommodation also takes place as the newcomers learn institutional and cultural practices and how to interact in the new environment. It is then easier for future waves of conationals, be they refugees or economic immigrants, to find their way around. The old-timers may become a bridge for newcomers.

One of the crucial factors in this process of adaptation is the formation of a critical mass of residents. For the newcomers, the presence of "old-timers," both prior exiles and other countrymen, can lessen alienation and contribute to reconstructing some sense of normalcy and community in the diaspora. The existence of such human bridges has encouraged the growth of massive transnational labor migratory waves through the region and beyond, mostly into Mexico and the United States.

In the early 2000s the Central American Commission of Migration Directorates estimated the migrant population of the region to be nearly 5 million. More than 100,000 Guatemalan agricultural workers are employed in Mexico annually as temporary agricultural workers, with many more heading north to Mexico, the United States, and Belize. It is estimated that 108,000 Hondurans transit through Guatemala annually. Hondurans comprised 36 percent of all border apprehensions in Mexico in 1999 and 46 percent of Central American illegal immigrants apprehended in the United States between 1999 and 2001. These percentages are complemented by significant numbers of Salvadorans and Guatemalans apprehended while crossing these two borders illegally. Salvadorans have migrated to Guatemala as temporary agricultural workers, with many conationals moving from Guatemala to Mexico, the United States, and Belize. Hondurans have migrated either directly or through El Salvador and Mexico to Guatemala, Belize, and the United States. In Belize and Guatemala many Hondurans have found work as temporary agricultural laborers. Nicaraguans have migrated to Costa Rica, where they currently comprise about 8 percent of the population, as well as to destinations in Central America and—through transnational chains of migration—also to Mexico and the United States, albeit in smaller numbers than others, at least as measured by the number of individuals apprehended by U.S. immigration authorities while attempting to enter the country illegally from Mexico.[7]

Table 11.1, elaborated by David Guinn and Elissa Steglich, sums up these migration flows both within the isthmus and beyond, indicating the main destinations and transit areas in the late twentieth and early twenty-first centuries. According to estimates, by the early 2000s more than 2 million Central Americans were living in the United States, over 50 percent of them from El Salvador. Salvadorans also constituted up to 12 percent of the population of Belize, while Nicaraguans comprised about 10 percent of the population of Costa Rica.[8]

In the United States many of the hundreds of thousands of Central Americans have remained undocumented or illegal residents. In 1990 Salvadorans were the first group to be eligible for "temporary protected status" (TPS) later

Table 11.1. General migration flows in Central America

Origin	Nicaragua	Honduras	El Salvador	Guatemala	Costa Rica	Belize	Mexico	USA
Nicaragua	X	T	T	T D	D	D	T	D
Honduras	X	X	T	T D	X	D	T	D
El Salvador	T	T	X	T	X	D	T	D
Guatemala	X	X	X	X	X	D	D	D

Source: Adapted from Guinn and Steglich, *In Modern Bondage* (2003), 25.
Notes: T = Transit
D = Destination

to be granted to others such as Nicaraguans and Hondurans. Without recognizing asylum, TPS status has provided legal temporary residency and the possibility of getting employment authorization. This system, created as part of the Immigration Act of 1990 and modified in March 2003, was designed for aliens who are temporarily unable to safely return to their home countries because of ongoing armed conflict, environmental disaster, or other extraordinary conditions. It does not entitle migrants to permanent residency, and it leaves its bearers in a state of uncertainty, pondering time and again whether the status will be extended or derogated for them. Many of those residing in the United States and Mexico do not have such protective status. Thus, for instance, recently the United States, Mexico, and Guatemala have been deporting tens of thousands of Hondurans and others to their home countries.

The ambiguous status of many of these migrants in the countries of relocation has created what Adrian Bailey and associates have defined as a condition of "permanent temporariness."[9] Engaging in geographical mobility due to the political situation in their home countries or as a strategy to achieve social mobility, these individuals have become deterritorialized and reterritorialized at the same time.

Living across different space-time spans, their life experiences have generated new transnational projects and a varied economic impact both in the countries of origin and in the places of relocation. Such wide impact includes areas such as home ("nostalgic") tourism, attempts at family reunification, the emergence of new devices, expanding markets for inexpensive telecommunication, new markets for produce, food, and beverages from the home countries, as well as the weight of remittances in the Central American economies.[10] The proliferation of these ventures also involves the active consideration by individuals of their present experiences in terms of the past and the projection of future plans in terms of present dilemmas, prospects, and constraints.[11] The economic contributions of transnational networks and the strong numbers of migrants have given them a strategic visibility recognized by the politicians in the home country who have campaigned among them in recent years and have courted their financial support. At the same time, even as they have access to more resources and new technologies, they have faced tremendous difficulties as they tried to integrate in the new environment, evading being captured and deported, trying in some cases to have credentials recognized, and keeping their living costs at a minimum in order to send remittances to their families. The undocumented status of many and their stigmatization in the United States have generated situations of marginalization, rising crime, and exploitation by local employers.

Even communities of migrants who can trace their origins back many decades and who have relocated within the isthmus, as is the case of Nicaraguans in Costa Rica, have felt subject to stigmatization and criminalization. Being the focus of a racial discourse that "whitened" Costa Ricans and "darkened" Nicaraguans, the Nicaraguans became the "internal other," being held responsible in the 1990s for the rise of criminality and the spread of diseases such as cholera. These processes did occur but were only tangentially related to the immigrants. As of 2000, more than 226,000 Nicaraguans were living in Costa Rica. During harvest times, their numbers grew even larger and reached close to 8 percent of the population. The Nicaraguans thus became a substantial minority, being "inside the country but outside the nation" in Carlos Sandoval-García's characterization.[12] Processes of racial discrimination and criminalization of Nicaraguans have been under way for a long time. Nicaraguans are thought by Costa Ricans to be darker in skin and have a more indigenous physiognomy, which is matched in talk and behavior, as they supposedly exhibit distinct colloquialisms and violence-prone behavior. These stereotyped images have symbolically transformed Nicaraguans into a perceived social threat. In the early 2000s Costa Ricans already suspected Nicaraguans of affecting the attractiveness of their country to tourists, which, according to locals, had been clean and "ecological" until the immigrant Nicaraguans polluted its spatial and social texture. Following the same logic, in 2008 the Costa Rican authorities adopted more stern criteria for granting legal residency to aliens in the country.

Migration did not decline with the end of the conditions that had triggered forced migration in the first place. With the end of the regional wars and repression and until the economic crisis of the late 2000s, many individuals continued to flow in the direction of the poles of attraction in search of higher incomes and livelihood, and other Central Americans were repat-riated, especially from the United States. Their experiences in the United States were mixed. Many were hard-working individuals who used their so-journs to support their families and send remittances and were empowered individually and collectively by the experience, as reflected, for instance, in the emerging Hispanic presence and press in the United States or in the pan-Maya movement in Central America. Still, others lived marginal and insecure lives, some of them joining illicit networks and learning the ways and know-how of criminality, with a transnational impact that was fully re-vealed once civil wars ended and the isthmian countries democratized and liberalized their markets.

12

Transnational Illicit Markets and Criminality

Paradoxically, the transition to democracy and the relative liberalization of society, until then regulated by authoritarian controls, created a background that could easily be misused by economic interests related to transnational illicit markets undermining the normative bases of society. Toward the end of the 1990s the transit routes of U.S.-destined drugs, primarily cocaine, shifted from the Caribbean islands to Central America and Mexico, mostly by maritime lines.[1] This shift fed into a rising scenario of criminality, violence, and public insecurity in the societies of the region, particularly in those of the so-called Northern Triangle, that is, Honduras, Guatemala, and El Salvador.

The rising presence of criminal and transnational illicit networks has been recognized by individuals close to the reins of power. Federico Brevé-Travieso, minister of defense of Honduras between 2002 and 2006, has stated that gangs and illicit networks have been growing faster than the economies, a situation calling for immediate action to stop the snowball effect that has already begun.[2] In Honduras, the country with the highest number of gangs both per capita and in absolute numbers, a Perception of Human Development national survey conducted in 2005 found that over 40 percent of respondents in the two major cities reported having been victims of theft, while 8 percent of the rural respondents, 11 percent of those living in minor cities, and 13 and 16 percent of residents in the Central District and San Pedro Sula, respectively, indicated they had family members who were murdered. In the metropolitan areas, the theft rate reached 54 percent in the higher socioeconomic status, 47 percent in the middle strata, and 33 percent in the low status. Violence had reportedly become more extreme and spread across all social strata. In the main cities of Honduras, more than 65 percent of the people asserted that they no longer walked the streets, 60 percent reported having limited the places where they shopped, 62 percent reduced their recreational activities, and over 40 percent stopped visiting somebody they cared about, due to the generalized sense of insecurity.[3] The

UNDP Human Development Report for 2006, from which the above figures are taken, indicated disturbing findings of such dynamics of rising public insecurity and deinstitutionalization of social life:

> Parallel to, or as a consequence of, a relative weakness in the institutional response to this problem and to the need of consolidating a legal state, a culture of informality, illegality and illegitimacy tends to evolve, particularly influencing certain population segments. Violence becomes a phenomenon that has become part of daily lives, norms and laws are discretionally respected, and for many the solution is found by taking justice into their own hands. The other side of the coin is a sensation of fear and insecurity in citizens that seriously affects life quality and in where citizenship building faces vast obstacles . . . resulting in high levels of residential segregation and social breakup consistently on the rise.[4]

More recently, in September 2008 the National Commissioner for the Protection of Human Rights, Ramón Custodio López, reported that the rate of homicide in Honduras for 2007 stood at 49.9 per 100,000 inhabitants (N=3,262 individuals murdered). He added that this rate was about 2.4 times the rate for the Americas—which stood at 18 percent per 100,000 inhabitants, according to data for 2002—and 5.25 times the world average, which was 8.8 per 100,000 inhabitants in 2000. As one reads these statistics, it is important to recall that world organizations consider 10 per 100,000 to be a dangerously high number of homicides.[5]

In Guatemala, however, rural zones are much more peaceful now than during the conflict. At least there the insecurity and violence now penetrating the country are based far more in urban spaces, while during the conflict violence targeted the rural population in particular.[6]

Unsurprisingly, recent years have witnessed throughout the isthmus a growing number of firms hiring private security services. This trend conceals as well the fact that while there is a generalized sense of public insecurity, most rank-and-file citizens are unable to buy private security services, contrasting with economic corporations and firms that can take care of such services. This implies that many individuals are precluded by these conditions from fully exercising their citizenship rights, thus reproducing segmented ways of life and fragmenting the texture of participation in society.

The high incidence of violence has many sources, yet it is increasingly connected to the struggle over control of access to the illicit transnational trade of humans, substances, and arms and control of illicit markets. In

Central America citizens have increasingly related the rising crime to the presence of gangs, known as *maras*.[7] According to the Salvadoran National Police, there are nearly 70,000 gang members in the Central American region, with a breakdown roughly as follows: 36,000 in Honduras, 14,000 in Guatemala, 11,000 in El Salvador, 4,500 in Nicaragua, 2,700 in Costa Rica, 1,400 in Panama, and 100 in Belize. Although the Salvadoran MS-18 and MS-13 are the largest of the groups, many more exist. The list includes Los Nicas (Nicaraguans), Los Batos Locos (Crazy Boys), and Los Cholos (the Half-Breeds), all in Guatemala. La Máquina (The Machine) and La Mau Mau (the name of a 1950s New York gang and Kenyan rebels) are also in El Salvador. In Honduras one finds both La Mau Mau and Los Batos Locos in addition to Los Rockeros (Rockers). Finally, in Nicaragua there are the Gerber Boys and Los Charly. These gangs are relatively young, the oldest probably ten to fifteen years old, and yet, some of them have become connected to transnational illicit activities and networks.

Juvenile "corner networks" or "barrio cliques" have existed for a long time. They would rob or assault people passing through their "territory," rob small businesses, and write graffiti on walls. Yet, transnational displacement has created a process of uprooting and projecting such dysfunctional behavior into an interface with organized crime and illicit markets.

The violence connected to illicit markets and circuits of transportation and commercialization of drugs and human trafficking has been boosted by individuals deported or returning from the United States who transferred their criminal know-how and networks to their countries of origin, particularly but not only into Honduras and El Salvador. Hand in hand with the increased centrality of Central America as a passage of drug and human trafficking to the United States there has been also a rise in arms trade, violence, extortion, and murder, burgeoning in the framework of state weakness and conflicts over control of access to illicit trade routes and markets, often reinforcing public corruption, and always disseminating fear among the population.

During the violence of the civil wars and repression of the 1980s, thousands of inhabitants fled their countries, mainly to the United States and Mexico. Many of those fleeing were individuals who had fought and/or had suffered persecution in the home countries and moved abroad looking for a site of asylum or refuge. Among those relocating to the United States, many moved to large cities where, due to language barriers, lack of education, and the slow adaptation process, they faced problems in finding employment and housing. Some were left on the streets living in poverty. For instance, many found themselves in Los Angeles, a city known to be home to numerous gangs, most of them racially and ethnically divided. These immigrants had come mostly from war zones and had been fighting either in the military or the guerrillas; they already had knowledge of weapons, and quickly they or their children got sucked into the gang life in the city. Some Salvadorans joined the multi-ethnic yet Mexican-dominated 18th Street Gang (M-18), while a large group of other Salvadorans founded the Mara Salvatrucha (MS or M-13), located on 13th Street, calling those who had joined M-18 traitors.[8] Those migrants and children of migrants who joined these gangs developed criminal skills.

The changes in U.S. federal immigration policies introduced after the 1992 violent riots in Los Angeles determined that imprisoned gang members were increasingly deported to their home countries after having served their jail time. As these individuals involved in gang and illicit activities were repatriated, the gang networks were consolidated in Central America in the direction of transnational illicit markets. Upon returning to their home countries, many ex-cons and gang members felt alienated in the new environment, some of them having never lived there or having been gone for many years. Once back, they could envision controlling part of the transnational circuits of drug transportation and illicit markets of human trafficking and arms, in addition to more localized selling of drugs, protection, and extortion. Soon some of them transferred acquired skills in organized crime, which they would put to use in the country of origin, recruiting new members in societies where economic opportunities were limited, states had started to "retreat" from assuming public functions, and many families had disintegrated or were malfunctioning due to these and other structural constraints.[9] By the late 1980s, MS-13 appeared in El Salvador and Honduras and later on in Guatemala, adding local members and evolving into more and more organized networks, partly connected to transnational illicit interests.

One decisive factor in the entrenchment and radicalization of gang violence has been the substratum of violence that turned routine in previous decades. After the civil wars, societies such as those of El Salvador, Guatemala, and Honduras remained traumatized by routine violence. Prolonged civil strife generated cultures of violence of variable historical depth throughout the isthmus. In Guatemala and El Salvador the widespread occurrence of post-traumatic disorders and the routinization of violence in everyday life could not be easily eradicated once peace agreements were signed, and—as in the case of El Salvador—the radical left was incorporated into political life. In El Salvador the expectations of violence were additionally enshrined in the collective memory traced back to at least the massive massacre of 1932. In other cases, violence became generalized in later stages of the cold war. In Honduras the more recent spread of violence equally affected daily lives and expectations, disseminating fear and creating serious obstacles for building active citizenship and civic participation geared to the institutionalization of citizenship rights. Less affected in this respect in recent years seems to be Nicaragua, although the problem is neither completely absent there.

Next is the fact that along with the dismantling of the repressive policies, states also weakened their regulative presence in society, creating vacuums that were filled by the illicit networks in their interface with local gangs and maras. When the maras showed up and became connected to organized crime and illicit circuits and markets, they managed to consolidate their economic power and violent control over territories, re-creating the gang atmosphere they had experienced in the United States. They were easily able to recruit new members due to the situation of poverty, unemployment, and public distrust of police and enforcement agencies that prevailed in most countries, the latter with the partial exception of Nicaragua and Costa Rica.

Due to a myriad of national and transnational factors, the countries in the region have continued to be haunted by serious problems, which one observer enumerated as "rampant corruption, gang warfare, drug smuggling, intense urban poverty and overpopulation, and neglect from the international community."[10] Gang networks in particular have arisen through the region, causing unrest and insecurity. Although there has been a tendency to demonize and criminalize gangs all across the board, it is the interface between the gangs and illicit markets, leading to struggles over control of territories and circuits of transport and commercialization of drugs, arms, and human trafficking, that has generated warfare, violence, and public insecurity in the region.

The illicit movement of drugs, people, and arms across borders using sea and air transportation as major venues has turned maras into operating networks. The countries in the region have served as transshipment passages to drug markets in Mexico and the United States. One of the methods used combined land-based drug smuggling with short-range aerial operations, with clandestine planes making stops in Central America before either transferring their cargo to a land vehicle or making another short flight toward Mexico. This brought drug-trafficking organizations to maintain a presence inside Central America.[11]

More recently, the increased pressure and surveillance on the Guatemalan border with Mexico has turned the former into a kind of storing house for drugs, with drugs being increasingly pushed to those social sectors with purchasing power within the country. A similar phenomenon is reportedly under way in El Salvador and Honduras.[12] There is a rising influence and transfer of Mexican cartels' activities all over Central America, especially after President Felipe Calderón increasingly applied military force in Mexico. Consequently, the region has also witnessed new levels of intergang violence hitherto unknown.[13]

There is debate on the transnational significance of the maras. Some observers indicate that maras function as networks with extensive transnational linkages. "MS-13, for example, reportedly has 20,000 members in the United States, 4,000 members in Canada, and a large presence in Mexico."[14] Others, most prominently a Centro de Estudios y Programas Interamericanos (CEPI) study in 2007 and an empirical study commissioned by the Swedish Agency of International Cooperation (ASDI) and the Central American Bank of Economic Integration (BCIE) and carried out on the basis of in-depth interviews with mara members, networks in civil society, and state officials, have claimed that only a small proportion of the maras have transnational links with organized crime and narco-trafficking networks.[15] For instance, in Guatemala most gang networks are neighborhood-based and only tangentially connected to the transnational trafficking circuits, while various cases disclosed seem to indicate that networks of policemen, former military, and strongmen rather than gang members have been at the core of some narco-trafficking networks and the so-called *poderes paralelos*, or de facto para-institutional powers.[16]

Mara members are first and foremost members of social networks, which alludes to the importance of interpersonal factors explaining the expanding impact of maras and the regional variance in the salience and organizational variability of such networks across countries and localities. Often, joining a gang has meant for many youngsters gaining respect in their neighborhoods, developing a social identity,[17] and hopefully attaining an economically lucrative position denied them otherwise. Many were attracted to a mara as a means of escaping the lack of protection in a violent environment, yet mara membership has paradoxically heightened the likelihood of facing violence for those joining a gang. Violence is the code of initiation and access to membership and is even more prominent as these gangs face other gangs and the authorities. Different gangs continuously get into fights over control of territories and drugs. The maras do not only "rough each other up" but have been known to decapitate and mutilate their victims. Less conflictive has been the access to perks and monetary benefits available by selling marijuana and cocaine on the streets or making homemade firearms, selling protection, or assaulting people and businesses in or beyond their territory, and so forth. Once maras became established, they have sold protection to people in their territories, making street vendors or small-business owners pay for their security. They have also entered the prostitution and human-trafficking markets. Connected to these activities, they carried out many acts of violence, including homicide.[18] In turn, these activities have created a sharp sense of fear and a deep stigmatization of the population living in the popular sectors, which has reinforced the sense of abandonment and exclusion felt by many young people from lower and middle-lower strata and created a reduction of employment avenues for them, increasing the likelihood of their becoming part of criminal circles, in a kind of self-fulfilling prophecy.

The maras thrive in institutional environments in which there are pockets of corruption, at the level of enforcement forces as well as high-ranking officials with vested interests in transnational illicit commercialization of drugs and other commodities. Ana Arana describes a series of factors facilitating the growth of maras and their increasing use by illicit networks: the corruption of government officials, the existence of dense jungles, clandestine airstrips left over from civil wars, and the countries' lack of high-tech border controls have all allowed criminal mafias to form transnational links and operate regionally.[19] Likewise, the most comprehensive recent study by Demoscopía (2008) has found that with some exceptions, the police are perceived as corrupt and not trustworthy. The exceptions are in Nicaragua, where citizens report being assisted by the police and helping them in turn, and Costa Rica, where there are medium levels of trust in the police, albeit with rather high levels of dissatisfaction with their performance. In the other countries, a significant minority of the interviewed individuals—reaching more than half in Honduras—perceived the enforcement officers as corrupt and conniving with the criminal networks, to which they provide arms and protection in return for illicit profit.

Reinforcing such perceptions is the lack of effectiveness and the weakness of law enforcement forces, which is partly technical—due to insufficient human power, vehicles, helicopters, intelligence systems, and communication equipment—and partly due to weak traditions of commitment to civil service. This brings people in these Central American countries to assume that state authorities are corrupt and have vested interests in not reinforcing institutional effectiveness, leaving rank-and-file citizens on their own to solve problems and face the rising criminality and public insecurity. A survey of the police force in Belize, even if extreme, is representative. Belize has a comparatively high crime rate in the region, even though it is only populated by a mere 260,000 people. A research team interviewed officers, policemen, and men training in the academy, as well as citizens and visited prison facilities in order to get an accurate assessment of the situation. The study shows the extent of ineffectiveness of law enforcement in that country. First of all, "the Belize City Traffic Branch had just one automobile and four motorcycles at its disposal. . . . [The officers] are not encouraged to engage in high-speed pursuits of fleeing felons" out of fear of harming one of their very small stock.[20] Due to lack of transport and to complacent attitudes, they usually do not reach crime scenes until hours after the crime has occurred, even days sometimes, allowing plenty of time for the scene to be changed and tampered with. Morale is not very high. Morale goes down rapidly as the police officers conclude the training program and enter the field, due to low pay, the weekly shifts and location transfers, and mostly the public criticism and general lack of respect for police effectiveness. Accordingly, there are high rates of turnover, reinforced by a government regulation that provides a one-time gratuity of $1,000 to those officers serving ten years in the force. Having police experience gives individuals a preferred standing in immigration to the USA, where most go upon receiving their thousand dollars.[21] The maras and their criminal activities have caused the crime rates throughout the region to grow exponentially to the point that researchers closely following this development have recognized the deterioration of personal security. In recent years El Salvador, Honduras, and Guatemala have surpassed Colombia as the "homicide capitals" of Latin America. According to reports, around 60 percent of the murders committed in El Salvador in 2004 and 2005 were gang-related. Violence is threatening the very foundations of the democratic public spheres in these nations, eroding institutional trust, and generating a correlate loss in state legitimacy. The maras are instilling much fear, reinforcing the willingness of individuals to migrate from the home countries, and thus perpetuating in new ways the vicious cycle that caused the rise of these gangs in the first place. High crime and homicide rates also cause countries to be less alluring to tourists, and with tourism being one of the main sources of income, this affects the economy, deteriorating the situation of many and causing impoverished people to be more likely to join the maras. Besides their social effects, the maras' activities interfere with free markets, particularly affecting small businesses by threats, extortion, and violence.

Within each country, states have been enforcing various changes hoping to successfully battle the maras, yet many of the measures have been repressive, often resulting in the reinforcement of organized crime rather than in the creation of alternatives for the reinsertion of gang members in the formal economy and work. In Honduras the sentence for gang membership was increased in 2003 in the penal code to twelve years and increased again soon thereafter to thirty years. The army was put back on the streets in order to aid the small police force of merely 8,000, and the law that anyone with a gang-identifying tattoo would be thrown in jail was enacted. The prison system in Honduras is, however, not geared to rehabilitation and is overcrowded, creating serious problems of management and reinforcing the control of organized crime within the prisons. On May 17, 2004, 103 inmates—most of them heavily tattooed young members suspected of belonging to gangs—were burned to death when a fire swept through a wing of the prison in San Pedro Sula, Honduras' second-largest city.[22] This incident damaged the government's image, while it drew public sympathy for the gang members who died in the fire. It brought attention to the dismal prison situation in Honduras and throughout Central America since it occurred in a prison that was designated to hold 800 inmates but had 2,200 inmates at the time.[23]

More recently, Honduras launched programs of rehabilitation and work insertion for former mara members with the support of USAID and local business owners. Likewise, El Salvador developed the aforementioned Super Mano Dura programs while also developing with the FBI several rehabilitation and prevention programs. Panama has developed a program called Mano Amiga (Friendly Hand), which aimed to provide access to theater and sports activities for some 10,000 Panamanian youths as an alternative to joining gangs. Guatemala instituted several programs aimed at preventing crime and working with youths who have the potential to join gangs and former gang members. It put 4,000 of its reserve army troops on the streets to aid the struggling police.

Rehabilitation is a major challenge not lacking in contradictions, as the issue of access to arms indicates. Gangs tend to have and use weapons, securing a constant supply of good ones, not to mention the training to operate them. The maras were ahead of the game in this respect even before many of them joined gangs in Los Angeles and brought their gang knowledge back home. Since many had either been guerrillas or in the military during the 1970s and early 1980s, they were all well trained in combat and the use of weaponry. This generation provided a strong base of trainers for the proliferating gangs. The younger generation has been found to be employing a new strategy for access and training. With the growth of the gangs, the countries that have militaries are always eager for new recruits. Clearly, they will not knowingly allow a gang member into the army, though they do accept some former gang members who have been rehabilitated, though still hesitantly. However, there have been rumors of active mara members infiltrating the army in search for easy access to weaponry (or at least to find storage locations) and for training while getting paid by the very government that is trying to eradicate them. Central American countries have started envisioning ways to cooperate on a transnational level to be able to control the wider disrupting effects of these illicit and criminal networks pervading to various degrees most of the isthmian countries. In order to combat them, Central American countries started entering agreements aimed to carry out transnational practices of containment and regulation. In January 2004 Nicaragua, Honduras, Guatemala, El Salvador, and the Dominican Republic's officials started building a criminal database to better track the movements of the criminal organizations within the region. In June 2004 at a Summit of Presidents, the Salvadoran president proposed a Central American Security Plan (Plan Centro América Segura), to be conceived as part of the Integration System of Central America (SICA) and aimed at combating the perils of terrorism, narco-trafficking, and related crimes. In April 2005 an "anti-mara summit" was held at SICA, attended also by representatives from the United States and Mexico. Police forces of El Salvador and Guatemala have started cooperating along the border, coordinating actions aimed at the arrest of gang members irrespective of where the crimes have been committed. There is increasing recognition of the need to launch transnational mechanisms to fight the rising crime and the growth of illicit markets through the cooperation of the isthmian nations and the endorsement, guidance, and funding of other countries. Thus, the United States has established a security cooperation program of several hundred million dollars with the Central American countries as part of the so-called Mérida Initiative, or Plan México (2008–10), aimed at fighting the smuggling of drugs, arms, and people, transnational crime, and money laundering. The plan has been designed to finance training, intelligence, and provision of surveillance and other equipment, strengthening law enforcement, enhancing border inspection, preventing crime, and controlling gang activities.[24]

Correlated with these initiatives has been the renewed U.S. concern with counter-terrorism, which led to a significant increase in military funding and assistance to security forces, particularly since 2003, and to the reinvigoration of the Central American Armed Forces Conference (CFAC), a regional council of the military commanders of Guatemala, El Salvador,

Honduras, and Nicaragua. In 2005 the Central American presidents endorsed a CFAC proposal "to create a regional fast-deployment military task force whose main objective would be to fight terrorism, organized crime, and their related activities." According to Mark Rosenberg and Luis Solís, the presidential decision "ended the short-lived but formal effort to separate public security from national defense that was codified through the Treaty of Central American Democratic Security of 1995."[25]

Countries agreed to joint actions performed within countries, pooling resources and overcoming in this manner limitations imposed by each country's internal laws and limited resources. It has been argued that only such coordination and external funding could be effective and elicit a sense of unity and team spirit in the face of transnational illicit networks and the deficit in public security. Since funding is a major obstacle for these countries and in the spirit of leaving the state only a regulatory function, it has been suggested as well to involve nongovernmental organizations and religious mission groups in creating rehabilitation programs to help former mara members re-enter society, in addition to programs of mandatory rehabilitation designed to enable the future recruitment of mara members into the armed forces.[26]

The rise in transnational illicit markets and criminality in the isthmus—with youngsters joining in impoverished communities—has a direct correlation with the process of globalization and the problems of institutionalization that the new democracies of the region have experienced particularly since the 1990s.

13

Globalization and Transnational Dynamics in Contemporary Central America

The democratization of Central American states went hand in hand with increasing global linkages and new transnational trends. Production processes became debordered, creating a web of interdependence between sites of production and assembly and circuits of commercialization, both of legal and illicit markets. Many products consumed in the United States and the European nations are manufactured in Third World countries, where production processes have taken place, with foreign investment growing in correlation to the existence of cheap labor, which also often goes hand in hand with a lack of social security for workers. From there, many of these products are transported in legal and illicit circuits into the developed countries, supplying the demand of more affluent consumers than the average consumers in the countries of origin. All this reflects the growing role of globalization. Many recognize, as stressed by William Robinson, that

> the core of globalization, theoretically conceived, is the near culmination of a centuries-long process of the spread of capitalist production around the world and its displacement of all pre-capitalist relations ("modernization"). . . . In the process of creating a single, and increasingly undifferentiated field for world capitalism, [it] integrates the various polities, cultures and institutions of national societies into an emergent transnational or global society.[1]

A major move in that direction was achieved in the 1980s by the General Agreement on Tariffs and Trade (GATT), which allowed the following: "1) freedom of investment and capital movements; 2) the liberalization of services, including banks; 3) intellectual property rights; and 4) a free movement of goods."[2] Later stages included prescribed neoliberal programs of liberalization of trade and finances; "flexibilization" of the labor force; deregulation, which supposedly limits the state's involvement in economic decision making; and privatization of public services. New approaches, however, add that the process is one of mutual imbrications, which in parallel to the inclusion of peripheral areas in the global circuit of accumulation, carry with it also social, political, and cultural effects and is translated not only in the manner of a growing economic convergence—around the so-called Washington consensus—but leads as strongly to conflict, fragmentation, and redefinition of collective identities.[3]

When international investors and businesses came to Central America, these nations' economies became export-led. At first it was mainly traditional exports such as coffee, bananas, and sugar that spurred growth. With the translocation of capital for mass production purposes, many nontraditional exports became the main sources of income in the isthmus countries. Assembly plants and nontraditional agricultural exports, or NTAEs—such as fruits, flowers, winter vegetables, spices, and ornamental plants—grew in importance. There are two modes of NTAE production. The first is known as "estate plantation farming" in which a company buys a large plot of land and hires local workers to do all of the work on it. The second is called "satellite production" in which the company contracts local farmers to produce the crop it wants. One of the advantages of satellite production for investors is that they could exploit unpaid family labor since the farmers are paid according to the crop they yield and not by the labor that went into it. It is not simply the farmer doing all of the work, but his entire family ends up helping as well, giving investors a large component of free labor.[4] In addition to remittances and tourism, these sectors became leading engines of growth in the second half of the twentieth century in each and every one of the Central American nations.

In spite of such transformations and shifts in economic activity, the basic position of Central Americans as "price takers" rather than "price makers" in the global domain did not change radically. Moreover, while the income from NTAEs has had a positive effect on these nations, its social implications have not been bright. Due to foreign companies buying up much of the land to farm these products, the process has triggered a steep rise in the price of land, which has in turn resulted in the decline of small farming.

Maquiladora is the Spanish term for an assembly plant, that is, what is in essence a sweatshop. American and other international companies began placing factories, mainly garment-related, in Central American nations due to the availability of cheap labor as well as of work environments not regulated by the states, so that employers could demand long hours without being subject to the constraints of labor regulations and capital performance back home. During the 1990s and 2000s these assembly plants clearly grew in economic significance, as can be seen in graphs 13.1 and 13.2.

The remarkable growth of maquiladoras taking place between the 1980s and the late 1990s is a striking example of a more general process associated with globalization, namely, that some of the productive forces contributing greatly to globalization enjoy only meager benefits. From a sociological

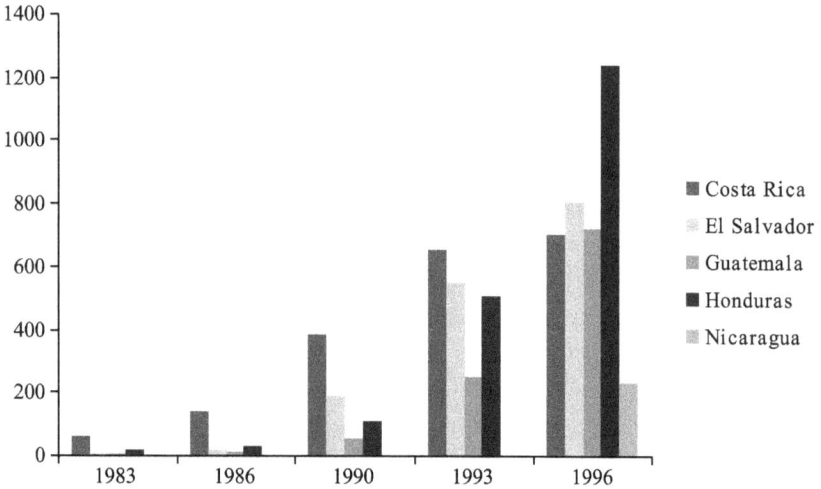

Graph 13.1. Garment assembly in Central America (measured by U.S. imports, millions of U.S.$). Adapted from William Robinson, *Transnational Conflicts*, 163, table 3.8, based on U.S. Department of Commerce data.

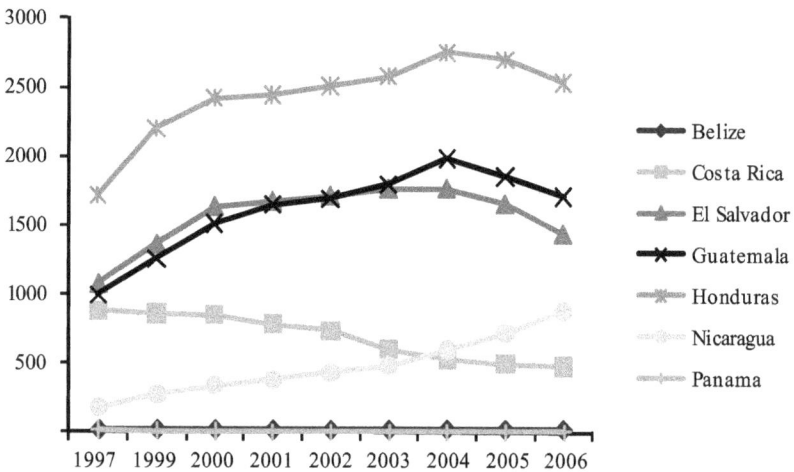

Graph 13.2. U.S. Imports of textiles, apparel, and footwear from Central America (millions of U.S.$). Adapted from USAID, *Latin America and the Caribbean: Selected Economic and Social Data 2007*, chapter 8, http://pdf.usaid.gov/pdf_docs/PNADK100.pdf.

perspective, these Central American workers have been marginalized, being forced to relocate, losing the protective shield of their families and neighbors, and being subject to various forms of abuse and violence, especially critical in the case of young women. Both in Central America as elsewhere, such as in Africa, many of these workers are "poor people scratching a living in poor countries" in the definition of James Dunkerley,[5] which has turned them into inner migrants relocating to the locations where these plants operate. In recent years the international community has given more attention to the need to regulate working conditions. In the case of Central America, the differentiated rate of salaries across countries has implied the decreased profitability of expanding activities in the more developed countries of the region such as Costa Rica and Panama. The other Central American states, being more impoverished, still count greatly on the assembly plants for their gross domestic product (GDP) and are reluctant to regulate the working conditions prevailing in their territory.

Starting in the 1990s, Central American countries have engaged in a series of state reforms, mostly in the economic and administrative domains, linked to trends of globalization. Economic reforms have included structural adjustment reforms aimed at reducing custom taxes and protective tariffs, liberalizing financial markets, eliminating state intervention in marketing and price setting, adding flexibility to the currency market, and privatizing utilities while aiming at increasing service provision. The macro-institutional aspects introduced were seen by many as harmful or, at best, as irrelevant to their daily lives and experiences and not conducive to the improvement of their living standards and prospects. Such perceptions of state reforms have reinforced public distrust toward democracy and its institutions. When questioned, Honduran migrants to the United States reflected critically on the home country they had left behind:

> Where is the democracy for a person that does not have one Lempira (US $0.05) to get on a bus that will take him 20 miles to look for a doctor? In other words, what good is a presumed democracy if a person cannot provide for the most basic and important thing in his life, the life of his child?[6]

Poverty has been perceived as a sign of institutional dysfunctional performance as much as lack of public safety. Although poverty in Honduras and most of Central America is not nearly as extreme as in Africa, it is a tremendous problem, especially in terms of the profound socioeconomic gap separating the wealthy from the poor in these countries, with far-reaching social and cultural consequences that affect the texture of public life, as will be discussed later. In Guatemala, for example, estimates are that nearly 50 percent of children under age five have suffered from chronic malnutrition, with the percentage becoming even higher among the indigenous population of the country.

The human development ranking, as assessed by international agencies, reflects this lack of convergence between policies of economic reform and social benefits. The UNDP releases Human Development Reports that include a human development index (HDI) measuring "the average achievements in a country in three basic dimensions of human development: a long and healthy life; access to knowledge; and a decent standard of living,"[7] These dimensions are measured by various indicators, which include per capita GDP, life expectancy at birth, percentage of people living below a poverty line (defined as those making less than a couple of U.S. dollars a day), and gross enrollment in schools. Using those indicators, countries are ranked according to their scores in the index of human development. According to this ranking, Panama and Costa Rica have been placed in the High Human Development category, while the rest of the isthmian countries fall into the Medium Human Development category. Table 13.1 shows the relative world ranking of these countries among 177 countries. Table 13.2 indicates their standing in terms of some of the main indicators of human development, and graph 13.3 shows their development since the 1980s. In this regard, and with the exception of Belize coming out of a crisis in recent years, the changes in these countries' achievements in human development as compared to other countries in the world during the fifteen years between 1990 and 2005 have been detrimental, in sharp contrast with the rising expectations that accompanied the heralded return of democracy and the ensuing state and economic reforms.

The poverty statistics for the region provided by UNDP (graph 13.4) and derived from other sources such as USAID attest to the sense of many living

Table 13.1. Human Development Index rankings 1990–2009

Country	1990	1997	2004	2006	2009
Belize	—	—	95	90	93
Costa Rica	28	33	48	53	54
El Salvador	72	112	101	106	106
Guatemala	80	116	118	123	122
Honduras	76	117	117	112	112
Nicaragua	60	127	112	124	124
Panama	—	—	58	61	60

Source: Robinson, *Transnational Conflicts*, 310, table 5.10, expanded through UNDP, *Human Development Report 2007/2008*, http://hdrstats.undp.org/en/indicators/82.html, and *Human Development Report 2009*, http://hdr.undp.org/en/statistics/2009.

Table 13.2. Human development profile 2004 (in U.S.$) and HDI rank 2004–2007

Country	GDP per capita	Life expectancy at birth	Adult literacy rate	Gross enrollment ratio	Gender development index	HDI rank 2004	HDI rank 2005
Belize	6,747	71.8	75.1	81.0	n.a.	95	80 (2007
Costa Rica	9,481	78.3	94.9	72.0	0.831	48	48
El Salvador	5,041	71.1	79.7	70.0	0.725	101	103
Guatemala	4,313	67.6	69.1	66.0	0.659	118	118
Honduras	2,876	68.1	80.0	71.0	0.676	117	115
Nicaragua	3,634	70.0	76.7	70.0	0.684	112	110
Panama	7,278	75.0	91.9	80.0	0.806	58	62
Average	5,437	71.7	82.5	71.5	0.730		

Source: USAID, *Latin America and the Caribbean: Selected Economic and Social Data 2007*, http://pdf.usaid.gov/pdf_docs/PNADK100.pdf.

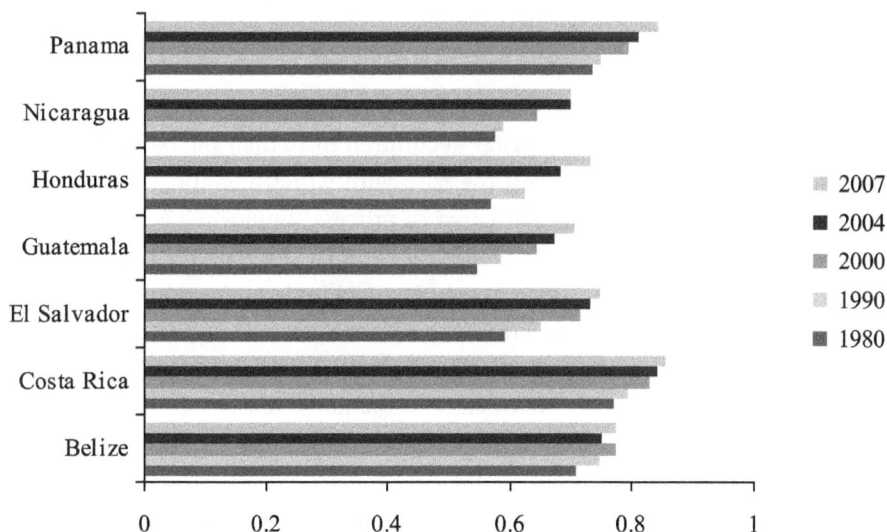

Graph 13.3. UN Human Development Index value, 1980–2007. Data from USAID, *Latin America and the Caribbean: Selected Economic and Social Data 2007*, 14, http://pdf.usaid.gov/pdf_docs/PNADK100.pdf; UNDP, *Human Development Report 2007/2008*, http://hdrstats.undp.org/indicators/25.html; UNDP, *Human Development Report 2009*, http://hdrstats.undp.org/en/statistics (accessed June 9, 2010).

in uncertainty and under conditions of deteriorating daily life in spite of good macro-economic performance. One immediate social consequence has been that these countries have become a focus for legal and illegal adoptions, that is, the adoption of newborns and children abducted from their parents or sold by their parents for a profit and in the hope of the children's relocation

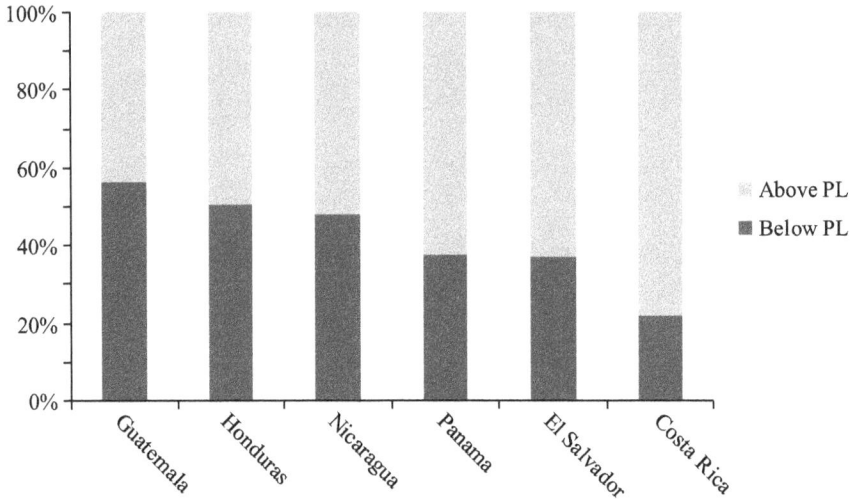

Graph 13.4. Population living below the national poverty line (percent). Adapted from UNDP, *Human Development Report 2007/2008*, http://hdrstats.undp.org/indicators/25.html.

to wealthy families abroad. Guatemala created in January 2008 a Council of Adoptions to regulate the transfer of children from their biological to adoptive parents and has curtailed the ease with which the abusive track was conducted by demanding that cases in process should be completed only upon a full declaration by the biological parents. Unsurprisingly, more than a hundred attorneys making a living from facilitating adoption papers tried to challenge the constitutionality of this well-conceived regulatory policy.

Compounding poverty is the unemployment rate within the nations. Table 13.3 offers a conservative view of the labor market. Indeed, while it shows the unemployment rates, it fails to account for the population that is underemployed or for unpaid family work, particularly in the informal sector. Moreover, too many within the poorer population work multiple jobs in order to scrape by and also account for those making less than $1 a day and are thus counted in the sector of the population living in poverty as well. Compounding this gloomy picture is a substantial problem of illiteracy in many quarters. Even in El Salvador, where authorities conveyed optimism, more than 682,000 adults over the age of twenty-five—close to one-fifth of that population—could not read or write, according to the Ministry of Education. While there has been an improvement since 1992, when that rate stood at nearly 26 percent, only recently efforts have been partially successful in further reducing illiteracy, mainly due to the lack of state resources and the constraints of poverty.[8] If these countries do not invest strongly in supporting the educational capacities and improving the occupational skills of

Table 13.3. Unemployment in Central America (percentage of labor force) 1980–2008

	1980s	1990s	2000	2005	2008
Belize	n.a.	9.8 (1993)	9.1 (2001)	11.0	8.2
Costa Rica	5.9 (1980)	4.6 (1990)	5.2	6.6	4.9
El Salvador	12.9 (1980)	10.0 (1990)	7.0	7.2	6.4 (2007)
Guatemala	3.5 (1987)	3.2 (1991)	1.4	3.1 (2004)	1.8 (2006)
Honduras	7.3 (1982)	4.8 (1990)	3.9 (2001)	4.1	2.9 (2007)
Nicaragua	11.1 (1980)	11.1 (1990)	9.8	12.2 (2002)	n.a.

Sources: USAID, *Latin America and the Caribbean: Selected Economic and Social Data 2007*, http://qesdb.
cdie.org/lac/docdownload.html; *LABORSTA Internet*, http://laborsta.ilo.org (accessed June 9, 2010).

Table 13.4. Share of income, poorest and richest, in Central America (percent)

	Year	Poorest 10%	20%	Richest 20%	10%
Belize	2003	1.6			48.0
Costa Rica	2003	1.0	3.5	54.1	37.4
El Salvador	2002	0.7	2.7	55.9	38.8
Guatemala	2002	0.9	2.9	59.5	43.4
Honduras	2003	1.2	3.4	58.3	42.2
Nicaragua	2001	2.2	5.6	49.3	33.8
Panama	2003	0.7	2.5	59.9	43.0

Sources: USAID, *Latin America and the Caribbean: Selected Economic and Social Data 2007*, http://qesdb.
cdie.org/lac/docdownload.html; *IndexMundi*, http://indexmundi.com/belize/unemployment_rate.html
(accessed July 29, 2008).

their populations, such skewed structure turns even more critical in terms of the prospects of their long-term development.

As indicated above, income distribution is highly unequal in these countries, which have been characterized by a huge gap between the rich and the poor and a comparatively reduced middle class. Table 13.4 shows data reflecting the highly skewed structure of income distribution.

The socioeconomic gap reflected in the distribution of income among the different percentiles can be more clearly seen in the Gini coefficient of these countries. The Gini coefficient measures the inequality of income distribution of a country. It varies from 0, which represents perfect equality, with every household earning exactly the same, to 1, representing absolute inequality, with a single household earning a country's entire income. Central and South America, with a persisting Gini coefficient of around 0.50–0.60 (graph 13.5), have been found to be among the world's most unequal regions, perhaps only surpassed by Africa.[9]

Several social and cultural factors reinforce the skewed income structure, including the structure of the labor market—where significant sectors with little education work for low or minimum wages—and racist attitudes on the part of employers. As is well known, better education leads to higher levels

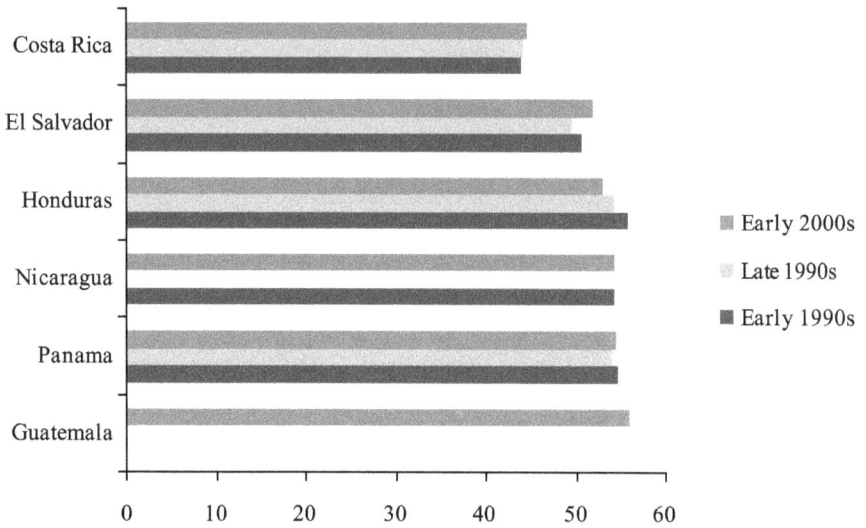

Graph 13.5. Gini coefficients of Central American societies. Adapted from *Inequality in Latin America and the Caribbean: Breaking with History?*, advance conference edition, (Washington, D.C.: International Bank for Reconstruction and Development/World Bank Latin American and Caribbean Studies, 2003), 373, table A6.

of income. One cannot expect the GDP per capita to increase and be more equally distributed without an increase in the general enrollment through secondary school in each of the nations. Even in a country with a relatively good ranking in literacy, as Nicaragua has, there are thousands of individuals who are functionally illiterate. That is, even if they went through the educational system and are counted as literate, they can barely read or write freely. However, educational improvements require funding, which is sorely insufficient in most of these nations. Moreover, as problems such as poverty and lack of public safety became acute throughout the region in the past generation, the well-advertised "retreat of the state" has caused anxiety and led to a low degree of civil and political involvement and distrust in public arenas.

Transnational, intraregional trade has expanded in recent decades, almost tripling since 1980. In spite of its name, the signing of the Central American Free Trade Agreement (CAFTA) in May 2004, coming into effect in March 2006, was not geared to expand further this transnational connection but rather to promote a better insertion in global trade and markets. Specifically, it was aimed to balance the preferential treatment of Mexico since the institution of the North American Free Trade Agreement (NAFTA), which came into effect in 2004, and to enable Central American producers to compete with producers in China for a share of mainly the clothing market. Resistance to the agreement has been documented by Rose Spalding for El

Salvador. Spalding has found enthusiasts represented by the business sector organized in the American Chamber of Commerce of El Salvador and a varied set of opposition coalitions. Among the latter were groups interested in critically negotiating the terms of the agreement Iniciativa Mesoamericana de Comercio, Integración y Desarollo (Iniciativa CID) and groups rejecting any compromise, defined by the author as "transgressive resisters," organized through the Foro Mesoamericano. The CID proponents were not entirely opposed to the terms of CAFTA but believed that much of it should be altered. Its members combined active drafting of policy proposals with cross-regional lobbying and allied with many NGOs and oppositional groups in the other Central American countries. The group conducted research to identify the treaty's impact on vulnerable sectors, developed proposals for amendments and additions to the agreement, pushed for and participated actively in the "side room" process during the negotiation rounds, lobbied unofficial decision makers, and in an effort to influence public opinion disseminated information at public forums through the CID Web site and in the local press.[10]

Some of the issues they found controversial in CAFTA were labor rights, concern for small and medium-size businesses, and environmental implications. In spite of their civil engagement, they failed to promote their agenda. In July 2003 they called unsuccessfully for a moratorium aimed to "permit Central American countries to step back from the frenetic negotiations, complete research on the socioeconomic impact of various concessions, [and] allow Central American legislatures to define a baseline of institutional and economic conditions needed for a successful free trade transition."[11] Contrastingly, the Foro Mesoamericano—originating in Mexico and spreading from there to the isthmus—strongly rejected the CAFTA project. Its members believed that CAFTA would flood the market with U.S. goods and ruin small and medium-size producers, cause a collapse of basic grain production due to shipments to the United States, and create a deepening fiscal crisis, all of which would result in massive emigration. Considering CAFTA fully detrimental to sustained development, with the support of groups of followers from among the poorer and indigenous population, Foro Mesoamericano resorted to tactics such as "highway and border crossing blockades, authorized and unauthorized marches tinged with transgressive acts, and the physical takeover of legislative chambers."[12] The group's strategy of mass public confrontation failed, too, in preventing the signing of the Central American–Dominican Republic Free Trade Agreement (CAFTA-DR).

Between August 2005 and April 2006, El Salvador, Guatemala, Honduras, and Nicaragua ratified the 2004 CAFTA-DR agreement of free trade with the United States. The incorporation of Costa Rica was a protracted one. With parties and citizens strongly divided, the issue went to a vote in October 2007. After over 51 percent of votes were cast in favor of the free trade agreement, the president signed the agreement and the parliament moved to promulgate laws for its implementation, a process completed by early 2009. Thus far, the prediction that the agreement would do little to ease poverty and reduce the socioeconomic gap has not been proven wrong, even though there are country variations. Whether the problems that have been found—such as know-how in handling the bureaucratic procedures required by the United States—will be solved remains to be seen.[13]

Notwithstanding this agreement and the negotiations being conducted by the Central American Common Market (CACM) with other commercial blocks such as the European Union and Mercosur, the Central American countries have faced difficulties in coordinating joint external positions in negotiations. As a result, there has been a tendency to sign bilateral rather than multilateral free trade agreements. For instance, even though there was a framework for free trade between these countries and Mexico, signed in 1991, only El Salvador, Guatemala, and Honduras have signed a formal agreement; Costa Rica has negotiated individually a free trade agreement, CARICOM, with Mexico, Canada, and the Caribbean; Guatemala and Nicaragua have signed agreements with Taiwan; Nicaragua has done the same with Mexico and Guatemala; El Salvador, Costa Rica, and Guatemala have signed agreements with Chile; and Panama has signed agreements with Taiwan, Singapore, the United States, and Costa Rica while carrying out bilateral negotiations with Honduras. Other negotiations involve El Salvador, Guatemala, Honduras, and Nicaragua with Canada; Nicaragua with Chile; and El Salvador and Honduras with Taiwan.[14] Unsurprisingly, in spite of some growth in intraregional trade, extraregional trade far outdoes it, as graph 13.6 indicates.

Related major trends are the movement of many Central Americans to more developed countries in search of higher incomes and better futures for their children and the significant growth of remittances this wave of immigrants has sent back to their home countries.

The growth in migration flows has been translated into a surge of remittances, which have become a most important component of national domestic growth, as shown in graph 13.7. In 2004 remittances were a far larger component of domestic GDP than tourism in most Central American countries. They constituted from less than 2 percent of the GDP in Costa Rica and Panama to at least 10 percent of GDP in the rest of the region: Guatemala (10 percent), El Salvador (12.1 percent), Honduras (15.1 percent), and Nicaragua (17.8 percent).

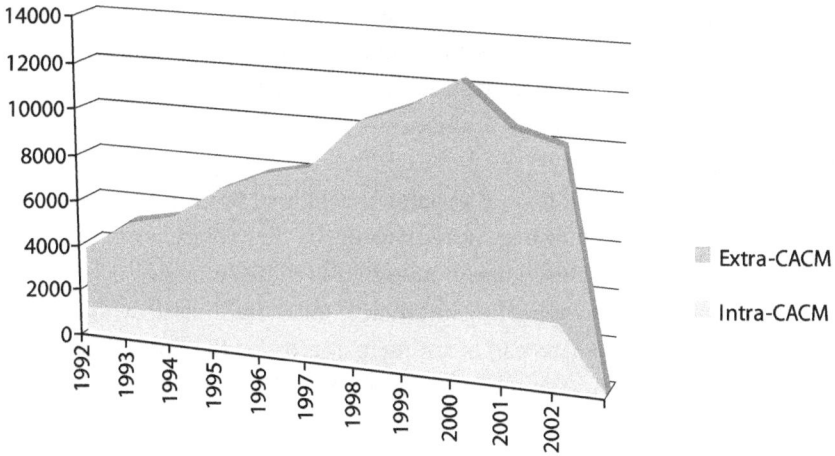

Graph 13.6. Intraregional and extraregional exports (millions of U.S.$). Adapted from *SICE/OAS Foreign Trade Information System*, http://www.sice.oas.org/SICA.

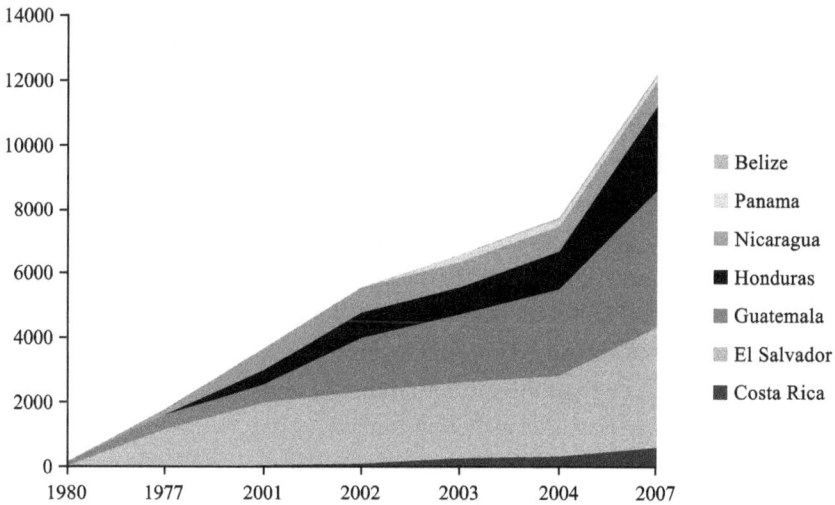

Graph 13.7. Remittances to Central America 1980–2007 (millions of U.S.$). Adapted from Economic Commission for Latin America and the Caribbean (ECLAC), on the basis of data from the Inter-American Development Bank/Multilateral Investment Fund (IADB/MIF); Inter-American Development Bank, 2005, 2007, http://www.iadb.org/mif/remesas_map.cfm and http://hdrstats.undp.org/en/countries (accessed June 9, 2010).

These figures do not even reflect the remittances that are not sent through legal channels or are sent as bulk gifts instead of money. Once again, one can see that the reliance on remittances was lower in Costa Rica and Panama, due to their more elevated and prosperous economies, which contributed to higher percentages of workforce retention and lower numbers of migration to other countries. In the other countries, remittances added to the

purchasing power of impoverished strata but also contributed to reinforcing internal imbalances in the distribution of income, price of commodities,
and access to markets of different strata in the population. The financial and
commercial crisis of 2008–10 dramatically lowered the transfer of remittances to Central America.[15]

Tourism is the other source of revenue that gained prominence since the
1980s, with increasing numbers of tourists of the First World traveling and
exploring the isthmus. Hotels began investing in these countries as ecotourism was conceived as an appealing alternative for those tourists who wished
to explore exotic nations instead of sitting in a resort by the pool. Costa Rica
has been the country in the region to profit most from tourism and where
ecotourism has started booming as well. The country benefited from the
existence of a network of national parks promoted by biologists interested in
conservation as well as from a series of museums such as the Jade Museum
and the pre-Columbian Gold Museum, which were instrumental to the tourist boom of the 1990s. Costa Rica also benefited from its reputation as an
economically sound and politically stable country, while many associated
civil unrest and poverty with the other Central American nations, hinder-
ing the development of the tourism industry there. Panama follows closely
behind Costa Rica, mainly due to the presence of the Panama Canal, a focus
of tourist attraction, with other locations in Panama becoming equally at-
tractive in recent years, particularly once the country regained control of
the canal. Still, some remote areas in the eastern jungle of Panama have been
marked by criminal activities that constituted a hindrance to their effective
inclusion in tourist circuits. Graph 13.8 shows the economic benefits from
tourism and the growth of the tourism industry between 1970 and 2007.

It is important to note that although tourism brings many more people to
the region spending money in the different countries, a substantial part of
the income generated by tourism goes to the airlines and foreign-run hotels
instead of directly into the country itself. This trend is even more accentu-
ated in the case of a country such as Belize, in which around 15 percent of
the GDP has been generated by tourism in general and increasingly by cruise
tourism, a type of tourism that impinges the country very selectively and
partially in the form of enclaves related mainly to the reef circuits.

Research has also found that in addition to ecotourism and sometimes
combined with it, there has been a growing surge of human trafficking for
purposes of sexual exploitation. The range of such exploitation includes
women and minors, female stripping, and female and child pornography.
In recent years, softened border controls have eased the activities of the

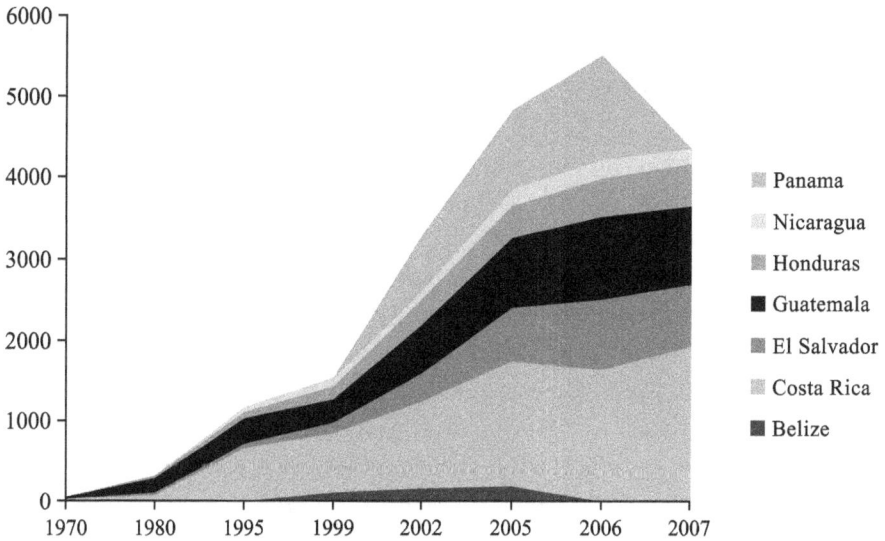

Graph 13.8. Income from tourism in Central America, selected years (millions of U.S.$). Adapted from Secretaría Técnica del SCCCT, Consejo Centroamericano de Turismo, http://www.sica.int/cct.

trafficking networks, especially those leading north from Nicaragua through Honduras and possibly El Salvador and ending in Guatemala, Belize, and Honduras and in different forms toward the south, attempting to enter the more affluent environments of Costa Rica and Panama. Throughout Central America such phenomena emerged in the framework of "zones of tolerance" in tourist areas, ports, casinos, and transnational trucking routes. Prostitution also occurs in border areas and public markets as well as in certain agricultural areas populated by temporary male agricultural workers.

Under the allure of tourist dollars, bar owners, taxi drivers, hotel staff, market vendors, and independent pimps all provide brokering services to clients. In the poorest regions one can even find family-controlled prostitution (as in Honduras) or gang-related prostitution (as in Salvador and Honduras), while in more affluent areas such as Costa Rica and Panama marriage fraud and deception have been reported. Moreover, abduction and misadventure seem to be generalized paths of human trafficking throughout the countries of the isthmus without exception. A group of researchers studying this phenomenon has pointed out that under the heightened immigration requirements in Costa Rica and Mexico, the Guatemala-Mexico border has increasingly become a thriving hub and fertile environment for transnational human trafficking and prostitution. This development is explained by a number of factors:

First, the availability of women and children is extremely high. . . . Migrating women and children will often find themselves at the border with insufficient funds to secure their further progress. In addition, the Central Americans who have crossed without success and returned to the Guatemalan side of the border, rather than to their countries of origin. Many [individuals] desire to try again, for which money is necessary. Male migrants, finding themselves in similar situations of waiting at the border to cross into Mexico, create a demand for sexual services. . . . Innumerable criminal networks function in the area [of Tecún Umán], trading in persons, cattle, vehicles, drugs and other illicit goods. The trafficking of women and children into prostitution is easy business. The networks involved in the trafficking include establishment owners, rickshaw drivers (*tricicleros*), and migrant smugglers. Corruption of municipal officials, and police and immigration authorities is reported as being extremely high. The corruption—in the form of bribes, payment through sexual services, and direct participation—has secured total impunity for traffickers.[16]

Transnational border arrangements and globalization have thus contributed to some improvements in macro-economic performance, and yet, they had mixed implications for these societies, failing to be instrumental in creating inclusive economic growth or in reducing institutional fragility. Economic reforms have done little to reduce poverty, socioeconomic gaps, and social exclusion. Criminality, illicit markets, social violence, and the lack of public safety have added roadblocks on the way to creating a sense of universal development and active citizenship.

14

Interstate Institutions
and Transnational Involvement

A New Stage?

Following the advance in the peace process initiated in the late 1980s and perhaps building upon the important regional cooperation leading to its success, interstate institutions have gained momentum in recent decades. In the 1990s and 2000s there was substantial institutional development. Regional institutions have proliferated, yet we should ask whether the growing number of Central American institutions also reflects a growing trust in their capability to cope with the problems of these countries and improve the quality of institutional and social life or whether they replicate some of the long-standing institutional problems of state institutions, primarily their performance and deficit of public trust, and whether the regional institutions have reflected regional identity or contributed to it.

Institutional development built upon some earlier antecedents that can be traced back to the 1950s and 1960s. After a hiatus during the depression of the 1930s and World War II, transnational efforts resumed starting in September 1951 with meetings that created the Organization of Central American States (ODECA), comprised of Costa Rica, El Salvador, Guatemala, Honduras, and Nicaragua. This move led to a series of subsequent initiatives oriented toward peaceful cooperation and construction of transnational institutions.

These initiatives, launched since the 1960s, differed from the early projects of reunification, as they were geared toward creating mechanisms of transnational cooperation rather than political union, as in the past. They involved the creation of the Central American Common Market (MCCA or CACM) in 1960. Other institutional frameworks created in that period included the Central American Bank of Economic Integration (1961), the Central American Monetary Council created to coordinate the development of a monetary union (1964), the Central American Council of Defense, or CONDECA, that included Guatemala, El Salvador, Honduras, and Nicaragua, with a symbolic adherence of Costa Rica and the addition of Panama in 1972; and the Central American Council of Superintendents of Banks, Insurance, and Other Financial Institutions, created in 1974 to foster cooperation and the exchange of information.

The Central American Common Market served as an economic alliance of El Salvador, Guatemala, Honduras, and Nicaragua—and Costa Rica joining in 1962—aiming to attract foreign investment into the region and promote free trade among the member states. Though its overarching goal was to produce a "balanced regional growth," outside investors favored the core and more advanced states, El Salvador and Guatemala, over the underdeveloped ones such as Honduras. This, along with Honduras' military confrontation with El Salvador in the Soccer War of 1969,[1] led Honduras to demand that the Central American Common Market be reorganized. When El Salvador and Guatemala rejected this demand, Honduras left the alliance, which then collapsed. Central American regional trade decreased throughout the 1970s.[2]

The initiatives of regional institutional cooperation gained momentum again in the 1990s, reinforced by the intervention of the countries in the peace agreements that took off with Esquipulas II in August 1987 and were instrumental in leading to the end of the civil wars in El Salvador and Guatemala as well as in establishing various mechanisms for cooperation. Schematically, this phase of reconnection includes among others the following initiatives:

A meeting of Central American presidents in June 1990, involving the five countries, with the president of Panama as observer, agreeing on starting an economic plan of action for Central America (PAECA). This plan of action was aimed at dismantling customs between countries in the region while establishing a multilateral, regional program with a greater stake in promoting international commerce, tourism, and attraction of investments. The program foresaw cooperation in many areas, including coordination of agrarian policies, negotiations concerning foreign debt, and a regional policy for science and technology.

The establishment of a Central American Parliament (PARLACEN), projected since 1986 and carried out in 1991, with its location in Guatemala City.

The establishment in 1991 of the System of Central American Integration

(SICA), composed by the countries of the region with the Dominican Republic as an associate member, with headquarters in San Salvador. Among its aims were the strengthening of democracy and
the respect for human rights; the creation of a regional system of
security that would reinforce civilian rule and overcome poverty,
violence, corruption, terrorism, narco-traffic, and traffic of arms;
the promotion of economic union and strengthening of a Central
American financial system; reinforcement of the regional economic
block; the promotion of a single foreign policy aimed at achieving
comparatively greater weight in international relations; the promotion of the harmonic and sustained economic, social, cultural, and
political development of the member states and the region; and overall creation of institutions that would rely on the mutual respect of
the member states.

The creation in 1992 of a Central American Court of Justice, located
in Nicaragua.

The signing in 1993 of a protocol to the 1960 Treaty of Economic Integration, launching free trade in the region. This was reinforced by
the establishment of a common external tariff in February 2001.

The Central American Alliance for Sustainable Development (ALIDES)
in 1994.

The Treaty of Central American Social Integration (TISCA) in 1995.

The Treaty for the establishment of a Framework of Central American
Democratic Security (TMSDA), also in 1995. This treaty formally left
the doctrines of national security of the cold war behind, to be replaced by a regional vision of democratic and civil security, adopting
an integrated view recognizing and aiming to heal the social roots
of insecurity.[3]

In this new stage, institutional steps aiming at coordinated action proliferated and broadened to include dozens of regional institutional mechanisms
such as a confederation of public universities, a disaster agency, and a regional transportation council. Such institutional development has been dictated by, among other processes, trends of globalizing economic circuits and
the transnationalization of migration, whether of a legal, an informal, or an
illicit nature.[4] These institutional steps have been embedded rhetorically in
professed declarations of a seeming existence of "an economic-political community that aspires to the integration of Central America" and to claims that,
while respecting the individuality of the societies composing the isthmus,

the steps that have been taken support the notion of a Central American nation with an "integrationist culture" rooted in multiple historical bonds and driven by shared interests in the present.[5]

In spite of the idealistic overtones of transnational solidarity and future reunification of the states of Central America professed often by drafters of agreements and observers, recent decades have witnessed the move toward institutional coordination as derived from the structural imperatives that all these independent states face in parallel and that led to the coordination of efforts and creation of mechanisms such as the derogation of international tariffs, the eased controls of national documents and vehicles at border crossings, and the joint prevention of international gang activity.

Participation in these bodies has been voluntary and partial. For instance, while the seven countries of the region participate in SICA (together with the Dominican Republic as an associate member), membership in other agencies has been partial. Only Nicaragua, El Salvador, and Honduras have joined the Central American Court of Justice. Belize did not sign the Treaty of Social Integration or the security treaty. The Dominican Republic has joined the latter, but Panama and Costa Rica have signed the treaty with reservations, claiming they have no army.

Vehemently criticized has been PARLACEN, the regional parliament comprised of twenty-two lawmakers from each of the member countries—Guatemala, Honduras, El Salvador, Nicaragua, Panama, and the Dominican Republic.[6] Costa Rica's government has chosen to remain out of the Central American parliament, claiming it is a costly institution that brings little benefit. With a budget of twenty million dollars a year, the organization has come under fire, since it has come up with few results and those are nonbinding. In addition, PARLACEN has been criticized for providing immunity from prosecution for politicians accused of corruption. In 2000 Guatemala threatened to withdraw from the body. More recently, it was Honduras' turn to hint in that direction. In December 2003 Honduran Attorney General Sergio Zavala labeled the regional legislature dysfunctional, telling reporters that his government had the political will to retire from the institution and from the Central American Court of Justice as well. "It is painful to pay so much money to be a member of these regional institutions," he said. Each of the six member countries was paying then a reported $1.7 million annually to support the organization and, according to Zavala, got precious little in return, especially as member countries are not obligated to comply with any act or decision of the body.[7] PARLACEN has faced increasing criticism due to its inability to deal with the dilemma of either maintaining the current system that grants immunity from criminal prosecution to its parliamentarians, including former heads of state who serve ex officio in its ranks, or overriding the immunity and thus allowing for Central American bodies such as the Court of Justice to bring to trial current and former power holders, overriding member states' sovereignty.

PARLACEN's institutional deficit of trust reflects closely a transnational phenomenon: the disillusionment of many Central Americans with the workings of their national and interstate institutions. As the area entered fully the process of structural reform, particularly in the domain of economic globalization, the idea was to accompany these reforms with institutional reforms aimed at making the states more democratic, efficient, and responsive to citizens' expectations and needs. Yet, the economic reforms, primarily those oriented to the deregulation of state intervention in the economy and the privatization of key services, were actively promoted, while the envisaged improvement of the public administration lagged far behind. Provision of justice has been still slow and inefficient, corruption was still found and widely expected, and citizens often remained skeptical of public institutions.

These problems are compounded by the practices followed by many of those in power. With democratization there were great expectations, but in practice major groups and sectors continued to be concerned with their discrete interests and expressed little interest in promoting citizen participation and little commitment to solidarity, bridging to other groups in order to sustain social cohesion, and the well-being of society. Accordingly, the constellation of forces holding power has bred alienation, while no new values or norms were introduced into the dominant political cultures. Immigrant entrepreneurs and foreign investors joined those benefiting from a coercive and extractive socioeconomic environment in the rural areas. Privileged concessions and personal contacts have been the key to contracts and riches.

Even if this trend cannot be generalized to the entire region, it is rather wide. Even the Sandinista revolution, which constituted a radical shift in elites, did not produce a clear-cut break in public norms and legality. Neither did the revolution produce a change in the customary appropriation by power holders of public resources, something known popularly as La Piñata, as if it was the prize of sweets children used to get in certain festivities. In their case, the appropriation of resources by the revolutionary leadership continued unabated. Even with political turnover in 1990, not much changed in Nicaragua in the general respect for public legality and norms.[8] Perhaps standing out in this respect is the Nicaraguan police force, which seems less corrupt than other forces; some attribute this to their socialization in the period of the Sandinista revolution. Nonetheless, regarding overall transparency, Nicaragua still has much to do. As recently as June 2009, $64 million in U.S. foreign aid channeled through the Millennium Challenge Corporation to contribute to sustainable development in Nicaragua was halted, due to seeming electoral fraud in the municipal elections of November 2008 and the lack of appropriate inquiries by the Nicaraguan administration.[9]

One can also find a persisting trend of ignoring administrative and legal procedures for the sake of partisan interests and meta-social goals, which may vary from place to place and across time, be they those of progress, industrialization, development, revolution, national security, or structural adjustment. Throughout constant instability, one can find persistence of particularistic politics, corruption, and nepotism, favors to family and social networks, authoritarian mentalities, and failing political openings that often cut across party lines and ideological divisions. One of the most blatant cases of allegations of corruption, impunity, and political maneuvering seems to have unfolded in Nicaragua in the late 1990s and early 2000s. In 1996 the former mayor of Managua and president of the Liberal Alliance, Arnoldo Alemán, defeated Daniel Ortega in the presidential elections. In March 1998 Ortega's thirty-year-old stepdaughter Zoilamérica Narváez accused him of having sexually abused her for nine years, between 1979 and 1988, beginning when she was eleven. When Narváez filed a civil suit against him, Ortega claimed parliamentary immunity. Soon thereafter, when Hurricane Mitch hit Nicaragua in late 1998, President Alemán was accused of profiting while he was on the public payroll as mayor of the capital in the 1990s. Under such a background, with the reputation of their most prominent leaders blemished, liberals and Sandinistas reached a power-sharing agreement in June 1999. According to the agreement, these two political forces would divide among themselves the seats of the supreme court and the electoral council. This clearly would allow them to achieve control over key institutions responsible for overseeing both judicial and electoral accountability while excluding minor parties from access to power.

The 2001 presidential elections brought seventy-three-year-old vice president Enrique Bolaños to power on an anti-corruption platform. Yet, then the situation became even more entangled. Both Alemán and Ortega received seats in the assembly and were thus assured impunity from the respective charges of illicit enrichment and molestation. Eventually, Alemán and some of his close relatives and associates were charged and convicted on counts of embezzlement and money laundering. The former president was sentenced to twenty years in prison and started serving his sentence in March 2004.

While in prison, however, his supporters joined the Sandinistas in the parliament in an attempt to impeach President Bolaños. Many saw this move as motivated by the combined wish for revenge of the Alemanistas and the fear of the Sandinistas that Ortega could be the next target on the agenda of the administration. Although the impeachment threat came to nothing, in January 2005 Alemanistas and Sandinistas joined forces to curtail by legislation Bolaños' appointment powers. Soon the crisis ended, as Daniel Ortega—who was soon to announce his candidacy in the 2006 presidential elections—declared he would support Bolaños remaining in office until the end of his term, thus gaining political capital for the forthcoming elections. By all counts, while not based on repression, post-Sandinista democracy seemed to remain as manipulative and corrupt as during previous administrations, thus bringing citizens to think that little had changed in that respect in spite of the dramatic political shifts that Nicaragua underwent since the days of Somoza and the subsequent rule of Sandinistas.

These trends suggest the resilience of certain political patterns beyond changes in power and ruling coalition. A major problem accounting for such resilience is the divergence between the letter of the law and political practice, which has been a common thread of political culture in the isthmus for decades. Connected to it, one can trace many cases of theatrical staging and talking about the public good—in high-brow rhetoric, or *grandilocuencia*—which provided ground for social cynicism on public issues and has remained salient in the region. In the past, elites drafted liberal constitutions but did not abide by them, creating a gap between the formalities of public administration and politics on the one hand and their use of clientelistic favors and repression as means of controlling societies. Even in Costa Rica electoral fraud was the norm until 1948, the assumption being that it was a means of defending institutionalism against the ignorant masses, which were not ready for self-government. Representative institutions could not serve to mediate in conflicts, and authoritarianism was justified to avoid the deviation from the goals of the rulers.[10] Networks were more important than institutions, and political actors repeatedly changed sides. It was not uncommon for people to be helped by those selected to imprison them due to personal sympathies or respect for social background. Likewise, partisan commitments and personal animosities continued to color interactions to the point of institutional failure and internal war. The rule of law has been applied selectively, and political fraud is widespread. Those in power have used it to monopolize control of institutions and the access to positions and markets selectively to sustain personal followings and political alliances. An institutional conundrum developed in Honduras following President José Manuel Zelaya's decision of calling a referendum on the convention of an assembly to reform the constitution. The personalist style of Zelaya, coupled with financial nepotism, and corruption scandals that led to very low levels of popular support,[11] and moreover his confrontational rule in discarding warnings of constitutional misconduct by the attorney general, the supreme court, and the congress, as well as his dismissal of the head of the armed forces who declined to support the presidential initiative, prompted a coup that led to Zelaya's ostracism and exile. While the OAS Permanent Council strongly condemned the coup under the Inter-American Democratic Charter and demanded the immediate and unconditional return of President Zelaya to his constitutional duties, a move supported by the United States and Venezuela alike, a mediating initiative of Costa Rican President Oscar Arias was ineffective due to the intransigent positions of both the government of de facto President Roberto Micheletti and of Zelaya and his Bolivarian Alliance for the Americas (ALBA) supporters. The sequence of Zelaya secretly crossing the border to remain secluded in the Brazilian embassy until after the elections followed by his departure into exile are well known. Beyond the unfolding details of this dramatic case and its emblematic status in terms of democratic continuity or discontinuity throughout the Americas, it has been doubly significant for what it reveals in terms of political practices that are predicated on bare power and the will to impose decisions unilaterally by whatever means are available to those in power. Under such conditions, a clash of branches of government can lead to the breakdown of procedural rule and the ostracism and political exile of opponents.

Many of these practices have persisted even though they are under increasing pressure due to the publicity of normative regulations and the growing openness of these societies to the global domain. Failing to meet normative expectations, many of these instances are colored by the discourse of corruption and illegality. This, in turn, has stained the image of institutions and has reverberated in society, reinforcing institutional distrust and anomic behavior at the popular level.

Many of these drawbacks are projected into the regional institutions. As indicated earlier, the Central American parliament has been viewed with widespread scorn throughout the region due to its high costs and the lack of a binding nature of its deliberations, together with the rising number of irksome scandals involving some of its members. A recent source mentions the following stream of problematic cases: "The arrest of Honduran PARLACEN Deputy César A. Díaz Flores in Nicaragua with 7.2 kilos of heroin; the arrest of Jorge A. Cáceres, a PARLACEN functionary, for trafficking in cocaine at PARLACEN's Honduras facility; the sentencing of former Nicaraguan President Arnoldo Alemán to a 20-year term for money laundering and fraud. Alemán's immunity from prosecution as an ex-officio PARLACEN member figured prominently in the case, protracting it for years; the indictment in Panama of Deputy Bernardo Díaz De Icaza on domestic violence and child abuse charges; and the investigation of Panamanian ex-President Ernesto Pérez Balladares (1994–1999), another deputy by virtue of past presidency, for illicit enrichment. He remains shielded by his immunity."[12]

The structure of regional institutions composed of representatives of states has further hampered the possibility of developing a distinct institutional track for those institutions, which could avoid the drawbacks of the lack of trust in national institutions.

Providing further obstacles to reform is the lack of conditions assuring the free and critical performance by the media. According to a National Report on the Media, Politics, and Democracy released by the United Nations Program for Development (UNDP) in 2008, these conditions were particularly problematic in Guatemala and Honduras, where journalism was defined as a "high-risk" occupation. Throughout the isthmus, journalists who have been critical of the political or social system have often received death threats, which, even if carried out only selectively, have forced others to flee their countries, while inducing a more reserved and less critical attitude by the "fourth power."[13]

Whether the above cases are the tip of the iceberg of a widespread phenomenon of lack of normative behavior on the part of representatives or, alternatively, scandals triggered by partisan attacks launched by competing political forces is to be assessed in a case-by-case manner, which is beyond the purview of this work. Nonetheless, whatever the case, it is clear that such scandals seriously affect the image and capacity of institutions to become beacons of transnational identity, contributing a sense of transnational pride and raising the levels of generalized trust in these societies.

The above trends are reflected in the image of institutions and the public trust they engender. Transparency International's Corruption Perception Index, the CPI, provides an index of measuring the perception of institutional performance, although its index is built upon a distinction among countries. The CPI uses a scale from 1 to 10 to rank a country's overall corruption, as derived from the amalgamation of expert polls and surveys provided by selected institutions. A score of 1 is considered the most corrupt, and a score of 10 is considered the least corrupt. Transparency International has

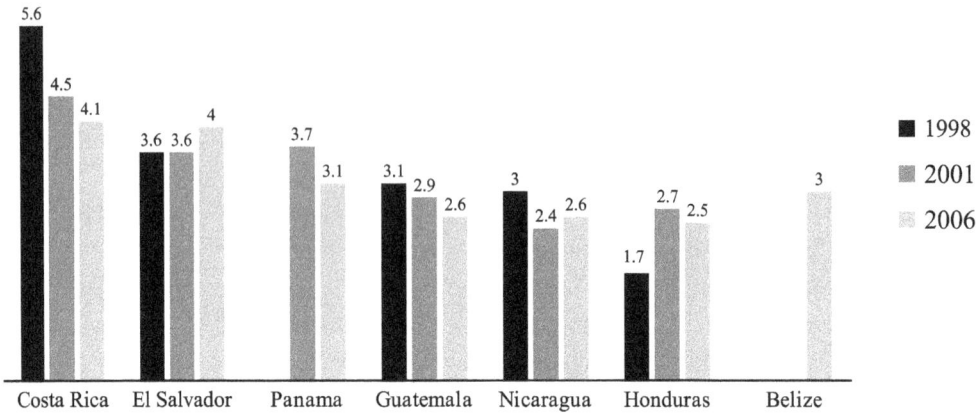

Graph 14.1. CPI data for 1998, 2001, and 2006. Adapted from Transparency International, "Corruptions Perceptions Index" (2008), http://www.transparency.org/policy_research/surveys_indices/cpi/2001 (accessed September 16, 2008).

established that countries scoring below a 5 are considered to have a problem of corruption, and those scoring below a 3 are considered to have a severe corruption problem. Overall, Latin American and Caribbean countries score an average CPI of 3.5. As can be seen by looking at graph 14.1, in 2006 all of the Central American countries scored below a 5. Moreover, only Costa Rica and El Salvador had scores that placed them out of the realm of having an extensive corruption problem. Compared to other countries in Latin America and beyond, the corruption scores of Central American countries varied widely. As can be seen in graph 14.1, Costa Rica scored the highest of the Central American countries, ranking 7th highest (that is, 7th least corrupt) out of all Latin American countries. Costa Rica was followed closely by El Salvador, which came in 8th. Honduras ranked the lowest, scoring 26th out of all Latin American countries. Worldwide, however, Costa Rica only ranked 55th, while Honduras ranked 121st.

Interestingly, four out of the six countries' CPI rates have fallen since 1998 or, in Panama's case, since 2001. In 1998 Costa Rica had a score of 5.6, which meant it was not considered to have a corruption problem. El Salvador and Honduras are the only two countries that have actually increased their CPI ratings after 1998. Honduras' rating, however, has dropped since 2001, although it is still higher than its 1998 rate (graph 14.2). For the most part, it seems that Central American countries have been faced with higher corruption rates in recent years.[14]

Because the CPI is based on perceptions of corruption, it is also important to look at the experience of those victimized by corruption in each country in Central America per year, which can be traced through the work of

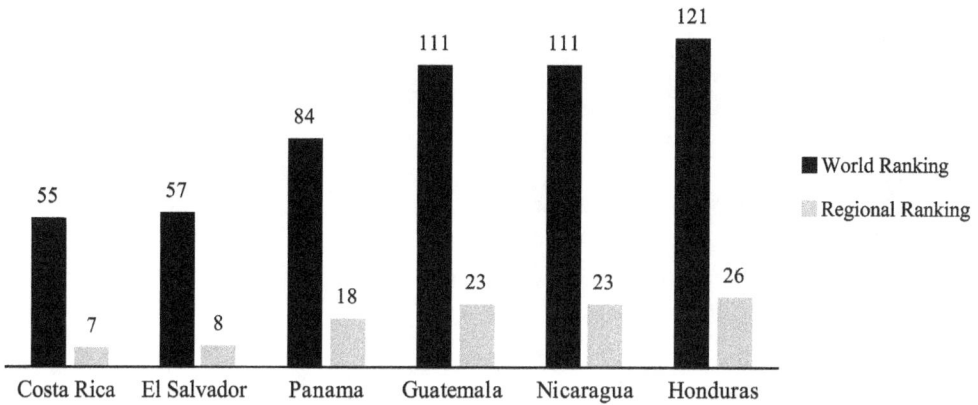

Graph 14.2. CPI world and regional rankings 2006. Data from Transparency International, "Corruptions Perceptions Index," (2008), http://www.transparency.org/policy_research/surveys_indices/cpi/2001.

the Americas Barometer carried out by the Latin American Public Opinion Project (LAPOP), directed by Mitchell Seligson.[15] Based on representative surveys, the LAPOP researchers found for 2006–07 that the percentage of the population that reported having been victims of corruption in each country did not closely align with reports of perceived corruption by the CPI. As far as victimization is concerned, Panama had the lowest rate, with 11.8 percent of its population reporting being victimized by corruption. Costa Rica, Guatemala, and Nicaragua had the highest, at 19.3, 18.0, and 18.0 percent, respectively (graph 14.3). That is, while Costa Rica is shown by the CPI as having one of the lowest levels of perceived corruption, in terms of reported victimization by corruption Costa Rica even surpassed the level of corruption of Guatemala or Nicaragua, among the highest in the region. This discrepancy may be due to the fact that even though Costa Rican institutions still scored average, there was a significant decline in institutional trust from 2004 to 2006, as shown in graph 14.4.[16] While Costa Rica may have more corruption than the CPI indicates, other countries may have less according to the Corruption Victimization Index. Accordingly, "in fact, in Central America, Guatemala, Honduras, and Nicaragua had been placed among the countries with 'generalized' or alarming perceived levels of corruption but exhibit intermediate levels of victimization." It is generally perceived that the Corruption Victimization Index is closer to the reality of the level of local corruption in a country because it deals with people's day-to-day experiences with corruption, while the CPI is measured by the opinions of regional and international experts and often addresses perceptions of high-level cor-

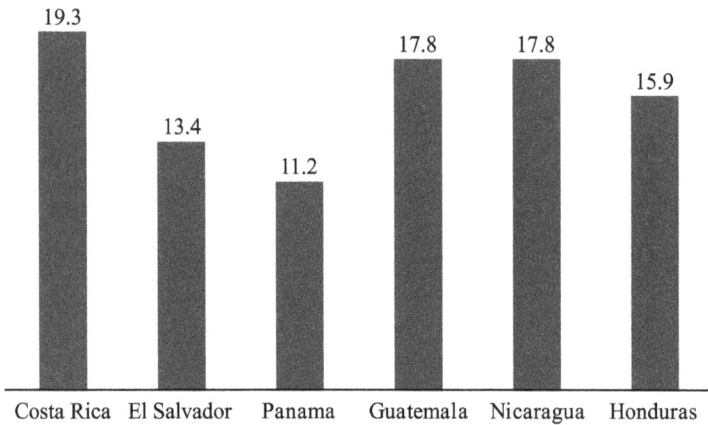

Graph 14.3. Population reportedly victimized by corruption (percent). Data from Dominique Zéphir, "Corruption and Its Impact in Latin American Democratic Stability," in Mitchell A. Seligson, ed., *Challenges to Democracy in Latin American and the Caribbean: Evidence from the AmericasBarometer 2006–2007* (USAID, LAPOP [Latin American Public Opinion Project], AmericasBarometer, and Vanderbilt University: 2008), 256.

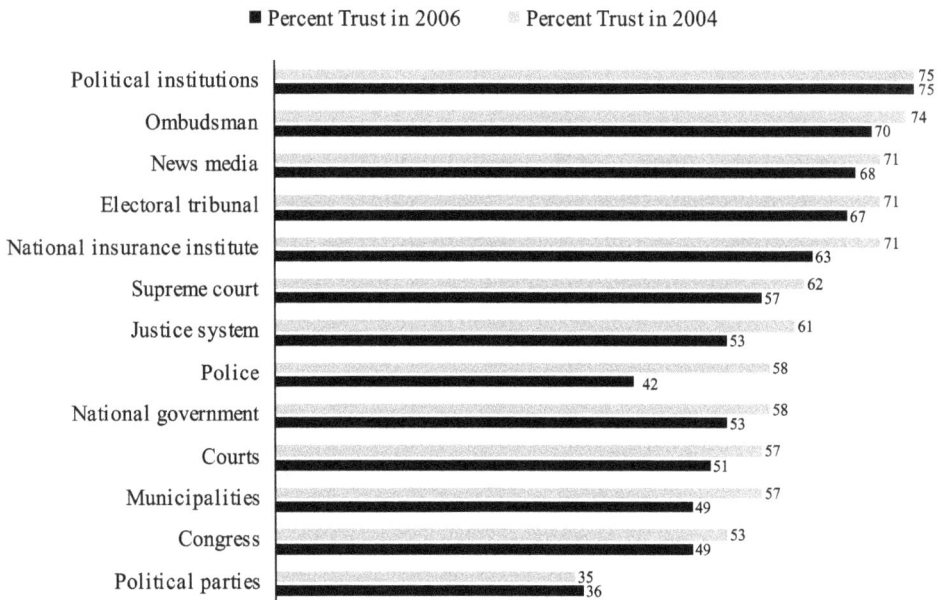

Graph 14.4. Institutional trust of Costa Ricans 2004 and 2006. Data from Jorge Vargas-Cullell and Luis Rosero-Bixby, "The Political Culture of Democracy in Costa Rica: 2006," Mitchell A. Seligson, ed. (The AmericasBarometer by LAPOP, Vanderbilt University: 2008), 65, *www.vanderbilt.edu/lapop/ab2006/costa-rica1-en.pdf* (accessed September 16, 2008).

ruption.[17] Nonetheless, both sources should be taken into account, as they provide a complementary perspective on the extent of the problem.

Institutional trust reflects citizens' assessment as to whether state agencies meet their expectations, which in turn implies both the perception of institutions as committed to citizens as well as about their efficacy in meeting their professed functions. According to data collected through LAPOP, the principal sites of corruption in the countries seem to be the municipal governments and the courts.[18] Interestingly, while Panama is shown as having the least proportion of its population victimized by corruption, it also has the second-highest percentage of bribes in institutions reported. And among citizens of the Central American countries, Salvadorians and Costa Ricans report being the least affected by corruption of the judicial system and professed to have the highest trust in it, as shown in graphs 14.5 and 14.6. When comparing the percentage of citizens who trust municipal authorities vis-à-vis the rate of those trusting the national government, only Costa Rica and Panama showed more popular trust in the national government than in the municipalities. In Honduras and El Salvador, however, even though the people trust their municipalities more, it has been found that they show a greater support for a centralized state (graph 14.5). There seems to be a

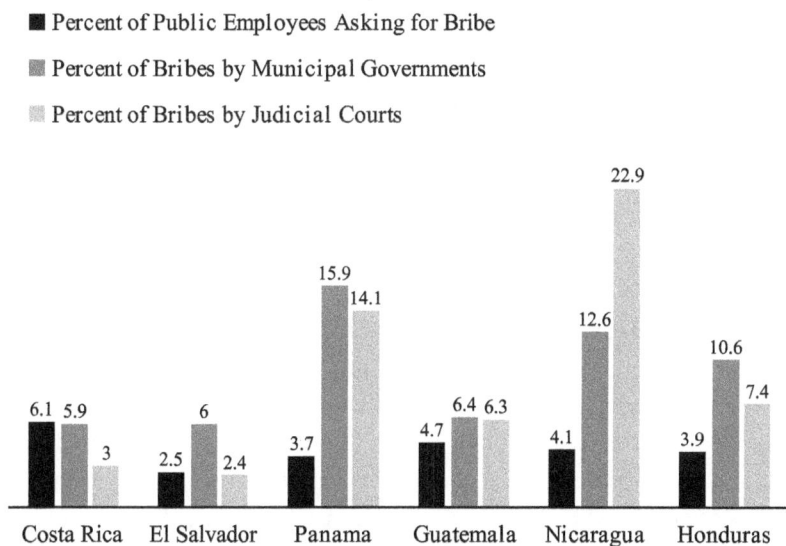

Graph 14.5. Bribes in public institutions. Data from Dominique Zéphir, "Corruption and Its Impact in Latin American Democratic Stability," in Mitchell A. Seligson, ed., *Challenges to Democracy in Latin American and the Caribbean: Evidence from the AmericasBarometer 2006–2007* (USAID, LAPOP, AmericasBarometer, and Vanderbilt University: 2008), 200.

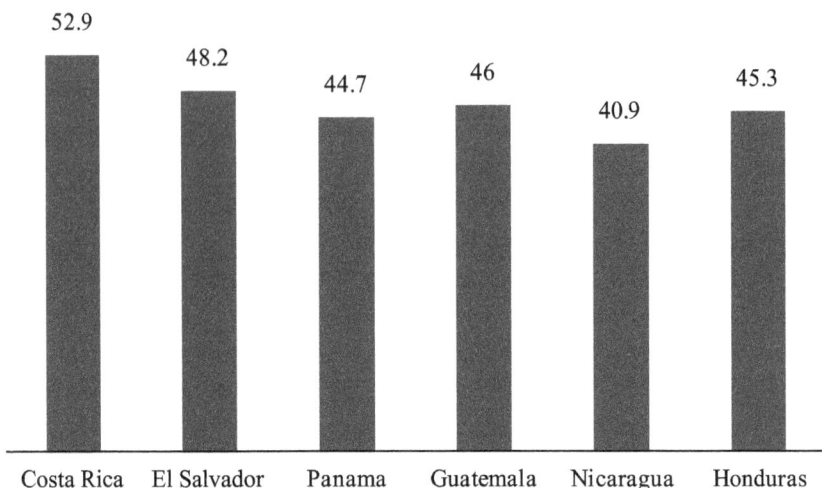

Graph 14.6. Citizens who trust the judicial system (percent). Data from Juan Carlos Donoso, "Justicia y democracia: El estado de derecho en las Américas," in Mitchell A. Seligson, ed., *Desafíos para la democracia en Latinoamérica y el Caribe: evidencias desde el Barómetro de las Américas 2006–2007* (USAID, LAPOP, AmericasBarometer, and Vanderbilt University: 2008), 292.

correlation, if not exact, between the extent of perceived and reported corruption and the popular trust in institutions and government in these countries. For instance, the CPI ranked Nicaragua as having severe institutional corruption and the highest number of reported bribes of the judicial system, with Nicaraguans having the lowest percent of public trust for the country's judicial system.[19]

The importance of reducing corruption and images of corruption cannot be overestimated. Trust in institutions often affects the trust in a country's democracy as a whole. A deficit in public trust seriously affects the reputation and efficacy of institutions while re-creating cynicism and a reliance on those same practices as means of access to public agencies and resources. Yet, even if conducted publicly for purposes of image cleansing, anti-corruption campaigns may sometimes worsen the situation by disseminating the perception of corruption as seemingly generalized in the public domain. Such perceptions are detrimental in overcoming state fragility, as shown in the difficulties of enforcing truthful tax collection and reducing the scope of tax evasion.

From a regional perspective, such a vicious cycle also affects the functionality of the transnational institutions in working to deepen a regional commitment with popular resonance in the isthmus. This is particularly troublesome as Central America faces myriad problems that compromise public security and the sense of well-being of the population.

The very concept of public security has changed from the cold war concept of national security to a more multidimensional approach that contemplates the mutual interplay of the social, economic, political, and cultural dimensions involved as the need arises to face previously unknown levels of criminality, drug trafficking, and proliferation of weapons in society. This new understanding contemplates a wide array of factors as contributing to public security:

> New and broader concepts of security, such as "common," "mutual," "comprehensive," "cooperative," and "human" have added a multidimensional character to traditional security relations. A broader concept of security might include, in addition to the obvious military dimension, diplomatic, political, economic, and cultural aspects. The diplomatic dimension is subordinated to the idea of national sovereignty within the context of a regional vision of security. The political aspect refers to the type of political regime; for instance, nowadays, a threat to democracy is considered a threat to regional security. With the structural economic reforms of the 1980s and 1990s and the current plans for economic integration at the regional and sub-regional levels, the economic dimension has been reincorporated into the general scheme of security. Finally, the cultural dimension refers to the normative dimension of sharing common values within the Latin American international society.[20]

With the reduction of the old "conventional" security threats, the countries of the region are facing new security risks and more diverse threats. By broadening the concept of security, countries also contemplate issues such as increasing unemployment and poverty, the marginality of many sectors of the population, drug trafficking, terrorism, organized crime, violations of human rights, environmental degradation, and threats to democratic development and economic well-being, which have been analyzed in previous sections. As we have seen, many of these issues have had a transnational impact in the current stage of globalization and need comprehensive treatment. It is still uncertain whether the regional institutions, with a mandate delegated by member states, will be able to cope with these issues, especially in times of global crisis.

Conclusions

Small Nations and Transnationalism in a Globalizing Era

Transnationalism is bound to contemporary processes of deterritorialization, porosity of national borders, new ways of cross-border interaction, and reconstruction of collective identities. These final pages "shift gears" from analysis into discussing the prospects of regional transnationalism under the growing impact of globalizing processes in the region, suggesting the need to consolidate interstate coordination in various domains, but also to make regional institutions accountable and relevant to rank-and-file citizens, reinvigorating public trust, a crucial component of both citizen participation and institutional success on a transnational level. We need to look at these issues from the perspective of economic trends as well as sociologically, politically, and culturally.

Macro-economically, until recently, the countries of the region had stabilized their economies and adopted market-oriented reforms that have contributed to growth, trade integration, and financial liberalization, being praised by the International Monetary Fund on these grounds. Nonetheless, these policies failed mainly in reducing poverty and the huge socioeconomic gaps that characterize the societies.

The change affected not only vertical integration into world markets but also intraregional linkages. Thus, for instance, the countries adopted an open trade tariff system structured around a common external tariff (CET) that stands at less than 5 percent. Due to preferential access to the U.S. market, first in the context of a Caribbean Basin Initiative and since 2004 in the framework of CAFTA-DR, trade increased with the United States and among the countries of the region as well. Intraregional financial sector linkages have also grown. The countries maintained consultation among their central banks as well as trade harmonization, even though policy coordination is still incipient.[1]

Even more recently, exports from the most diversified economies of the region have been increasingly funneled into new markets, specifically in the case of Costa Rica to China, including Hong Kong. Without large internal markets for their goods, this tendency will probably be reinforced if the current trend of supporting diversification of exports, including nontraditional products, deepens in the region and due to the impact of the financial crisis in the west. Costa Rica has attracted direct investments by Intel to build plants for the production of computer parts and has managed to diversify its economic structure further than other countries. In 2007, 77 percent of Costa Rican exports (from a total of $9.3 billion) were in the rubrics of electronics and electrics, medical devices, chemicals and pharmaceuticals, and metals for cars and machinery parts. Investments by Lear, a U.S.-based automotive company specializing in car interior systems and components, has similarly led to the opening of assembly plants producing electrical wire harnesses in northwestern Honduras, adding to the textile plants operating in that country.[2]

The current pattern of macro-economic development suggests the possible deepening of supply of chain linkages, yet this pattern may pose serious bottlenecks on the way to poverty reduction and income redistribution, two of the most imposing challenges these countries currently face. Imbalances among the countries are still to be expected. Apparel products dominate exports in most countries of the region, with El Salvador and Honduras (in addition to the Dominican Republic) providing around 75 percent of all exports in that rubric.

From a regional perspective, such trends are already under way, and countries have started a needed process of policy coordination. Otherwise, countries could induce, in the words of economists, a "race to the bottom," that is, to compete with one another for flows of direct investment by offering a rising cycle of tax incentives and other incentives in a race to outdo the other countries. Likewise, mechanisms of financial integration can reduce the volatility of financial markets. Such volatility, triggered by short-term relocation of investments, is still to be feared, as it is detrimental to sustainable development, affecting particularly the welfare of the lower strata. Also instrumental in promoting sustained development are projects such as the publicized Dry Channel that may provide a land-corridor highway between Salvadoran and Nicaraguan ports on the Pacific coast and Honduras and Guatemalan ports on the Caribbean coast, shortening to a third the time currently needed to transport products through the Panama Canal.

The successful translation of market-oriented reforms—consonant with globalization and short-term growth—into long-term development leads to reflection on the quality of institutions and regulatory agencies as well as on citizen participation and respect for the rule of law. In the case of Central America, as discussed earlier, such policy reforms are mostly still to be undertaken. Observers have indicated that although the countries in the region have been able to liberalize their trade regimes, they face the need to implement structural reforms in various areas, among them institutional domains relating to state efficiency and regulatory capabilities that may lead to the protection of property rights and transparency and regulatory frameworks.[3] All these issues are increasingly affected by the transnational crossings and aspects analyzed in this work.

Sociologically, politically, and culturally, the region has faced increasing pressures derived from transnational illicit networks, social violence, and immense socioeconomic gaps. Corruption and administrative inefficiency have added to public distrust, while public insecurity has led to citizens' retreat from public spheres, widespread reliance on private security services, and a growing fragmentation of civil society. Many have left their countries to escape the vicious circle of unemployment, poverty, and lack of prospects of life improvement. Many more had dreamt of taking the road of migration too, at least until the economic crisis hit the United States and Mexico in the late 2000s. Even the image of Costa Rica, a country systematically found to be rather exceptional in terms of its self-image and long-standing democratic performance, has been tainted in the eyes of its own citizens. Already in the 1990s there were signs of draining of public support reflected in a decline of voter turnout.[4] Even though phrased with some exaggeration, the following assessment by Tatiana Lobo reflects the growing criticisms of many citizens about what they see as their society's unfounded self-satisfaction and feeling of attainment, defied by social and institutional problems:

> When we think of Costa Rica we represent it as a white society . . . [with] a simple individualism. . . . The *tico* is [supposedly] the farmer acclaimed by our national anthem. But it happens that the farmer has turned delinquent, narco-trafficker, robbing politician, swindler banker, violating *macho*, incestuous father, psychopath abusing children, killing husband and aggressor, corrupt policeman.[5]

Even though this trend is reversible, it is important to note that in spite of its historical exceptionalism, Costa Rica has been increasingly perceived not as the Switzerland of the Tropics, as its elites wanted it to be, but rather as part of Central America, sharing with the other countries many of the problems and challenges they face in this globalizing era.

In the past decade, social disenchantment has taken hold of vast sectors, particularly among the younger generations, who have become critical of the decline in economic growth, the growing inflation and trade deficit, heightened poverty, declining literacy, and widespread xenophobic attitudes. Accordingly, they have endorsed revisionist readings of their societies and more recently have moved the political pendulum to the left, for instance in Nicaragua and El Salvador, thus betting on an alternative way of transformation of their societies.

Globalization processes have already transformed the territorial domains of the nation-states of the region. Treaties and agreements have been signed that have defined in new forms the need to coordinate actions and achieve higher forms of economic integration, harmonization, and regulation. The question is how the regional layer becomes incorporated and supported by the national and subnational levels and whether the development of non-state civil networks and multilevel governance can be attained.[6] There are structural constraints that lend credibility to the idea of supporting regional coordination and transnational cooperation. Small countries face particularly difficult problems in terms of the limitations of their internal markets, the threat posed by transnational criminal networks, and the lack of resources needed to redefine the public arena in terms of alternative models of developments, public confidence, and the emergence of civic accountability and diminishing corruption. Pooling resources and easing the formation of regional transnational strengths thus makes sense. The question is whether the current layer of public agencies at the regional level is working to generate the institutional trust needed to support any further move in the direction of coordinated strategies, particularly now that these strategies cannot be reduced to economic and trade integration but, to be effective, need to address a broader range of transnational issues, so to support an ethos of increasing democratization, citizen participation, and multilevel governance in the region.

The isthmian countries have agreed to coordinate actions and have even created a series of institutions at the regional level and promulgated making these institutions accountable—and projecting this image of accountability widely—to make them relevant to the citizens of the different countries. Likewise, national and regional differences must be taken into account in social governance, and regional goals must be translated into specific national plans to be monitored in turn both by participatory mechanisms at the local and subnational levels and by the evaluation of international agencies and arenas.

The combination of such horizontal and vertical forms of accountability is the key to a successful reinvigoration of public trust so necessary for the next stages of democratization and transnational regionalization in the isthmus. One excellent illustration of such developments is the recently launched International Commission against Impunity in Guatemala (CICIG), an initiative to fight corruption and the incompetent justice sector there; the commission has been brought about by a broad coalition of Guatemalan NGOs with transnational connections. The CICIG was established by an agreement between the United Nations and the Guatemalan government and approved by the Guatemalan congress in August 2007, but that initiative could not have been achieved without the massive transnational and national work of a coalition of Guatemalan NGOs and external NGOs such as the Washington Office for Latin America, or WOLA.[7] Leading to this unusual development to tackle state-related violence were several factors of clear transnational transfer and implications: first, the paradigmatic example of the Salvadoran experience in launching an investigative commission connected to the United Nations. Roger Atwood, the communications director at WOLA, indicates in his report that

> the Salvadoran government agreed to create the Joint Group for the Investigation of Illegal Armed Groups with Political Motivation in El Salvador, or *Grupo Conjunto*, in late 1993. The group was led by four commissioners, two named by the Salvadoran president and two named by the United Nations, which would also fund the initiative. The group's jurisdictional scope was quite limited. It had no power to arrest or prosecute suspects, but it could organize and supervise a team of investigators comprised of Salvadoran and international experts that could present evidence to prosecutors. The group was also charged with presenting a report on its findings, with recommendations, to the Salvadoran government.[8]

Even though the Salvadoran report did not lead to a single prosecution, it showed that sectors of civil society could project their activism in new directions in a postwar environment.

The Salvadoran example inspired Guatemalan activists to join forces and generate transnational support through dense advocacy networks and reach momentum in pushing their own government to act. Key actors and social forces within the country were also led to understand that only by seeking the help of the international community in confronting internal security and state-related violence could they circumvent the compromised work of national institutions. In the final stages of putting pressure on congressional representatives to approve the CICIG, another transnational event would ultimately lead to its approval, namely, the embarrassing involvement of Guatemalan police in the murder of three Salvadoran politicians and their driver on the outskirts of the Guatemalan capital in February 2007, followed by the assassination of the imprisoned suspects in a Guatemalan prison. This turned into the final push, as it signaled the inability to reach accountability by addressing the problem of state-related violence within national boundaries and under the often professed allegations of national sovereignty. Adopted in 2007 with a two-year provision, the CICIG's mandate was extended in 2009 for another two years. Since its inception, the head of the International Commission against Impunity in Guatemala, Carlos Castresana Fernández, has taken front-stage criticizing state agencies and government procedures openly in an attempt to put pressure on existing institutions with the professed aim of strengthening them.

The present work has discussed transnationalism beyond the institutional level in terms of historical memories and narratives, cross-border practices, and networks and movements of ideas and peoples. We have followed these various aspects interconnecting the states and societies of the isthmus within a long-term perspective, showing that transnationalism existed long before the current stages of globalization and beyond the domain of economics. Accordingly, we stressed that globalization and transnationalism are not coterminous, although they may impinge upon one another, as is the case in the current stage of development. We have focused particular attention on the domains of politics, public life, and the construction of collective identities, tracing the tension-ridden interplay between the process of constitution and consolidation of states and distinctive national identities on the one hand and, on the other, the lingering presence of alternative projects of reconstruction of broader, transnational commitments and identities entangled with one another in shifting ebbs and flows at different historical moments.

Throughout this work, Central America is not reified as an entity that has existed unchanged. Rather, I have traced a series of processes of region making and region dismantling, identifying sociopolitical, economic, and cultural forces working in favor of transnationalism or against it, with actors making choices within a framework of historical legacies and contemporary challenges. They acted so in an open-ended process of political engineering that involves interpretive and discursive practices, identity politics, and the active reconstruction of public spheres.

The idea of Central America persisted beyond the short-lived attempt at political unification in the early nineteenth century. For some, that experience became a source of inspiration of later transnational projects, while for others its memory solidified the will to take a distinctive path of disengagement. At times, the region was conceived as part of constructive political formulas designed by elites. At other times, it was the core idea of popular movements, informed by the experiences of exiles, migrants, and intellectuals crossing state borders and willing to generate a sense of isthmian brotherhood. There were times when the resistance to foreign interventions triggered a sense of transnational solidarity, while under other circumstances it was the United States as hegemonic power that supported the idea of regional coordination and integration.

In sum, in different periods and under varied circumstances there were diverse ways of envisaging the future of Central America, many of them geared to the logic of consolidation of nation-states but others oriented toward projecting transnational connections, as traced in the past two centuries in diverse political initiatives, civil society networks, belligerent actions, cross-border coalitions, and transnational practices. Rather than claiming that Central America has existed as an objective entity, the book has analyzed some of these major processes and forces that have promoted transnational commitments or fought them in the past two centuries. I see as equally important contributing to the realization that along with important demographic and economic foundations, the region has witnessed transnational processes involving politics, public life, and the shaping of collective identities led by social and political actors and elites whose actions were strongly embedded in historical visions, cultural ideas, and alternative political projects. It is this embedded character that can fully explain the persistent presence of transnational politics, movements, and networks in Central America long after a federative state broke down in early independence and balkanization led to fragmented sovereignties in the isthmus.

In this book we have followed the ebbs and flows of the transnational dimensions of political action, construction of collective identities, and constitution of public spheres in Central America. While focusing on a specific region with a distinctive development, the transnational perspective followed in this book can be important not only for students of this region known as the isthmus but also for those interested in analyzing the interconnectivity of societies and highlighting the interplay of the local and national and the regional, international, and global arenas in other geopolitical contexts and historical periods as well. Examining these relations and the tension between these realms in the constitution of societies and states indicates the importance of a nuanced approach to the active role played by political actors, social movements, and organizations resulting in institutions—such as "nation-states"—that many have tended to take for granted yet whose development needs to be analyzed systematically. Studying the transnational axis is a necessary step on the road to achieving understanding of human activities and processes that extend across national boundaries and state borders, particularly in this era of increasing globalization and anti-globalizing mobilization.

Notes

Preface

1. Ralph Lee Woodward Jr., "Unity and Diversity in Central American History," *Latin American Research Review* 27, 3 (1992): 255.

2. An outstanding work in that direction, written from the perspective of international relations, is Mark B. Rosenberg and Luis G. Solís, *The United States and Central America* (New York: Routledge, 2007).

3. Forrest D. Colburn and Arturo Cruz, *Varieties of Liberalism in Central America* (Austin: University of Texas Press, 2007), 27.

Chapter 1. Nation-States and Transnational Theories: The State of the Art

1. Adam Lupel, "Tasks of a Global Civil Society: Held, Habermas, and Democratic Legitimacy beyond the Nation-State," *Globalizations* 2, 1 (2005): 117–33; Saskia Sassen, *Territory, Authority, Rights: From Medieval to Global Assemblages* (Princeton: Princeton University Press, 2006).

2. Donatella DellaPorta and Sidney Tarrow, eds. *Transnational Protest and Global Activism* (Lanham, Md.: Rowman and Littlefield, 2005).

3. See among others, Jan Nederveen Pieterse, "Globalization as Hybridization," in Mike Featherstone, Scott Lash, and Roland Robertson, eds., *Global Modernities* (London: Sage, 1995); Néstor García Canclini, *Culturas híbridas. Estrategias para entrar y salir de la modernidad* (Mexico City: Grijalbo, 1990), and "Globalización e interculturalidad: Próximos escenarios en América Latina," in Alfonso de Toro, ed., *Cartografías y estrategias de la "postmodernidad" y la "postcolonialidad" en Latinoamérica* (Frankfurt: Iberoamericana-Vervuert, 2006), 129–41.

4. See, e.g., Luis Roniger and Mario Sznajder, *The Legacy of Human Rights Violations in the Southern Cone* (Oxford: Oxford University Press, 1999); Lauren Langman, "From Virtual Public Spheres to Global Justice: A Critical Theory of Internetworked Social Movements," *Sociological Theory* 23, 1 (2005): 42–74; Micheline R. Ishay, *The History of Human Rights. From Ancient Times to the Globalization Era* (Berkeley: University of California Press, 2004); and Amparo Menéndez-Carrión, "Revisiting the *Polis* amidst Shifting Sands: The Places and Spaces of Citizenship and the Public in the New Global Era," paper presented at the World Congress of the International Political Science Association, Santiago, Chile, July 2009.

5. Steven Vertovec, "Conceiving and Researching Transnationalism," *Ethnic and Racial Studies* 22, 2 (1999): 447–62.

6. Eva Østergaard-Nielsen, "The Politics of Migrants' Transnational Political Practices," *International Migration Review* 37, 3 (2003): 760–86.

7. Peter Evans, "Fighting Marginalization with Transnational Networks: Counter-Hegemonic Globalization," *Contemporary Sociology* 29, 1 (2000): 230–41.

8. Claus Leggewie, "Transnational Citizenship: Cultural Concerns," in *International Encyclopedia of the Behavioral and Social Sciences* (Elsevier, ltd.: 2001), 15857–62 (quotation on p. 15858).

9. Ulf Hannerz, *Transnational Connections* (London: Routledge, 1996); Ulrich Beck, *World Risk Society* (Cambridge: Polity Press, 1998).

10. Alejandro Portes, ed., *The Economic Sociology of Immigration: Essays on Networks, Ethnicity, and Entrepreneurship* (New York: Russell Sage, 1995); Khachig Tölölyan, "Rethinking Diasporas: Stateless Power in the Transnational Moment," *Diaspora* 5 (1996): 3–36; Gabriel Sheffer, *Diaspora Politics: At Home Abroad* (Cambridge: Cambridge University Press, 2003).

11. See Roger Waldinger, Howard E. Aldrich, and Robin Ward, *Ethnic Entrepreneurs: Immigrant Business in Industrial Societies* (Newbury Park: Sage, 1990) and Steven C. Boraz and Thomas C. Bruneau, "Are the 'Maras' Overwhelming Governments in Central America?" *Military Technology* 31, 1 (2007): 54–56.

12. Arif Dirlik, "Globalization as the End and the Beginning of History," forthcoming in Georgi M. Derlugian and Walter Goldfrank, eds., *The Changing Geopolitics and Geoculture of The World System* (tentative title) (New York: Greenwood: forthcoming).

13. William Bunge, *Theoretical Geography* (Lund: S. W. Gleerup, 1966).

14. Federica Morelli, "Territorial Hierarchies and Collective Identities in Late Colonial and Early Independent Quito," in Luis Roniger and Tamar Herzog, eds., *The Collective and the Public in Latin America* (Brighton: Sussex Academic Press, 2002), 37–56.

15. Adrian Bailey, Richard A. Wright, Alison Mountz, and Ines M. Miyares, "(Re)producing Salvadoran Transnational Geographies," *Annals of the Association of American Geographers* 92, 1 (2002): 125–44.

16. Shmuel N. Eisenstadt, *Multiple Modernities* (New Brunswick, N.J.: Transaction Books, 2002) and "The First Multiple Modernities: Collective Identities, Public Spheres, and Political Order in the Americas," in Luis Roniger and Carlos H. Waisman, eds., *Globality and Multiple Modernities, Comparative North American and Latin American Perspectives* (Brighton, England: Sussex Academic Press, 2002), 7–28.

17. See, e.g., Jasmin Soysal, *Limits of Citizenship* (Chicago: University of Chicago Press, 1994) and Arjun Appadurai, *Modernity at Large* (Minneapolis: University of Minnesota Press, 1996).

18. See Bruce Mazlish and Ralph Buultjens, *Conceptualizing Global History* (Boulder, Colo.: Westview, 1993) and Victor Lieberman, introduction to the special issue "Eurasian Context of Early Modern History of Mainland Southeast Asia, 1400–1800," *Modern Asian Studies* 31, 3 (1997): 449–61.

19. Dirlik, "Globalization as the End and the Beginning of History."

20. Sanjay Subrahmanyam, "Connected Histories: Notes towards a Reconfiguration of Early Modern Eurasia," *Modern Asian Studies* 31, 3 (1997): 735–62 and *Explorations in Connected History: From the Tagus to the Ganges* (Oxford: Oxford University Press, 2005).

21. Michael Werner and Bénédicte Zimmermann, "Beyond Comparison: *Histoire Croisée* and the Challenge of Reflexivity," *History and Theory* 45 (February 2006): 30–50.

22. Werner and Zimmermann, "Beyond Comparison," 38–43 (quotation on p. 43). These scholars develop their approach more fully in "Vergleich, Transfer, Verflechtung: Der Ansatz

der *Histoire croisée* und die Herausforderung des Transnationalen," *Geschichte und Gesellschaft* 28 (2002): 607–36.

23. Micol Seigel, "Beyond Compare: Comparative Method and the Transnational Turn," *Radical History Review* 91 (2005): 62–92. See also "The Nation and Beyond: Transnational Perspectives on United States History. A Special Issue," *Journal of American History* 86 (1999), especially 965–75.

24. Martin Marcussen and Jacob Torfing, *Democratic Network Governance in Europe* (New York: Palgrave-Macmillan, 2006).

25. Lupel, "Tasks of a Global Civil Society," 119–27.

26. Robert O'Brien, Anne Marie Goetz, Jan Aart Scholte, and Marc Williams, *Contesting Global Governance. Multilateral Economic Institutions and Global Social Movements* (Cambridge: Cambridge University Press, 2000). See also Thomas Risse, "Transnational Actors and World Politics," in Walter Carlsnaes, Thomas Risse, and Beth A Simmons, eds., *Handbook of International Relations* (London: Sage, 2002), 255–74.

27. Andrew F. Cooper and Thomas Legler, *Intervention without Intervening? The OAS Defense and Promotion of Democracy in the Americas* (New York: Palgrave Macmillan, 2006). See also Thomas Legler, Sharon F. Lean, and Dexter S. Boniface, eds., *Promoting Democracy in the Americas* (Baltimore: Johns Hopkins University Press, 2007), 1–18.

28. Margaret E. Keck and Kathryn Sikkink, *Activists beyond Borders: Advocacy Networks in International Politics* (Ithaca, N.Y.: Cornell University Press, 1998). On the impact of such networks on the development of human rights see also Roniger and Sznajder, *Legacy of Human Rights Violations*, 1–50 and 129–35; Claudio Fuentes, *Contesting the Iron Fist: Advocacy Networks and Police Violence in Democratic Argentina and Chile* (New York: Routledge, 2005); and Mario Sznajder and Luis Roniger, *The Politics of Exile in Latin America* (New York: Cambridge University Press, 2009), chapters 5–6.

29. Louise Fawcett and Andrew Hurrell, *Regionalism in World Politics* (New York: Oxford University Press, 1995); Andrew Hurrell, "Norms and Ethics in International Relations," in Carlsnaes et al., *Handbook of International Relations*, 137–44; Arie Kacowicz, *The Impact of Norms in International Society: The Latin American Experience, 1881–2001* (Notre Dame, Ind.: University of Notre Dame Press, 2005).

30. Marianne H. Marchand, Morten Boas, and Timothy Shaw. "The Political Economy of New Regionalisms," *Third World Quarterly* 20, 5 (1999): 897–910.

31. See, for instance, Hans Ulrich Jessurun d'Oliveira, "Union Citizenship: Pie in the Sky?," 58–84 in Allan Rosas and Esko Antola, eds., *A Citizen's Europe: In Search of a New Order* (London: Sage, 1995); Andrew Gamble and Anthony Payne, eds., *Regionalism and World Order* (London: Macmillan, 1996); Björn Hettne and Fredrik Soderbaum, "Theorizing the Rise of Regionness," *New Political Economy* 5, 3 (2000): 457–74; and Randall Hansen and Patrick Weil, eds., *Towards a European Nationality* (Houndmills, England: Palgrave, 2001).

32. Hettne and Soderbaum, "Theorizing the Rise of Regionness," 462.

33. Michelle Pace, *Politics of Regional Identity* (London: Routledge, 2006).

34. A. Hasenclever, P. Mayer, and V. Rittberger, "Integrating Theories of International Regimes," *Review of International Studies* 26, 1 (2000): 3–33.

35. Ander Gurrutxaga Abad, *El presente del estado-nación* (Bilbao: Universidad del País Vasco, 2004).

36. Daniel M. Goldstein, comment on Clifford Geertz' views in "What Is a State If It Is Not a Sovereign?: Reflections on Politics in Complicated Places," *Current Anthropology* 45, 5 (2004): 587–88.

Chapter 2. Central America as a Region

1. Noelle Demyk, "Los territorios del estado-nación en América Central: Una problemática regional," in Arturo Taracena and Jean Piel, eds., *Identidades nacionales y estado moderno en Centroamérica* (San José: EDUCA, *1995), 13–30.*

2. See Justin Wolfe, *The Everyday Nation-State. Community and Ethnicity in Nineteenth Century Nicaragua* (London: University of Nebraska Press, 2007).

3. Paul D. Escott, *"What Shall We Do with the Negro?" Lincoln, White Racism, and Civil War America* (Charlottesville: University of Virginia Press, 2009), 26–59.

4. *Centro-América* 2, 4 (1910): 492–93. Unless otherwise indicated, translations from Spanish to English throughout the book are mine.

5. Mario Rodríguez, *El experimento de Cádiz en Centroamérica 1808–1826* (Mexico City: FCE, 1984).

6. Eventually, Chiapas—the sixth domain mentioned—turned into one of Mexico's states, as will be discussed.

Chapter 3. Balkanization as Formative Experience

1. Morelli, "Territorial Hierarchies and Collective Identities," 37–56.

2. Angel Rama, *The Lettered City* (Durham, N.C.: Duke University Press, 1996); María Elena Martínez, "Space, Order, and Group Identities in a Spanish Colonial Town: Puebla de los Angeles," in Roniger and Herzog, *The Collective and the Public in Latin America,* 13–36.

3. Tamar Herzog, "Communities Becoming a Nation: Spain and Spanish America in the Wake of Modernity (and Thereafter)," *Citizenship Studies* 11, 2 (2007): 151–72.

4. See Jordana Dym, *From Sovereign Villages to National States. City, State, and Federation in Central America, 1759–1839* (Albuquerque: University of New Mexico Press, 2006).

5. François-Xavier Guerra, "The Spanish-American Tradition of Representation and Its European Roots," *Journal of Latin American Studies* 26, 1 (1994): 1–35, and "The Implosion of the Spanish Empire: Emerging Statehood and Collective Identities," in Roniger and Herzog, *The Collective and the Public in Latin America,* 71–94.

6. Jordana Dym, "Central America," in Guntram H. Herb and David H. Kaplan, eds., *Nations and Nationalism. A Global Historical Overview* (Santa Barbara, Calif.: ABC-CLIO, 2008), 319.

7. Simón Bolívar, "Carta de Jamaica," in *Antología del Ensayo,* http://www.ensayistas.org/antologia/XIXA/bolivar, accessed May 1, 2009.

8. Manuel Montúfar y Coronado, *Memorias para la historia de la revolución de Centro Américaz* (Jalapa, 1832; Guatemala: Tipografía Sánchez & De Guise, 1934), 98–99, 293, quoted in Timothy Hawkins, "A War of Words: Manuel Montufar, Alejandro Marure, and the Politics of History in Guatemala," *Historian* 64, 3–4 (2002): 522, 526.

9. Carolyn Hall and Héctor Pérez Brignoli, *Historical Atlas of Central America* (Norman: University of Oklahoma Press, 2003), 175.

10. Dym, *From Sovereign Villages to National States,* xx.

11. Guerra, "Implosion of the Spanish Empire," 71–94.

12. José Carlos Chiaramonte, *Ciudades, provincias, estados. Orígenes de la nación argentina (1800–1846)* (Buenos Aires: Emecé, 2006).

13. See Manuel Correia de Andrade, *As raízes do separatismo no Brasil* (São Paulo: Editora UNESP and Editora de Universidade do Sagrado Coração, 1998).

14. The importance of such factors may vary cross-regionally. For Africa see Jeffrey I.

Herbst, *States and Power in Africa: Comparative Lessons in Authority and Control* (Princeton: Princeton University Press, 2000).

15. Tom Barry, *Panama: A Country Guide.* Inter-Hemispheric Education Resource Center, 1990, 20–22.

16. Ralph Lee Woodward Jr., *Central America. A Nation Divided* (New York: Oxford University Press, 1999), 256.

Chapter 4. State Logic and Nation Building

1. Ana María Alonso, "The Politics of Space, Time, and Substance: State Formation, Nationalism, and Ethnicity," *Annual Review of Anthropology* 23 (1994): 379–405.

2. See Anupama Mande, "Subaltern Studies and the Historiography of the Sandinista-Miskitu Conflict in Nicaragua, 1979–1990," paper presented at LASA 2000 Congress, http://lasa.international.pitt.edu/Lasa2000/Mande.pdf, accessed July 11, 2008.

3. See Guntram H. Herb and David H. Kaplan, eds., *Nations and Nationalisms in Global Perspective: An Encyclopedia of Origins, Development, and Contemporary Transitions* (Santa Barbara, Calif.: ABC-CLIO, 2008).

4. Benedict Anderson, *Imagined Communities* (London: Verso, 1991).

5. Robert H. Holden, *Armies without Nations. Public Violence and State Formation in Central America, 1821–1960* (New York: Oxford University Press, 2004).

6. Sarbello Navarrete, *La verdadera fecha de nuestra independencia* (San Salvador: Sociedad Bolivariana de El Salvador, Edición de la Corte Suprema de Justicia, 1996).

Chapter 5. Breaking Apart and Constructing Collective Identities

1. Sherry B. Ortner, "On Key Symbols," *American Anthropologist* 75 (1973): 1338–46; Anthony Smith, "The Symbolic Construction of National Identities," Euroconference on Collective Identity and Symbolic Representation, Paris, July 1996; Michael E. Geisler, ed., *National Symbols, Fractured Identities. Contesting the National Narrative* (Hanover, N.H.: University Press of New England, 2005).

2. Shmuel N. Eisenstadt and Berhard Giesen, "The Construction of Collective Identity," *Archives européennes de sociologie* 36 (1995): 85–93.

3. Ibid., 93–102.

4. Among important contributors is Steven Palmer, "Hacia la 'auto-inmigración.' El nacionalismo oficial en Costa Rica, 1870–1930," 75–86, in addition to contributors to Arturo Taracena and Jean Piel, *Identidades nacionales y estado moderno en Centroamérica* (San José: Editorial de la Universidad de Costa Rica, 1995. Also see Frances Kinloch Tijerino, ed., *Nicaragua en busca de su identidad* (Managua: Instituto de Historia de Nicaragua, Universidad Centroamericana, 1995); Marta Casaús Arzú and Oscar Guillermo Peláez Almengor, eds., *Historia intelectual de Guatemala* (Guatemala: CEUR/UAM/AECI, 2001); Arturo Taracena Arriola, *Etnicidad, estado y nación en Guatemala, 1808–1944*, vol. 1 (Guatemala: CIRMA, 2002); and Darío A. Euraque, Jeffrey L. Gould, and Charles R. Hale, eds., *Memorias del mestizaje. Cultura política en Centroamérica de 1920 al presente* (Guatemala: CIRMA, 2005).

5. See Consuelo Cruz, "Identity and Persuasion: How Nations Remember Their Pasts and Make Their Futures," *World Politics* 52 (2000): 275–312 and *Political Culture and Institutional Development in Costa Rica and Nicaragua. World Making in the Tropics* (New York: Cambridge University Press, 2005).

6. Clifford Geertz, *The Interpretation of Cultures* (New York: Basic Books, 1973).

7. Cruz, "Identity and Persuasion," 278–79; emphasis in the original.

8. Cruz, "Identity and Persuasion," 298, and *Political Culture*, 69–111.

9. Cruz, "Identity and Persuasion," 298–99, and *Political Culture*, 87–90.

10. Pablo Antonio Cuadra, *El nicaragüense* (Managua: Hispamer, 2004), especially 203–5.

11. John A. Booth and Thomas W. Walker, *Understanding Central America*, 4th edition (Boulder, Colo.: Westview, 2007), 69.

12. Thomas M. Leonard, "Central America and the United States: Overlooked Foreign Policy Objectives," *The Americas* 50, 1: (1993): 6.

13. Charles W. Domville-Fife, *Guatemala and the Status of Central America* (London: Francis Griffiths, 1913).

14. *Gaceta de Nicaragua*, no. 38 (September 20, 1873), 140, quoted in Patricia Fumero Vargas, "De la iniciativa individual a la cultura oficial: El caso del General José Dolores Estrada, Nicaragua, década de 1870," in Kinloch Tijerino, *Nicaragua en busca de su identidad*, 324–25.

15. Víctor Hugo Acuña Ortega, "Autoritarismo y democracia en Centroamérica: La larga duración," 535–71 in Kinloch Tijerino, *Nicaragua en busca de su identidad*.

16. Another trend was the split between public popular ceremonies and the ceremonies conducted in the secluded environment of recently established "clubs" reserved for the elite. Vargas, "De la iniciativa individual."

17. Eric Hobsbawn and Terence Ranger, eds., *The Invention of Tradition* (Cambridge: Cambridge University Press, 1983); Eisenstadt and Giesen, "Construction of Collective Identity"; Anthony Smith, "Symbolic Construction of National Identities" and *The Nation in History. Historiographical Debates about Ethnicity and Nationalism* (Hanover, N.H.: University Press of New England, 2000).

Chapter 6. Breaking Apart: Political and Economic Foundations

1. Charles Tilly and Sidney Tarrow, *Contentious Politics* (Boulder, Colo.: Paradigm, 2007), 45–57.

2. José León Castillo, *América istmeña* (Guatemala City: Unión Tipográfica, 1928), 48–49.

3. Steven Palmer, "Central American Union or Guatemalan Republic? The National Question in Liberal Guatemala, 1871–1885," *The Americas* 49, 4 (1993): 519.

4. See Holden, *Armies without Nations*, and Luis Roniger and Mario Sznajder, *Legacy of Human Rights Violations*.

5. Hall and Pérez Brignoli, *Historical Atlas of Central America*, 172.

6. Marvin Barahona, "Honduras. El estado fragmentado (1839–1876)," in Taracena and Piel, *Identidades nacionales*, 97–111.

7. Carlos Sandoval García, *Threatening Others: Nicaraguans and the Formation of National Identities in Costa Rica* (Athens: Ohio University Press, 2004), 73–74.

8. Palmer, "Hacia la 'auto-inmigración,'". 77.

9. Holden, *Armies without Nations*, 72–73.

10. Max Weber, introduction to his *Theory of Social and Economic Organization* (New York: Free Press, 1968, 65. See also Edward Shils, *Center and Periphery. Essays in Macro-Sociology* (Chicago: University of Chicago Press, 1975) and Shmuel N. Eisenstadt, *Power, Trust, and Meaning. Essays in Sociological Theory and Analysis* (Chicago: University of Chicago Press, 1995).

11. Shmuel N. Eisenstadt and Luis Roniger, *Patrons, Clients, and Friends* (Cambridge: Cambridge University Press. 1984).

12. "Y que juntas las manos amigas/ y una ¡oh, Patria! Tus cinco naciones/ sea insignia en

sus nuevas legiones/ el olivo fecundo no más/ . . . . . . /Suene el dulce vocablo de hermano,/ bata el aire una enseña de unión,/ cinco dedos formando una mano/ alto agiten un cetro de honor."

In the early twentieth century the Central American Office organized a competition to select the anthem of Central America and received nearly twenty submissions, some of them surviving the demise of that organization and oblivion. In June 1971 the Organization of Central American States (ODECA) adopted the lyrics of another anthem, "La granadera," as the official anthem of the organization. The latter anthem also stresses the end of war and the attainment of peace, following an invocation to God, union, and liberty.

13. Ley de Instrucción Pública, article 300.

14. Hall and Pérez Brignoli, *Historical Atlas of Central America*, 181.

15. Darío A. Euraque, *Reinterpreting the Banana Republic. Region and State in Honduras 1870–1972* (Chapel Hill: University of North Carolina Press. 1996), 2–3.

16. Woodward, *Central America*, 132, 185.

17. Gregory Weeks, *U.S. and Latin American Relations* (New York: Pearson-Longman, 2008), 36.

18. Woodward, *Central America*, 146–47.

19. Hall and Pérez Brignoli, *Historical Atlas of Central America*, 191–203.

20. Laurence Whitehead, "Latin America as a Mausoleum of Modernities," 34–36 in Roniger and Waisman, *Globality and Multiple Modernities*.

21. Hall and Pérez Brignoli, *Historical Atlas of Central America*, 196.

22. Jorge Arias Gómez, *Farabundo Martí* (San Salvador: Editorial Abril Uno, 2005), 231–88.

23. Woodward, *Central America*, 155–76.

Chapter 7. Citizenship and Subnational and Transnational Identities

1. Palmer, "Hacia la 'auto-inmigración,'" 78–79.

2. Greg Grandin, *The Blood of Guatemala* (Durham, N.C.: Duke University Press, 2000), 99–102; John Hawkins, *Inverse Images* (Albuquerque: University of New Mexico Press, 1984), 80–83.

3. Douglas Sullivan-González, "'A Chosen People': Religious Discourse and the Making of the Republic of Guatemala, 1821–1871," *The Americas* 54 (1997): 18–29; Fredrick Stirton Weaver, "Reform and (Counter) Revolution in Post-Independence Guatemala: Liberalism, Conservatism, and Postmodern Controversies," *Latin American Perspectives* 26, 2 (1999): 138–39.

4. John Hawkins, *Inverse Images*, 81–82.

5. Waqi' Q'anil, *Configuración del pensamiento político del pueblo maya*, part 2 (Guatemala: Cholsamay and Seminario Permanente de Estudios Mayas, 1995), 21.

6. Palmer, "Central American Union or Guatemalan Republic?" 516; Carol Smith, "Las contradicciones del mestizaje en Centroamérica," in Euraque, Gould, and Hale, *Memorias del mestizaje*; and Arturo Taracena Arriola, "Liberalismo y poder político en Centroamérica (1870–1929)," 167–253 in Víctor Hugo Acuña Ortega, ed., *Las repúblicas agro exportadoras (1870–1945)*, vol. 4 of *Historia General de Centroamérica* (Madrid: Sociedad Estatal Quinto Centenario and FLACSO, 1993).

7. Palmer, "Hacia la 'auto-inmigración'"; Marta Casaús Arzú, "Las elites intelectuales y la Generación del 20 en Guatemala: Su visión del indio y su imaginario de nación," in Arzú and Peláez Almengor, *Historia intelectual de Guatemala*.

8. Marta Elena Casaús Arzú and Teresa García Giráldez, *Las redes intelectuales*

centroamericanas: Un siglo de imaginarios nacionales (1820–1920) (Guatemala: F&G Editores, 2005).

9. Marta Casaús Arzú, "Las redes intelectuales centroamericanas y sus imaginarios de nación (1890–1945)," *Circunstancia: Revista de Ciencias Sociales del Instituto Universitario de Investigación Ortega y Gasset*, no. 9 (2006).

10. Fray Bartolomé de las Casas (1484–1566), a sixteenth-century bishop of Chiapas, opposed the exploitive treatment of indigenous populations by the Spanish settlers and became identified as an archetypical figure of the fight against racism in the Americas.

11. F. Hernández de León, *El libro de las efemérides. Capítulos de la historia de la América Central*, vols. 5 and 6 (Guatemala: Tipografia Nacional, 1963), 355–59.

12. Marta Casaús Arzú, *Guatemala: Linaje y racismo* (San José: F&G Editores, 2005).

13. See, for example, Kay B. Warren, "Pan-Mayanism and the Guatemalan Peace Process," 145–66 in Christopher Chase-Dunn, Susanne Jonas, and Nelson Amaro, eds., *Globalization on the Ground. Postbellum Guatemalan Democracy and Development* (Oxford: Rowman and Littlefield, 2001).

14. Aldo A. Lauria-Santiago, *Agrarian Republic: Commercial Agriculture and the Politics of Peasant Communities in El Salvador, 1823–1914* (Pittsburgh: University of Pittsburgh Press, 1999).

15. Virginia Q. Tilley, "New Help or New Hegemony? The Transnational Indigenous Peoples' Movement and 'Being Indian' in El Salvador," *Journal of Latin American Studies* 34 (2002): 525–54.

16. Wolfe, *Everyday Nation-State*, 158–63.

17. E. Bradford Burns, *Patriarcas y pueblo. El surgimiento de Nicaragua, 1798–1858* (Managua: Instituto de Historia de Nicaragua y Centroamérica, 1998); Cuadra, *El nicaragüense*.

18. Euraque et al., *Memorias del mestizaje.*

19. Nicholas Rogers, "Caribbean Borderland: Empire, Ethnicity, and the Exotic on the Mosquito Coast," *Eighteenth-Century Life* 26, 3 (2002): 121–22.

20. Wolfe, *Everyday Nation-State*, 156–60.

21. Frutos Ruiz y Ruiz, *La Costa Atlántica de Nicaragua* (Managua: 1927), 113, 115, cited in Volker Wünderich, *Sandino en la costa: De las Segovias al litoral Atlántico* (Managua: Editorial Nueva Nicaragua, 1989), 156–57.

22. Claudia García, "The Past in the Present. The Social Construction of Miskitu Identity in Sandinista Nicaragua," 95–114 in Roniger and Herzog, *The Collective and the Public in Latin America.*

23. Mande, "Subaltern Studies," 20.

24. "The Minorities at Risk Project," http://www.cidcm.umd.edu/mar, accessed October 3, 2008.

25. Foundation for Sustainable Development, "Human Rights Issues in Nicaragua," http://www.fsdinternational.org, accessed October 7, 2008.

26. Sandra Brunnegger, "From Conflict to Autonomy in Nicaragua: Lessons Learnt," Minority Rights Group International, 2007, http://www2.ohchr.org/english/bodies/cescr/docs/info-ngos/mrginicaragua39wg.pdf, accessed October 7, 2008.

27. Foundation for Sustainable Development, "Human Rights Issues."

28. See Sandoval García, *Threatening Others,* especially pp. 84–86.

29. Richard Lapper and James Painter, *Honduras. State for Sale* (London: Latin American Bureau, 1985), 17.

30. William V. Davidson, "The Garifuna of Pearl Lagoon: Ethnohistory of an Afro-American Enclave in Nicaragua," *Ethnohistory* 27 (1980): 37.

31. See Eva T. Thorne, "Land Rights and Garifuna Identity," *NACLA Report of the Americas* (2004); Sarah W. Haug, "Ethnicity and Ethnically 'Mixed' Identity in Belize: A Study of Primary School-Age Children," *Anthropology and Education Quarterly* 29 (1998): 47.

32. Oliver N. Greene Jr., "Ethnicity, Modernity, and Retention in the Garifuna Punta," *Black Music Research Journal* 22 (2002): 191–92; Davidson, "Garifuna of Pearl Lagoon," 38.

33. Nancie L. González, "Garifuna Settlement in New York: A New Frontier," *International Migration Review* 13 (1979): 256; Thorne, "Land Rights," 23.

34. More recently, companies like the United Fruit Company no longer provided steady jobs like they had in the past, and fishing alone was not enough to sustain the population. See Paul C. Johnson, "Migrating Bodies, Circulating Signs: Brazilian Candomble, the Garifuna of the Caribbean, and the Category of Indigenous Religions," *History of Religions* 41 (2002): 301–27, especially p. 316. Moreover, many Garifuna left Central America due to the ever-growing tourism industry that was encroaching on the land the Garifuna had controlled for a long period. See Thorne, "Land Rights," 24, and Davidson, "Garifuna of Pearl Lagoon."

35. Yet, even in this "binational" war, other transnational connections were not completely absent: some eight hundred Guatemalan nationals who belonged to civilian paramilitary forces active in northwestern Guatemala joined Hondurans in their fight against the forces of El Salvador. Carlos Sabino, *Guatemala. La historia silenciada (1944–1989)*, vol. 2 (Guatemala: Fondo de Cultura Económica, 2008), 58. It is likely that Guatemala feared a spillover of the war on its territory, where it faced the presence of guerrillas and paramilitary forces, thus prompting its diplomatic intervention, which led to a ceasefire controlled by the Organization of American States that both Honduras and El Salvador eagerly accepted. See James Dunkerley, *Power in the Isthmus* (London: Verso, 1988), 359.

36. UNPO, http://www.unpo.org/content/view/8160/83, accessed September 30, 2008.

37. "The Minorities at Risk Project," http://www.cidcm.umd.edu/mar, accessed October 3, 2008.

38. Celestino Andrés Arauz et al., *La historia de Panamá en sus textos, tomo I: 1501–1903* (Panama City: Editorial Universitaria, 1980), 60–70.

39. Steve C. Ropp, "Panama. Militarism and Imposed Transition," 111–32 in Thomas W. Walker and Ariel C. Armony, eds., *Repression, Resistance and Democratic Transition in Central America* (Lanham, Md.: Rowman and Littlefield, 2000), especially 121–22.

40. See, for instance, Robert C. Harding, *The History of Panama* (Westport, Conn.: Greenwood Press, 2006).

41. Deborah Yashar, *Contesting Citizenship in Latin America: The Rise of Indigenous Movements and the Postliberal Challenge* (New York: Cambridge University Press, 2005), 6.

42. Yashar, *Contesting Citizenship*, 34, 308.

Chapter 8. Ebbs and Flows of Regional Dismemberment and Unification

1. Decree of 1885, in García Laguardia, *El pensamiento liberal de Guatemala. Antología* (San José: Editorial Universitaria Centroamericana, 1977), 292–95.

2. Montúfar y Coronado, *Memorias para la historia*, 98–99, quoted in Hawkins, "War of Words," 522.

3. See, for instance, William J. Griffith, "The Personal Archive of Francisco Morazán," *Philological and Documentary Studies* 2, publication 12 (New Orleans: Tulane University, Middle American Research Institute, 1977); Edmond Conrad, "Francisco Morazan in the Historiography of Central America," *Revista Interamericana de Bibliografía* 1–4 (1997), http://www.educoas.org/portal/bdigital/contenido/rib/rib_1997/articulo11.

4. Leonard, "Central America and the United States," 4.

5. In the period between President James Monroe's 1823 address and Theodore Roosevelt's era, the United States had expanded its territory through a series of successful moves, most notably the incorporation of Texas, the defeat of Mexico in the 1846–48 Mexican-American War, and the defeat of Spain in the so-called Spanish-American War of 1898. Beginning in 1898 Cuba was occupied by U.S. troops and had to accept the terms of the Platt Amendment that conditioned its sovereignty for more than thirty years. Puerto Rico remained dependent and connected to the United States. In 1904 President Theodore Roosevelt added a corollary to the Monroe Doctrine according to which the United States "would be forced" to intervene in the Western Hemisphere when chronic unrest and political corruption would demand it.

6. Weeks, *U.S. and Latin American Relations*, 45–51.

7. Jan Knippers Black, *Sentinels of Empire. The United States and Latin American Militarism* (New York: Greenwood, 1986), 27–28.

8. Hall and Pérez Brignoli, *Historical Atlas of Central America*, 225.

9. *Centro-América* 12, 2 (1920): 1.

10. *Centro-América* 9, 4 (1918): 506–7.

11. See, for example, Salvador Mendieta, *La enfermedad de Centro América*, 3 vols., *Descripción del sujeto y síntomas de la enfermedad*, *Diagnóstico y orígenes de la dolencia*, and *Terapéutica* (Barcelona: Tipografía Maucci, 1934).

12. See Margarita Silva H., "Salvador Mendieta y la unión centroamericana (1879–1958)," in Colegio de México, http://shial.colmex.mx/textos/Salvador_Mendieta_1.pdf, accessed May 2, 2009.

13. A. Luna, "San Salvador," *La Quincena*, June 1, 1906, 129–31; Alejandro Bermúdez, *Lucha de razas* (Mexico City: Tipografía Económica, 1912), 34; Carlos Serpas, *Diario de Hoy* (San Salvador), May 8, 1954, in Mario Monteforte Toledo, "Los intelectuales y la integración centroamericana," *Revista Mexicana de Sociología* 29, 4 (1967): 844–45.

14. Marta Casaús Arzú, "Las redes intelectuales centroamericanas."

15. Donald Clark Hodges, *Sandino's Communism: Spiritual Politics for the Twenty-First Century* (Austin: University of Texas Press, 1992).

16. Alberto Masferrer, "El minimum vital," in Masferrer, *Ensayos*. San Salvador: CONCULTURA, 1996.

17. Alberto Masferrer, "Cuartillas de Alberto Masferrer: Mandamientos unionistas," *Revista Vértice* (Quetzaltenango), December 25, 1939, in Casaús Arzú, "Las redes intelectuales centroamericanas," 7.

18. Teresa García Giráldez, "La patria grande centroamericana: La elaboración del proyecto nacional por las redes unionistas," in Casaús Arzú and García Giráldez, *Las redes intelectuales centroamericanas*, 123–205.

19. Wünderich, *Sandino en la costa*; Barry Carr, "A través de los mares y de las fronteras/ Across Seas and Borders around the Red Lake: Excavating the Webs of Radical Internationalism in the 'Red' Circum-Caribbean, 1910–1940," 27–28 in Luis Roniger, James N. Green, and Pablo Yankelevich, eds., *Exile and the Politics of Exclusion in the Americas* (manuscript, 2010).

20. As Sandino traveled in 1929 from Nicaragua to Mexico to try to secure military support, he used a Honduran passport and crossed the Salvadoran and Guatemalan territories under the understanding of the respective governments.

21. Hodges, *Sandino's Communism*. Hodges claims that Sandino supported a special form of communism, a claim that other scholars have disputed. On Sandino's complex positions in the late 1920s and early 1930s see also Cruz, *Political Culture*, 201–6. See also Gómez, *Farabundo Martí*, 149–64.

22. Joaquín Rodas, *Mis prisiones y peregrinación por Centroamérica*, 2nd edition (Guatemala: Tipografía Nacional, 1964), 188–89.

23. Gómez, *Farabundo Martí*, 35–42, 129–180; Carr, "A través de los mares," 26–27. Jeffrey L. Gould and Aldo A. Lauria-Santiago, *To Rise in Darkness. Revolution, Repression, and Memory in El Salvador, 1920–1932* (Durham, N.C.: Duke University Press, 2008); Héctor Lindo-Fuentes, Erik Ching, and Rafael A. Lara-Martínez, *Remembering a Massacre in El Salvador* (Albuquerque: University of New Mexico Press, 2007).

24. Among them were *La Tribuna, El Unionista, Tiempos Nuevos, Electra, Studium, Claridad, Vida, La Campaña*, and *La Hora*. See García Giráldez, "La patria grande centroamericana," especially 148.

25. *Centro-América* 4, 3 (1912): 322.

26. Ibid.

27. Leonard, "Central America and the United States," 13; see also Taracena Arriola, "Liberalismo y poder político," 223–25.

28. Holden, *Armies without Nations*.

29. *Constitución política de la República de Centroamérica de 1921*, in *Biblioteca virtual Miguel Cervantes*, http://www.cervantesvirtual.com/servlet/SirveObras/00367407811103873087857/p0000001.htm.

30. Taracena Arriola, "Liberalismo y poder político," 246.

31. Black, *Sentinels of Empire*, 4.

32. Mario Monteforte Toledo, "Los intelectuales y la integración centroamericana," 836, 850.

Chapter 9. Distinct Paths of Development and the Cold War Transnational Spillover

1. See, for example, volume 3, *De la Iiustración al liberalismo*, and volume 4, *Las Repúblicas agroexportadoras (1870-1945)*, of the *Historia general de Centroamérica*, edited by Héctor Pérez Brignoli and Victor Hugo Acuña Ortega, respectively, and Dunkerley, *Power in the Isthmus*, 1–53.

2. James Mahoney, "Path-Dependent Explanation of Regime Change: Central America in Comparative Perspective," *Studies in Comparative International Development* 36, 1 (2001): 111–41.

3. On the conceptualization of a path-shaping approach, implying that social and political forces can actively rearticulate path-dependence, see Klaus Nielsen, Bob Jessop, and Jerzy Hausner, "Institutional Change in Post-Socialism," 3–8 in Jerzy Hausner, Bob Jessop, and Klaus Nielsen, eds., *Strategic Choice and Path-Dependency in Post-Socialism* (Aldershot, England: Edward Elgar, 1995).

4. For an analysis see Sznajder and Roniger, *Politics of Exile in Latin America*.

5. Woodward, *Central America*, 192–93.

6. Dunkerley, *Power in the Isthmus*, 77, 84.

7. Charles D. Ameringer, *The Caribbean Legion Patriots, Politicians, Soldiers of Fortune, 1946–1950* (University Park: Pennsylvania State University Press, 1996).

8. Not only Somoza was after José Figueres. After 1956 Cuba's Fulgencio Batista and the Dominican Republic's Rafael Trujillo together plotted the assassination of Figueres, who supported the democratic left in exile. By 1957 Trujillo's agents were directing numerous intrigues in Mexico and Central America. See G. Pope Atkins, *Encyclopedia of the Inter-American System* (Westport, Conn.: Greenwood, 1997), 106.

9. Intellectual Isidoro Zarco reflected on the persistent impact and recurrence of political exile in Guatemala as he characterized the fate of his country's leading elites between the 1920s and the 1950s: "At least in the last 40 years, all former rulers—with the exception of Colonel Flores Avendaño—were either led with honors to the General Cemetery or had (or have) to live far away from the fatherland due to the misfortunes of politics. After suffering a military coup, Don Carlos Herrera had to travel 'freely by force' [*forcivoluntariamente*] abroad, where he died. His successor, General José María Orellana, passed to a better life long before he completed his presidential term. Don Lázaro Chacón practically gave his soul to the Almighty, pressured by the terrible load of governing this country. Don Baudilio Palma managed only to assume rule for three days before he was ousted and he later died in exile. General Manuel Orellana left with a consular position to Barcelona and was not allowed to die in his beloved fatherland. After 14 years of iron rule, General Ubico died in exile and only under Colonel Peralta's rule were his remains repatriated to Guatemalan lands. The only one who was permitted to return when dying was General Ponce Vaides. Of those still alive, Arévalo, Arbenz and Ydígoras are forced to stay far from their homeland. Some live with the threat of prison. Others must fear death." Isidoro Zarco, "El exilio: Ingrato destino de nuestros ex-gobernantes," 125–26 in César Brañas, ed., *El pensamiento vivo de Isidoro Zarco* (Guatemala: Editorial José de Pineda Ibarra, 1973).

10. This was taking place under a government democratically elected in 1958 that had supported actively the project of Central American integration, analyzed later in this book. See Sabino, *Guatemala*, 31.

11. Charles D. Ameringer, *The Democratic Left in Exile. The Anti-Dictatorial Struggle in the Caribbean, 1945–1959* (Miami: University of Miami Press, 1974), 161–220.

12. For detailed analysis see Dunkerley, *Power in the Isthmus*.

13. The United States did so especially since the discourse that attributed corruption to the civilian administrations in Latin America struck a chord in the minds of decision makers in Washington. See J. Johnson, *Latin America in Caricature* (Austin: University of Texas Press, 1980).

14. G. V. Correa, "Otros rasgos históricos de la derecha," *La Segunda* (Santiago, Chile), February 27, 1966.

15. A. Douglas Kincaid, "Demilitarization and Security in El Salvador and Guatemala: Convergences of Success and Crisis," 103–4 in Chase-Dunn, Jonas, and Amaro, *Globalization on the Ground*.

16. Sabino, *Guatemala*, 256–80.

17. There has been controversy over the number of victims in Guatemala. That controversy opened over the veracity of Rigoberta Menchú's testimony and has been projected more recently into an in-depth discussion of the criteria used to count murders and massacres. On these two stages of this important issue of representation and the construction of victimhood and genocide see in particular David Stoll, *Rigoberta Menchu and the Story of All Poor Guatemalans* (Boulder, Colo.: Westview Press, 1999); the special issue of *Human Rights Review* 1, 1 (1999), devoted to the Stoll-Menchú controversy; and Sabino, *Guatemala*, 365–94.

18. Dunkerley, *Power in the Isthmus*, 340–41.

19. See Donald E. Schultz and Douglas H. Graham, eds., *Revolution and Counterrevolution in Central America and the Caribbean* (Boulder, Colo.: Westview, 1984).

20. Thomas M. Leonard, "Search for Security: The United States and Central America in the Twentieth Century," *The Americas* 47, 4 (1991): 489.

21. Dunkerley, *Power in the Isthmus*, 377.

22. Randolph Siverson and Harvey Starr, "Opportunity, Willingness, and the Diffusion

of War 1816–1965," *American Political Science Review* 84 (1990): 47–67; Michael D. Ward and Kristian Gleditsch, "Location, Location, Location: An MCMC Approach to Modeling the Spatial Context of War and Peace," *Political Analysis* 10 (2002): 244–60.

23. Laurence Whitehead, "Three International Dimensions of Democratization," 3–26 in Laurence Whitehead, ed., *The International Dimensions of Democratization* (Oxford: Oxford University Press, 2001).

24. On peasant politics see Vinicio González, "La insurrección salvadoreña de 1932 y la gran huelga hondureña de 1954," *Revista Mexicana de Sociología* 60, 2 (1978): 563–606.

25. Kristian Skrede Gleditsch and Kyle Beardsley, "Nosy Neighbors: Third-Party Actors in Central American Conflicts," *Journal of Conflict Resolution* 48, 3 (2004): 385–86.

Chapter 10. Peace Making and the Challenges of Democratization and Liberalization

1. Susanne Jonas, *The Battle for Guatemala* (Boulder, Colo.: Westview, 1991), 80–81.

2. Woodward, *Central America*, 281.

3. James Dunkerley, *The Pacification of Central America* (London: Verso, 1994); Rachel Sieder, *Guatemala after the Peace Accords* (London: Institute of Latin American Studies, 1998); Margaret Popkin, *Peace without Justice. Obstacles to Building the Rule of Law in El Salvador* (University Park: Pennsylvania State University Press, 2000); Susanne Jonas, "Democratization through Peace," 49–81 in Chase-Dunn, Jonas, and Amaro, *Globalization on the Ground*; Cecilia Menjívar and Néstor Rodríguez, eds., *When States Kill* (Austin: University of Texas Press, 2005).

4. On these dilemmas see, for example, D. A. Crocker, "Reckoning with Past Wrongs. A Normative Framework," *Ethics and International Affairs* 13 (1999): 43–64; and Roniger and Sznajder, *Legacy of Human Rights Violations*.

5. Literally, "the vanished." The term was first used in Argentina under military rule (1976–83) and later widely adopted in Latin America to refer to individuals illegally abducted by state agents and whose whereabouts are unknown and whose bodies have not been recovered.

6. Menjívar and Rodríguez, *When States Kill*, especially Aldo A. Lauria-Santiago, "The Culture and Politics of State Terror and Repression in El Salvador," 85–114. See also Rachel Sieder, "War, Peace, and Memory Politics in Central America," 161–89 in Alexandra Barahona de Brito, Carmen González Enríquez, and Paloma Aguilar, eds., *The Politics of Memory. Transitional Justice in Democratizing Societies* (Oxford: Oxford University Press, 2001); and the revisionist estimates in Sabino, *Guatemala*, 365–93.

7. Mark Danner, *The Massacre at El Mozote* (New York: Vintage Books. 1994); and Popkin, *Peace without Justice*, 43–47.

8. Likewise, in Nicaragua, Father Fernando Cardenal indicted twenty-six members of the Nicaraguan Guardia with human rights violations including torture, the use of electric shock, and rape. Of the twenty-six accused, twenty-five were graduates of the SOA. Among renowned graduates of SOA were Omar Torrijos and Manuel Noriega of Panama, Humberto Regalado Hernández of Honduras, and Manuel Antonio Callejas of Guatemala.

9. Popkin, *Peace without Justice*, 115.

10. Tojo Balsells and Alfredo Edgar, *Olvido o memoria. El dilema de la sociedad guatemalteca* (Guatemala: F&G Editores, 2001), 91–92.

11. Marc Edelman, "Transnational Peasant Politics in Central America," *Latin American Research Review* 33, 3 (1998): 63–64, 72–74.

Chapter 11. Transnational Displacement: The Refugee Crisis and Migration

1. Celio Mármora, "Hacia la migración planificada interlatinoamericana. Salvadoreños en Argentina," *Estudios migratorios latinoamericanos* 1, 3 (1986): 275–93.

2. Hans Wollny, "Asylum Policy in Mexico: A Survey," *Journal of Refugee Studies* 4, 3 (1991): 228.

3. Keith W. Yundt, *Latin American States and Political Refugees* (New York: Praeger, 1988), 231.

4. Ibid., 135–39.

5. Laura O'Dogherty, "Mayas en el exilio: Los refugiados guatemaltecos en México," 213–17 in *Memorias del Segundo coloquio internacional de Mayistas,* Universidad Autónoma de México, Centro de Estudios Mayas, August 17–21, 1987.

6. Yundt, *Latin American States;* Menjívar and Rodríguez, *When States Kill.*

7. David E. Guinn and Elissa Steglich, *In Modern Bondage: Sex Trafficking in the Americas* (Chicago: De Paul University International Human Rights Law Institute and Transnational Publishers, 2003), 24–26.

8. Rosenberg and Solís, *The United States and Central America*, 72–73.

9. Bailey et al., "(Re)producing Salvadoran Transnational Geographies," 139.

10. Manuel Orozco, "Transnationalism and Development: Trends and Opportunities in Latin America," 307–30 in Samuel Munzele Maimbo and Dilip Ratha, eds., *Remittances: Development Impact and Future Prospects* (Washington, D.C.: World Bank, 2005).

11. Bailey et al. "(Re)producing Salvadoran Transnational Geographies," 128.

12. See Sandoval García, *Threatening Others.*

Chapter 12. Transnational Illicit Markets and Criminality

1. According to the United Nations Office of Drugs and Crime (UNODC), these trade circuits started during the civil war yet increased notably following it; UNODC, *World Drug Report 2007*, http://www.unodc.org/pdf/research/wdr07/WDR_2007.pdf. Deborah Yashar is currently studying the social and political consequences of this trend in the isthmus and South America. See Yashar, "Institutions and Citizenship: Reflections on the Illicit," forthcoming in Mario Sznajder, Luis Roniger, and Carlos Forment, eds. *Shifting Frontiers of Citizenship in Latin America* (Leiden: Brill, 2011).

2. Federico Brevé-Travieso, "The Maras," *Military Review* 87, 4 (2007): 88–96.

3. *Human Development Report, Honduras 2006. Towards the Expansion of Citizenship.* Tegucigalpa: United Nations Development Program, 2006.

4. Ibid., 23.

5. Comisionado Nacional de Derechos Humanos de Honduras, "Noticias," *September 9, 2008,* http://www.conadeh.hn/noticias/sicariato.htm, *accessed September 21, 2008.*

6. Lisbeth Zimmermann, Peace and Conflict Institute, Frankfurt, Germany, personal communication, February 19, 2010.

7. *Maras* means people rioting or out of control.

8. *Salvatrucha* is broken down into "salva," meaning Salvadoran, and "trucha," meaning streetwise or savvy, thus "streetwise Salvadorans."

9. Demoscopía, *Maras y pandillas, comunidad y policía en Centroamérica. Hallazgos de un estudio integral* (San José: Swedish Agency of International Cooperation [ASDI] and Central American Bank of Economic Integration [BCIE], 2008).

10. Ana Arana, "The New Battle for Central America," *Foreign Affairs* 80, 6 (2001): 88.

11. Stephen Meiners, "Central America: An Emerging Role in the Drug Trade," http://www.stratfor.com, March 26, 2009, accessed February 17, 2010.

12. Demoscopía, *Maras y pandillas.*

13. Council of Hemispheric Affairs, "COHA Responds to the UN World Drug Report," June 26, 2009, http://www.coha.org/2009/06/coha-responds-to-the-un-world-drug-report, accessed July 19, 2009.

14. Boraz and Bruneau, "Are the 'Maras' Overwhelming Governments in Central America?" 54.

15. Centro de Estudios y Programas Interamericanos (CEPI), *Pandillas juveniles transnacionales en Centroamérica, México y los Estados Unidos* (Mexico City: CEPI, 2007); Demoscopía, *Maras y pandillas.*

16. Lisbeth Zimmermann, personal communication, February 19, 2010.

17. The M-18 and MS-13 group members used to identify themselves with signature tattoos, hand signals, the graffiti they put on buildings, and even a special language whose vocabulary emphasizes violence and brutality. However, since El Salvador established anti-gang legislation called the Super Mano Dura, which gave authorities the authority to arrest anyone with a gang-related tattoo, a strategy that was quickly followed by Honduras and then Nicaragua, signature tattoos were discarded as identity markers.

18. The maras reportedly abuse individuals from all social classes, including from the middle and higher classes, who approach them in search of drugs and are sometimes recruited into the gang.

19. Ana Arana, "New Battle for Central America" and "How the Street Gangs Took Central America," *Foreign Affairs* 84, 3 (2005): 98–110.

20. Robert Hanson, Greg Warchol, and Linda Zupan, "Policing Paradise: Law and Disorder in Belize," *Police Practice and Research* 5, 3 (2004): 247.

21. Ibid., 250.

22. "Bringing It All Back Home," *The Economist*, May 22, 2004, 31.

23. Hanson, Warchol, and Zupan, "Policing Paradise," 248.

24. Its aid is added to other initiatives including aid through the Millennium Challenge Corporation (MCC), another U.S.-financed program geared to promoting sustainable economic growth and institutional transparency in some of the poorest countries, such as Nicaragua and Honduras.

25. Rosenberg and Solís, *United States and Central America*, 56–57.

26. Brevé-Travieso, "The Maras," 94; Demoscopía, *Maras y pandillas.*

Chapter 13. Globalization and Transnational Dynamics in Contemporary Central America

1. William I. Robinson, *Transnational Conflicts: Central America, Social Change, and Globalization* (London: Verso, 1999), 10, 13.

2. Ibid., 50–51.

3. Dirlik, "Globalization as the End and the Beginning of History."

4. This analysis of NTAEs draws on Robinson, *Transnational Conflicts.*

5. Dunkerley, *Pacification of Central America*, 5–6.

6. UNDP *Human Development Report, Honduras 2006*, 25.

7. UNDP *Human Development Report 2007/2008*, 225. http://hdrstats.undp.org/indicators/25.html.

8. See Alma Martínez, "Más de 680 mil son analfabetas en el país," *El Mundo* (San Salvador), September 9, 2008, http://www.elmundo.com.sv, accessed September 21, 2008. On the policies of President Mauricio Funes, in office since June 2009, see Alexander Brockwehl and Juan Pablo Pitarque, "Concessions of a Leftist Party: The FMLN's Dilemma in the Face of Funes' Centrist Policies," Council of Hemispheric Affairs, http://www.coha.org, accessed October 18, 2010.

9. See Claudia Biancotti, "A Polarization of Inequality? The Distribution of National Gini Coefficients," *Journal of Economic Inequality* 6, 1 (2006): 1–31.

10. Rose J. Spalding, "Civil Society Engagement in Trade Negotiations: CAFTA Opposition Movements in El Salvador," *Latin American Politics and Society* 49, 4 (2007): 90.

11. Ibid., 93.

12. Ibid., 96.

13. Alan M. Field, "CAFTA: Why It Is Spinning Its Wheels," *Florida Shipper* 33, 2 (January 14, 2008): 9–10.

14. Banco Interamericano de Desarrollo, Instituto para la Integración de América Latina y el Caribe, http://www.iadb.org/INTAL/cronologia, accessed September 8, 2008.

15. The Red de Centros de Pensamiento e Incidencia seems to have completed a report on this impact, *Crisis financiera mundial: Su impacto social y político en Centroamérica*, presented in Guatemala in February 2010. Information is available on the Web site of the Konrad Adenauer Foundation, http://www.kas.de/proj/home/events/55/1/veranstaltung_id-39393/index.html, accessed February 21, 2010.

16. Guinn and Steglich, *In Modern Bondage*, 39 and 35–37.

Chapter 14. Interstate Institutions and Transnational Involvement: A New Stage?

1. The war, fought by El Salvador and Honduras for a few days in July 1969, was triggered by riots during the second qualifying round for the 1970 FIFA (Fédération Internationale de Football Association) World Cup. The armed confrontation reflected deeper tensions following the expulsion of Salvadorans who had settled for years across the border in Honduran territories. Due to different population densities, about 300,000 Salvadorans had moved to Honduras in search of land. Following the enforcement of a land reform law by 1967, many of them—legal owners and squatters as well as temporary laborers—were displaced and forced to migrate back to El Salvador.

2. Jonas, *Battle for Guatemala*, 50–51; Sabino, *Guatemala,* 68.

3. *La integración centroamericana hoy* (Guatemala: INCEP, Instituto Centroamericano de Estudios Políticos, 2005).

4. Victor Bulmer-Thomas, ed., *Centroamérica en reestructuración: Integración regional en Centroamérica* (San José: FLACSO-Social Science Research Council, 1998).

5. Nicolle Carpio, Roberto Borrayo Reyes, and José Luis Borrayo Reyes, *Unión Centroamericana* (Guatemala: Ediciones Internacionales, 1998), 7.

6. "PARLACEN consists of 20 directly elected representatives from each member state plus the former presidents and vice presidents of Guatemala, El Salvador, Honduras, Nicaragua and Panama as well as 22 appointed representatives of the Dominican Republic." PARLACEN, http://www.parlacen.org.gt/documentos/PDF_english.pdf, accessed *February* 21, *2010.*

7. "Honduran Withdrawal from PARLACEN," http://goliath.ecnext.com/coms2/gi_0199–1265606/REGION-HONDURAN-WITHDRAWAL-FROM-PARLACEN.html, accessed July 27, 2008.

8. In this connection, perhaps a personal vignette may be telling. As my spouse and I visited the city of León in January 2007, we took a guided tour of the makeshift Museum of the Revolution. Located close to the central square, the museum told the story of the Sandinista resistance and revolution through newspaper articles, pictorial representations, and mostly blurred copies of photographs of key actors and events, in addition to a few material exhibits. Sandinista veterans, then out of power, provided free guided tours. We were told that we, as visitors, could contribute voluntarily to the common fund of the veterans at the end of the visit. Toward the end of the visit, I took a Nicaraguan bank note and handed it to our guide, who continued to talk, while—to our astonishment—he placed the bank note in his wallet and replaced it with another bank note, about a fourth of its value. As we all went to the exit, he placed the reduced contribution in the common box and commented to his fellow comrades that this was our contribution. While I may be wrong, my reading of the event tilts in the direction of a private appropriation of public funds, even on the part of those preaching a revolutionary gospel. I fear that this experience may be more emblematic than suspected and not limited to Nicaragua, as the aggregate data brought here indicate.

9. Council of Hemispheric Affairs, "Déjà Vu in Central America: Iran's Recent Push into Nicaragua," July 24, 2009, http://www.coha/2009/07/deja-vu-in-central-america-iran-recent-push-into-nicaragua, accessed July 27, 2009.

10. See Mario Samper, "Fuerzas políticas y procesos sociopolíticos en Costa Rica, 1921–1936," *Revista de Historia*, special issue (1988): 157–222.

11. These scandals included, according to a COHA report, "a number of hotly sought-after appointments to state-run companies that were ultimately steered to the brink of bankruptcy (Hondutel and ENEE), as well as his own questionable use of state funds for personal projects." "Caudillismo in Action: Looking Back at Honduras Plight," July 7, 2009, http://www.coha.org/2009/07/caudillismo-in-action-looking-back-on-honduras%E2%80%99-plight, accessed July 27, 2009.

12. "Honduran Withdrawal from PARLACEN," http://goliath.ecnext.com/coms2/gi_0199–1265606/REGION-HONDURAN-WITHDRAWAL-FROM-PARLACEN.html, accessed July 27, 2008.

13. National Report on the Media, Politics, and Democracy released by the United Nations Program for Development (UNDP) in 2008, http://hdrstats.undp.org/indicators/25.html.

14. See Transparency International, 2006, 2008, "Corruptions Perceptions Index," http://www.transparency.org/policy_research/surveys_indices/cpi/2001, accessed September 16, 2008.

15. Mitchell A. Seligson, ed., *Americas Barometer by Latin American Public Opinion Project: Challenges for Democracy in Latin America and the Caribbean* (Nashville: USAID and Vanderbilt University, 2008).

16. See Jorge Vargas-Cullell and Luis Rosero-Bixby, "The Political Culture of Democracy in Costa Rica: 2006," Mitchell A. Seligson, ed. (The AmericasBarometer by LAPOP, Vanderbilt University: 2008), 54, http://www.vanderbilt.edu/lapop/ab2006/costa-rica1-en.pdf (accessed September 16, 2008).

17. Seligson, *Americas Barometer,* 254–57 (quotation on p. 257).

18. Ibid., 272.

19. Ibid., especially 99–109.

20. Arie M. Kacowicz, "Economics and Security: The Counter-Intuitive Case of Latin America, 1945–2006," 3, paper prepared at the international conference Links between Economics and Security, Jerusalem, Leonard Davis Institute of International Relations, April

2006. See also Victor Bulmer-Thomas and A. Douglas-Kincaid, *Central America 2020: Towards a New Regional Development Model* (Hamburg: Institut für Iberoamerika-Kunde, 2000).

Conclusions: Small Nations and Transnationalism in a Globalizing Era

1. See Markus Rodlauer and Alfred Schipke, eds., *Central America: Global Integration and Regional Cooperation* (Washington, D.C.: International Monetary Fund, 2005).

2. See Marlon Hernández Muñoz, "Trade. Adios to 'Banana Republic.' Central America Diversifies its Exports," *Central America Today*, June–July 2008, http://www.centralamerica-today.com/e9/trade.html.

3. William C. Gruben, "Domestic Policy No Match for Trade Stance of Central American Countries," *Southwest Economy* (2005): 13–15.

4. See Mitchell A. Seligson, "Trouble in Paradise? The Erosion of System Support in Costa Rica, 1978–1999," *Latin American Research Review* 37 (2002): 160–85.

5. Tatiana Lobo, "Costa Rica imaginaria," Alexander Jiménez and Jesús Oyamburu, eds. *Costa Rica imaginaria* (Heredia: Editorial Fundación Una, 1998). 31.

6. See N. Phillips, "Regionalist Governance in the New Political Economy of Development: 'Relaunching' the Mercosur," *Third World Quarterly* 22, 4 (2001): 565–83; and Kanishka Jayasuriya, "Regionalising the State: Political Topography of Regulatory Regionalism," *Contemporary Politics* 14, 1 (2008): 21–35.

7. The coalition that started the initiative back in 2001 included the Center for Legal Action on Human Rights (Centro para la Acción Legal en Derechos Humanos, CALDH), the International Human Rights Research Center (Centro Internacional para Investigaciones en Derechos Humanos, CIIDH), the Myrna Mack Foundation (Fundación Myrna Mack, FMM), the Mutual Support Group (Grupo de Apoyo Mutuo, GAM), the Rigoberta Menchú Tum Foundation (Fundación Rigoberta Menchú Tum, FRMT), the Institute of Comparative Studies in Criminal Sciences of Guatemala (Instituto de Estudios Comparados en Ciencias Penales de Guatemala, ICCPG), the Human Rights Office of the Archdiocese of Guatemala (Oficina de Derechos Humanos del Arzobispado de Guatemala, ODHAG), and Security in Democracy (Seguridad en Democracia, SEDEM). By reaching out to international human rights organizations, "these eight organizations, often braving death threats and harassment, then sought to garner the support of Guatemalan government officials and representatives of aid-donor governments who were based in Guatemala, often at their respective countries' embassies, for this innovative proposal." Washington Office for Latin America, "Advocates against Impunity: A Case Study in Human Rights Organizing in Guatemala," December 2008, 4, http://www.wola.org/organized_crime/cicig/cicig_advocates_against_impunity.pdf, accessed February 24, 2010.

8. Ibid., 5.

Index

Luis Roniger is Reynolds Professor of Latin American Studies at Wake Forest University. A comparative political sociologist, he has made significant contributions to the study of clientelism and civil society, collective identities, and democratization and human rights. He is the author of numerous articles and books, among them *Globality and Multiple Modernities* (with Carlos H. Waisman) and *The Politics of Exile in Latin America* (with Mario Sznajder), and he is coeditor of *Exile and the Politics of Exclusion in the Americas.*

www.ingramcontent.com/pod-product-compliance
Lightning Source LLC
Chambersburg PA
CBHW031428270326
41930CB00007B/622